NEW ACCENTS

General editor: TERENCE HAWKES

Dialogue and Difference

IN THE SAME SERIES

Dialogue and Difference

English into the Nineties

EDITED BY
PETER BROOKER AND PETER HUMM

R

ROUTLEDGE
London and New York

First published 1989 by
Routledge
11 New Fetter Lane, London EC4P 4EE
29 West 35th Street, New York, NY 10001

Photoset by Rowland Phototypesetting Limited
Bury St Edmunds, Suffolk
Printed in Great Britain by
Richard Clay Limited, Bungay, Suffolk

British Library Cataloguing in Publication Data

Dialogue and difference: English into the nineties.—
    (New accents)
    1. Great Britain. Secondary Schools. Curriculum
    subjects: English literature. Teaching
    I. Brooker, Peter   II. Humm, Peter   III. Series
    820'.7'1241

    ISBN 0-415-01643-6
        0-415-01644-4 (pbk)

Library of Congress Cataloging in Publication Data

Dialogue and difference: English into the nineties/edited by
    Peter Brooker and Peter Humm.
        p. cm.—(New accents)
    Bibliography: p.
    Includes index.
    1. English philology—Study and teaching—Great Britain.
    I. Brooker, Peter.   II. Humm, Peter.   III. Series: New Accents
    (Routledge (Firm))
    PE68.G5D53   1989
    428'.007'041—dc19   89-3505

For
Dan and Joe and especially Will

Contents

General editor's preface

It is easy to see that we are living in a time of rapid and radical social change. It is much less easy to grasp the fact that such change will inevitably affect the nature of those disciplines that both reflect our society and help to shape it.

Yet this is nowhere more apparent than in the central field of what may, in general terms, be called literary studies. Here, among large numbers of students at all levels of education, the erosion of the assumptions and presuppositions that support the literary disciplines in their conventional form has proved fundamental. Modes and categories inherited from the past no longer seem to fit the reality experienced by a new generation.

New Accents is intended as a positive response to the initiative offered by such a situation. Each volume in the series will seek to encourage rather than resist the process of change; to stretch rather than reinforce the boundaries that currently define literature and its academic study.

Some important areas of interest immediately present themselves. In various parts of the world, new methods of analysis have been developed whose conclusions reveal the limitations of the Anglo-American outlook we inherit. New concepts of literary forms and modes have been proposed; new notions of the nature of literature itself and of how it communicates are current; new views of literature's role in relation to society flourish. *New Accents* will aim to expound and comment upon the most notable of these.

In the broad field of the study of human communication, more and more emphasis has been placed upon the nature and function of the new electronic media. *New Accents* will try to identify and discuss the challenge these offer to our traditional modes of critical response.

The same interest in communication suggests that the series should also concern itself with those wider anthropological and sociological areas of investigation which have begun to involve scrutiny of the nature of art itself and of its relation to our whole way of life. And this will ultimately require attention to be focused on some of those activities which in our society have hitherto been excluded from the prestigious realms of Culture. The disturbing realignment of values involved and the disconcerting nature of the pressures that work to bring it about both constitute areas that *New Accents* will seek to explore.

Finally, as its title suggests, one aspect of *New Accents* will be firmly located in contemporary approaches to language, and a continuing concern of the series will be to examine the extent to which relevant branches of linguistic studies can illuminate specific literary areas. The volumes with this particular interest will nevertheless presume no prior technical knowledge on the part of their readers, and will aim to rehearse the linguistics appropriate to the matter in hand, rather than to embark on general theoretical matters.

Each volume in the series will attempt an objective exposition of significant developments in its field up to the present as well as an account of its author's own views of the matter. Each will culminate in an informative bibliography as a guide to further study. And, while each will be primarily concerned with matters relevant to its own specific interests, we can hope that a kind of conversation will be heard to develop between them; one whose accents may perhaps suggest the distinctive discourse of the future.

TERENCE HAWKES

List of contributors

Margaret Beetham, Senior Lecturer, Department of English and History, Manchester Polytechnic.

Steve Bennison, Lecturer in English and Communication Studies, Filton Technical College, Bristol.

Sabrina Broadbent, Acting Head of English, Southfields School, London; committee member of the London Association for the Teaching of English.

Roger Bromley, Director of the School of Language and Literature, Faculty of Arts, The College of St Paul and St Mary, Cheltenham.

Peter Brooker, Senior Lecturer, Division of Literary and Cultural Studies, School of Humanities, Thames Polytechnic, London.

James Donald, Lecturer, School of Education, The Open University, Milton Keynes.

Zoë Fairbairns, novelist.

Liz Gerschel, ILEA Divisional Co-ordinator for Anti-Racist and Multi-Ethnic Education, Islington.

Denise Hayes, student, School of Humanities, Thames Polytechnic, London.

Peter Humm, Senior Lecturer, Head of the Division of Literary and Cultural Studies, School of Humanities, Thames Polytechnic, London.

Alison Light, Lecturer in English, Brighton Polytechnic, Brighton.

Alf Louvre, Senior Lecturer, Department of English and History, Manchester Polytechnic.

Brian Maidment, Principal Lecturer, Department of English and History, Manchester Polytechnic.

Lesley Massey, student, School of Humanities, Thames Polytechnic, London.

Ros Moger, Adviser for English, Enfield; committee member of the London Association for the Teaching of English.

Jan Montefiore, Lecturer, Board of English and American Studies, The University of Kent at Canterbury.

Paul Moran, part-time teacher, English Faculty, Beauchamp College, Leicester; research student, University of Leicester.

Susheila Nasta, Senior Lecturer in Multi-Cultural Education and Literary Studies, Portsmouth Polytechnic; Editor of *Wasafiri*.

Douglas Norsworthy, student, School of Humanities, Thames Polytechnic, London.

Margaret Peacock, Head of English, Kidbrooke School; now Deputy Head, Chestnut Grove School, London.

Nick Peim, Head of English Faculty, Beauchamp College, Leicester.

Jim Porteous, Head of English and Communication Studies, Brislington School, Bristol.

Penny Price, student, School of Humanities, Thames Polytechnic, London.

Jenny Rice, Lecturer, Youth Education Unit, Bournville College of Further Education, Birmingham.

Phil Rice, Senior Lecturer, Graphic Design and Communication Studies, Coventry Polytechnic.

Elaine Scarratt, English Department, Kidbrooke School, London.

Nikki Slater, student, School of Humanities, Thames Polytechnic, London.

Paul Stigant, Head of the School of Humanities, Thames Polytechnic, London.

Acknowledgements

The authors and publisher are grateful to the following for permission to reproduce copyright material: Karnak House for Grace Nichols (1983) *i is a long memoried woman* (London: Karnak House); Faber & Faber Ltd and Random House, Inc. for W. H. Auden (1972) 'Epistle to a godson' from *W. H. Auden. Collected Poems*, ed. Edward Mendelson (London: Faber & Faber); Oxford University Press for Edward Kamau Brath·waite (1987) 'Xango' from *X/Self* (Oxford: Oxford University Press). Unfortunately we have been unable to make contact with *The Sunday Gleaner*, Kingston, Jamaica for permission to reprint Edward Baugh's 'Truth and consequences'. We would appreciate any information which would enable us to do so.

We would especially like to thank Terry Hawkes for his sharp eye and judgement.

Introduction: Looking back and beyond

This selection of essays is an attempt to open up some of the as yet unsurveyed territory of English Studies and to introduce a new, more positive tone and greater range of voices to discussions of the future of the subject. Studies of the ideology of 'English' and explorations of new theory characteristic of work in Higher Education in recent years have, for all their integrity and value, tended to run free of the specific practices of English teaching and of the implications they might have for these. Indeed in some ways, rather than offering a new discourse and a common beginning which would take account of radical changes in policy, in curricula and pedagogy as well as in critical practice, they have reinforced a separation between sectors, perspectives, and opportunities. Too often teachers have been assumed to be the agents of a hegemony constructed by government edict, examination boards, and an inherited great tradition by those whose radicalism is in the thinnest sense 'theoretical', and confined to the very conventional form of the academic lecture, or written book or article. The answer to this is neither grander theory nor philistinism, neither more books nor a guilty (or guilt-free) battering away at the chalk face, but simply a more open and more informed exchange between teachers and institutions and forms of work, between theory and teaching practice, between what might be called the deconstruction and the progressive reconstruction that is going on throughout English education.

To envision this kind of exchange and transformation is as much to recall a delayed and obstructed agenda as it is to write a new one. In 1977, eleven years after the publication in France of Pierre Macherey's *Pour une Théorie de la production littéraire* and a year before its appearance in English (a period which also saw the translation of major texts by Lacan and Jacques Derrida) Macherey described his work up to that date as a way of testing Althusser's thesis that education was the dominant ideological apparatus. He argued that to explain literature in terms of its deformation by ideology, its conditions of possibility and reproduction would be to dispel its traditional theological aura and enlarge its range of meaning. If literary studies themselves were to be transformed, however, it was not enough, he said, to shift its domain and add in new material in the shape of an alternative canon. It would be necessary in fact to 'completely change the system in which the categories of literary study are thought out' (Macherey 1977: 9).

Proposals such as these, and Macherey and Balibar's work along these lines, have helped inspire the challenge to (as well as the defence of) 'English' as we have witnessed it over the last decade. This work of critique and reorientation has been conducted through commentary, guides, and criticism, through journals and conferences, and through the networks supporting, for example, *Literature, Teaching and Politics*, the National and the regional Associations for the Teaching of English as well as in the seminar and classroom. The *New Accents* series itself, also launched in 1977, has played a significant role in this process of redefinition. The 'General preface' to the series has reminded us over these years that the present period is one 'of rapid and radical social change', and of how this has inevitably affected the study of language, literature, and culture. Twelve years on we are only too painfully aware that this process of radical change has been steered by the Tory cabinet and the radical right rather than by a dissenting intelligentsia. As the Tory hatchet descends upon the neck of the dominant ideological apparatus, it is evident that the late 1980s are a demoralizing time for projects of progressive transformation. But yet the signs do not all point this way. In spite of everything, teachers have persisted in a practical critique of traditional categories and pedagogic modes in ways which draw on, as they draw out, a contrary experience of social change, moving against the grain of enforced national unity and towards cultural dispersal and difference.

The Olympian purview of Althusser and Macherey's scientific Marxism seems now neither available nor fit for these changed circumstances. There have been continuities as well as shifts over this period all the same, some of which we can only try to understand as we experience them. Macherey had spoken in 1977, for example, of how the transformation of literary studies depended not 'on a personal and independent decision', but 'upon a material and political conjuncture' and a type of decision which was 'necessarily collective' (Macherey 1977: 9). The left would probably still give ready and principled assent to this, though the raised hands would just as probably be accompanied by some furrowed brows. For increasingly the problem has been just what or who, in real terms, is meant by injunctions to 'collective' thought and action? Who or what *is* 'the left'? Without working assurances on these questions it is obviously difficult to envisage the character of future change, let alone the progressive transformation of literary studies.

At the end of 1987, in a much changed *Critical Quarterly*, Colin MacCabe addressed this same problem. The right's attempt to straitjacket a growing multi-ethnic society in the proposed National Curriculum, had, he felt, for all its 'muddle of fear and prejudice', produced two questions:

> How far does it continue to make sense to talk of a national culture in an era which sees a growing internationalisation and localisation of cultural production? And a further theoretical question: is it possible to construct a shared culture on differences rather than identities? Once these very important questions are properly couched, it is a difficult but perfectly feasible task to construct the appropriate syllabi and curricula.
>
> (MacCabe 1987: 8)

MacCabe's focus is a specific one, but he is posing here a key problem of our times; for how can we conceive of a structured or centred common identity in an age of deconstruction and unanchored *différence* which has edged such notions into the limbo of erasure and quotation marks? And how then can a new kind of unity be founded on intellectual and cultural diversity? What kind of narrative will give purpose and direction to changed subjectivities and a changing society, when – or so we are told – the 'grand narratives' that have hitherto structured human hopes and history have lost all credibility. James Donald takes up Colin MacCabe's argument in the opening chapter of the present volume. His answer to its central question is 'no', there cannot be a shared culture founded on differences rather than identities, because 'culture is *always* constructed on differences . . . MacCabe cannot have *both* a postmodernist free play of heterogeneity based on the denial of a normative consensus, *and* a consensual "shared" culture' (p. 26). Donald's own answer is one which informs the making of this present collection. What is needed, he writes, is 'a shift of emphasis away from the normative or consensual aspects of culture – order, authority, identity – to the dialogic processes out of which these are formed, and which they precariously organize and contain' (p. 26).

The indeterminacies of the present are not therefore so much, or only, a signal for eclectic play, as a call for flexible strategies of reorientation and restructuring. This does not mean abandoning ideals of common purpose so much as reconceiving them, and recomposing their constituents in newly responsive alliances. We cannot hope to reply in kind, that is to say, to present conservative policies which seek, as in the National Curriculum and the abolition of ILEA, to unify and control in their own interests (we might note that the right has stuck resolutely to its chosen 'metanarrative' for all that is said elsewhere of the impotence of such thinking); but we can, both professionally and politically, look to the formation of tactical alliances within and against the new institutional and ideological constraints this hegemony imposes. And we can attempt to introduce different tactics and networks to each other. Taken together, the arguments and reports we have assembled in this book do not amount to a grand narrative of single-minded change for 'English'. They debate with and contest traditional and conservative ideas and practices, but they respond to the general questions raised above in their own terms, bringing to this dialogue the differently accented experiences of school and college teaching, and the factors of gender, class, and race.

The structure of the book represents our sense of this darting dialectic. We have arranged the essays in three sections, not in order to stream high-flying theory separately from the realities of classroom practice, but to provide comprehensive evidence that teachers in all sectors of education are making use of theoretical insights in the reshaping of literary studies. Each section of essays brings together reports from schools, polytechnics, colleges, and universities which focus upon a distinct set of common interests.

The first four essays debate the present condition of 'English'. As Alison Light points out in chapter 2, 'what is so extraordinary about the 1980s is that it is the first ever period of educational decline' (p. 38). This has not happened quietly or through unbothered neglect but as the result of a series of bruising charges and mean assaults which have contrived to keep opposition divided and off balance. Ever since James Callaghan, as Labour Prime Minister, proposed a national debate on education, the interests and contributions of those in opposition to conservative trends have been sabotaged, misrepresented, or merely ignored.

Yet the essays in this first section do more than reveal opportunities missed: they suggest ways in which teachers can work collectively within and across institutions to change the agenda of educational policy. As Jenny and Phil Rice argue in chapter 4, teachers in secondary and further education are already experienced in working against the grain of the Government's efforts to promote an enterprise culture within education. And Sabrina Broadbent and Rosalind Moger in their account of LATE'S response to Kingman and other outriders of the National Curriculum similarly demonstrate the need for a collective reply to the implications of a conservative lexicon of excellence and relevance. Both essays therefore show how teachers can still recast the terms of educational debate.

The second section proves that this is more than wishful thinking. While the book as a whole reveals the influence of recent literary theory upon the aims and methods of teaching, the essays in this middle section concentrate upon those areas of study which have directly challenged the canon constructed by the long processes of what Roger Bromley calls 'patriarchal binary thought' (p. 152). Moreover, these accounts of the teaching of poststructuralist and feminist theory, of the still-marginalized areas of popular fiction and women's writing, and of attempts to implement anti-racist and multi-cultural perspectives, are relevant once again to more than post-school provision. Whether theory is being interpreted by postgraduates or by 14-year olds, the effect is to question not just the traditional construction of literary history but the pedagogic conventions and the curriculum which have comprised the power–knowledge relations of English as a discipline.

The final section provides case studies of specific courses illustrating the way in which both the subject and the teaching of English is being reconceived. This includes work on new kinds of texts, the introduction of more active modes of learning and writing in GCSE and A level, and the experience of teaching extra-mural courses in creative writing and access courses for mature students. All these are concerned with ways of expressing, knowing, and redefining the self, and show how criticism, autobiography, imitation, reconstruction in another medium, and exercises in the techniques of fiction can be employed to that end. In the process they bring us to question the conventional distinction between analytic and imaginative mentalities. Here, in an age of 'skills', are modes and techniques of writing traditionally associated with literature, but very rarely directly taught in 'English' courses and classes, and particularly not in higher education. The authors here do not share the same assumptions, nor should these case studies be taken to suggest that 'English' can, or ought to now move forward, unhindered and unrevised, along these lines. They do, however, introduce the prospect of more productive modes of learning, of new relations between pupils and teachers, and thus offer a new understanding of what the subject can mean.

One way to read these essays is as a series of reports on what urgently concerns teachers in their working lives, and as a practical response to present conditions. But yet it is important to scrutinize the idea of experience this implies. In one of the essays examining the value of autobiography as a problematic genre, Jim Porteous and Steve Bennison argue that 'uncovering and investigating both the generic and social processes of this construction marks the beginning of a politically useful knowledge, a conceptualized "making strange" of what appears to be natural and universal – the self' (p. 177). English has always been the subject most closely involved with the making of subjectivities and the case studies draw special attention to this. The problem is how to recognize and value the personal experience and personal voice which help comprise and articulate subjectivity while avoiding sentimental appeals to their absolute authenticity. For that particular English accent with its assumed model of the individual has served more often to deny than to value the experience of those who do not conform to it.

The authority of experience has also been an important if contested resource in the educational history of feminist criticism. The list of contributors divides almost equally between men and women, but although we were conscious of gendered differences of idiom and position, this has not resulted in a simple opposition between masterly surveys of the theoretical horizon and a feminine closeness to personal realities. Just as theory is of use to more people than the advanced undergraduate, so the debate on experience should be heard outside courses in women's studies or multi-cultural education. Over the last two decades, feminism has both discovered and lost a unity of direction. At the same time its present fragmentation and dispersal take us beyond false unities or simple binary divisions of gendered experience and discourse. Many of the essays register this, and we have also deliberately ordered the book's contents so as to check any (common) sense of a white, male academic norm to be enlivened every now and then by the latest dispatches from the feminist or the multicultural front.

It should be clear that we are not presenting these essays as exemplary, as the 'left's' model answers to conservative thinking and policy. In general terms, however, they do represent a democratic alternative, not least in the fact that over half of them have been co-produced and in many ways strike a blow at the sentimental, but finally demoralizing image of the lone teacher in command of the class. Taken together they represent a collective resistance to the present Government's determination to keep English education within the narrowing boundaries of discipline and heritage. What chapter 15 describes as 'the boundlessness' of cultural studies is – in its very imprecision – what alarms those who retain a dogmatic nostalgia for clearly understood distinctions between subjects on the timetable, between teachers' and students' contributions to a course, and between institutions so elaborately ranked that a mere two-tier system is no longer sufficient. The evidence of these essays is that throughout the state education system, teachers and students are making significant connections between the new approaches to English in schools and in tertiary education, between English and other critical discourses, and between theory and practice.

Yet, as the authors of the same chapter make clear, the collective work which puts together a course on cultural studies to challenge the familiar canon can easily exclude the students, who have not sat through the long processes of course design. Exhilaration at overcoming the inertia embedded in traditional definitions of literary studies can quickly be deflated at the realization that this risks 'substituting for the authority of the canon the equally repressive authority of the teacher' (p. 252). Any collection of case studies which excluded the contributions made by students would be incomplete and contradict the book's purpose. The essays in this final section therefore include direct comments by students or full quotations from their work. Students then take their part in the dialogues which make up the whole, as both the assessed and the assessors of educational change. At a time when Government policy in inner London and elsewhere forces the break-up of comprehensive authorities into divided and competing localities, at a time when English departments are being persuaded to 'sell themselves' and 'find new customers', these examples of co-operative work, of working alliances, of greater equality, remind us that there is a progressive alternative to the competitive ethos that drives modern 'enterprise culture'.

Our stress finally is upon the words of our title. As male teachers in a London polytechnic, we have learned from the solutions to problems in course innovation and in the classroom that other teachers have arrived at. We have benefited personally from this intellectual dialogue across differences, just as we have enjoyed, in the midst of some tension, bafflement, and frustration, the very different forms of real talk and correspondence we have had with contributors. The whole book has pulled people and arguments together in a provisional but 'necessarily collective' dialogic alliance. We hope it encourages others.

PART I
The Condition of English

Beyond our Ken:
English, Englishness, and
the National Curriculum

James Donald

Some feel we are in danger of losing our British heritage and
national pride and we do not intend to go down this path in
Berkshire.
(Tory councillors, on scrapping Berkshire's policy on racial
equality in education)

I walk in a landscape of ideological ruins.
(Juan Goytisolo, *Landscapes After The Battle*)

Did you notice how the idea of a *core* curriculum for secondary
schools went through a metamorphosis as it was incorporated
into the Education Reform Bill and emerged as the *National*
Curriculum? More Tory grandiloquence? Or does the change
represent something more sinister – a Bonapartist centraliz-
ation of control over knowledge, perhaps? There is an element
of that. The prescription of certain subjects for study enables
Education Secretary Kenneth Baker (or whoever) to proscribe
others he (or she) disapproves of. The testing of children at the
ages of 7, 11, 14, and 16 provides a mechanism for the ever more
detailed monitoring and surveillance of individual children. It
also allows tighter central control over a system nominally
diversified by giving some schools the chance to 'opt out' from
local education authority.

What about the cultural implications of the move? Is the
normative curriculum for the nation part of Mrs Thatcher's
regressive modernization,[1] her mission to change the soul of the
nation and produce a postindustrial enterprise culture imagined in terms of a peremptory 'Britishness'? It probably is,

although I don't want to sound too paranoid about it. For one thing, the tension between economic libertarianism and cultural authoritarianism may be what makes Thatcherism implode. For another, I am uneasy – or, rather, agnostic – about the notion of 'Englishness'.[2] I feel about it as Gertrude Stein felt about her home town of Oakland: 'there's no there there'. It only takes on substance as it is endlessly reproduced – not least by materialist cultural critics deconstructing its ideological instability and exposing its historical construction. But being an atheist doesn't mean you can ignore the power of the Church. So yes, 'Englishness' is part of the National Curriculum. But it is neither an expressive 'identity', nor an imagined unity foisted on a gullible population. 'Englishness' is a cultural *claim* or *demand* enforced through the institutional deployment of systems of representation.

Kenneth Baker has no such doubts about Englishness. In a lecture in November 1986, he declared:

> Next to our people, the English language is our greatest asset as a nation, it is the essential ingredient of the Englishness of England. . . . [I]t is the people of England who fashion the shape, create the flavour and determine the direction of our changing national consciousness. The thing that has held them together over the centuries and would still allow an Englishman transported back a hundred years or two hundred years or four hundred years, if you have a good ear for accent, to recognise that he was in the same country, is the English language.[3]

Here is Englishness as heritage, as mythical identity, as the almost sensual experience of an imagined past embodied not just in the language, but in the English countryside, in certain styles of architecture, and in English Literature. Behind this threadbare rhetoric of the Conservative nation lies not a lost historical Arcady (or even an organic community), but an ideology of Englishness sustained by traditions, rituals, and institutions 'invented' in the decades around the turn of the century. These were part of a new political strategy designed to contain the democratic extension of the suffrage and the rise of mass labour parties: its novelty lay in its emphasis on managing the *symbolic*.

In Britain the English language and English Literature, so ostentatiously dear to Mr Baker's heart, had a key role in this strategy. It is too abrupt to say that they also were invented at this time – of course, people spoke and wrote and published and read before – but this was when the categories took on their contemporary currency and their modern institutional forms.

The newly selected canon defined the literary idols of the English tribe, to be venerated by a clerisy in new university departments. George Gordon, one of the first professors of English at Oxford, captured Literature's messianic role: 'still, I suppose, to delight and instruct us, but also, and above all, to save our souls and heal the State' (cited in Eagleton 1983: 23). The ideological function of English in schools was made equally explicit – in the Newbolt Report on *The Teaching of English in England* (1921), for example, or in George Sampson's much-quoted warning in the 1925 preface to his *English for the English*: 'Deny to working class children any common share in the immaterial and presently they will grow into the men who will demand with menaces a communism of the material.' English, then, seems to have been invented to put the national whalebone into the cultural corset of the new curricula, to act as a moralizing and politically integrative force.

A similar ethic lay behind the standardization of the language evident, at around the same period, in the production of the *Oxford English Dictionary*. This was justified as a way of summoning Englishmen to a sense of England's glorious past and glorious destiny – an identification with the narrative of England and its continuity over time. Mr Baker still believes in this. 'Our children', he concluded his 1986 lecture, should emerge from being taught English 'with the confidence that comes from knowing that the language belongs to them and is in their keeping for the time being, and that is both a reassuring and awesome prospect.'

The imposition of a standard, national language can always be seen as both a symptom of, and a tactic within, the re-organization of cultural hegemony. To some extent, this involves an attempt to limit the polysemic nature of language and to fix a uniaccentual order of perception and expression. But it does not mean that everyone ends up speaking the same language in the same way. What is at stake is the reorganization and the revalorization of linguistic differences – less the imposition of identity than the organization of dissensus. The standard language legislates a norm, the consensual pole in this dissensus. In her studies of post-Revolutionary France, for example, Renée Balibar argues that the official French that was vigorously imposed allowed a *formal* equality at the same time as giving a new significance and value to the different dispositions towards it. What had previously been simply regional and dialectal differences were now incorporated into new patterns of discrimination (between 'correct' and 'incorrect' usages, between 'polite' and 'vulgar' forms). And familiarity with the newly-defined national Literature, which embodied the standard form, then marked off people of taste, judgement, and refinement from the rest.

That is how aesthetic training is passed off as a natural aptitude, and structural inequalities as individual differences. Children of the bourgeoisie experience the standard or literary language as their own: they learn that they have been speaking prose all their lives. Working-class children, taught the mechanical rules of 'grammar' in school, experience it as an external imposition and also as an exclusion from a superior language and culture: they learn they weren't talking proper.

English Literature and standard English thus form the twin pillars of a supposedly unifying national curriculum: 'unifying' because they claim an encompassing 'Englishness', 'supposedly' because they institute intricate patterns of cultural differentiation. The school curriculum, and its core discipline of English, set in place an academic culture – works that valorize certain categories of representation, perception, thought, and appreciation. They separate out 'culture' as something documentary and evaluative – Arnold's 'best that has been thought and said'. But this definition of 'culture' has to cohabit with another, more descriptive or ethnographic usage of 'culture': the patterns of perception and evaluation subjectively experienced in a set of social relations – Williams's 'whole way of life'. Although incommensurable, these two 'cultures' are intimately linked. The normative or consensual pole of the academic culture does not – cannot – produce an imagined identity. It does, however, produce different (and unequal) dispositions towards it within the lived culture.[4] The academic culture also helps to define the boundaries of the dissensual community that is the nation. The unity of the culture is always, inevitably, fragmented by differences and antagonisms which require strategies of management and containment.

Hence popular schooling, and hence English. In this sense, we have had a national curriculum for more than a century. So why the present fuss? What's new – and what's national – about Mr Baker's curriculum?

One obvious but important point is that strategies don't work. Any plan for popular schooling – usually in response to some immediate problem – always runs into resistances and produces consequences which, in time, themselves require a new strategic response. For Mr Baker, new needs need a new project, even if it is dressed up nostalgically as a return to old certainties. The National Curriculum should therefore be seen in the context of the 'modernization' of schooling – Mr Baker, a former Minister for Information Technology, is as starry-eyed about Britain's hi-tech destiny as he is about its glorious heritage. That is why the introduction of the 'new vocational-ism' into schools and colleges is presented in terms of servicing the labour requirements of industry and production. It does not achieve that, of course, but then that is not what it is designed for. The point is to replace the old idea of education for citizenship and democracy – which involved at least the possi-bility of critical reflection on social and political issues – with a strategy of socialization into the political and ideological imperatives of the enterprise culture. Thus, the new vocationalism turns out to be 'an ideology of production regulating education rather than an educational ideology servicing production' (Moore 1987: 241).

Not everyone is routed through this 'modernizing' in-strumental training. It is not a case of 'out with English, in with Communication Skills'. What we are getting is the new voca-tionalism *and* reassertion of the values of the old English. This reinscription of difference and hierarchy represents the regres-sive face of modernization. Such an uneasy duality also reflects other social changes. The symbolic unity of the nation cannot hold when it is penetrated from outside by multinational cultural industries and information media, and when it is increasingly fragmented internally by cultural differences. The community of the nation just does not figure in the way large numbers of people now imagine their identity and their affiliations (see Gilroy 1987: 247). One reaction to this loss of ideological innocence and certainty has been an anxious, sometimes vicious new Englishness; witness Dewsbury, witness 'anti-anti-racism'. Sadly, Mr Baker seems willing to be at least a fellow-traveller with this. The discussion document on the National Curriculum promises an all-embracing assimilationism: 'all pupils, regardless of sex, ethnic origin and geographical location, [will] have access to broadly the same good and relevant curriculum.' But that does not mean they will all have the same disposition towards it. The institution of the norm secures divisions, hierarchies, and inequalities. For many students, this proposal will mean access to a curriculum which is not only alien and exclusive, but one which obliterates the reality of their cultural formation and experience. 'We do not recognise the colour of the skins of any children in our education service,' said Kenneth Baker in January 1988, to his eternal shame.

Mr Baker also wants to reimpose a pseudo-traditional curriculum to punish the supposed *trahison* of the teaching *clercs*. There has always been a battle of ideas about the purposes of education and, therefore, about the legitimate aspirations and appropriate forms of English teaching. In this battle, and in many of the key institutions within education, the consensus has often run counter to a Tory hegemony.

The differentiation through standardization strategy has been around as long as popular education. Look closely at any of the more thoughtful conservative educationalists and usually you will find that this is what they are on about. Robert Lowe was a long-standing opponent of state-funded popular education until the extension of the suffrage changed his mind. In his *Primary and Classical Education* (1867), he spelt out the cultural and political logic of popular education. The newly enfranchised lower classes, he argued, should 'be educated that they may appreciate and defer to a higher cultivation when they meet it; and the higher classes ought to be educated in a very different manner, in order that they may exhibit to the lower classes that higher education to which, if it were shown to them, they would bow down and defer'. G. H. Bantock, drawing on the cultural thinking of T. S. Eliot, has been insisting for more than thirty years that the health of a culture, understood ethnographically as a way of life, depends on both the differentiation of classes and also their shared membership of the same (national) community. But for him the *evaluative* aspect of culture remains central: in Eliot's words, 'it is an essential condition of the preservation of the quality of the culture of the minority, that it should continue to be a minority culture'. Bantock has therefore proposed two different curricula, with the 'bottom 50 per cent of pupils' being freed from the demands of the academic culture and instead being offered a 'popular education' – Leavisite inoculation against the dangers of the mass media; physical and emotional discipline and expression; domestic studies for girls and technical studies for boys. The logic is taken to its conclusion by Roger Scruton. 'It is not possible to provide universal education,' he proclaims. 'Nor, indeed, is it desirable.' Education, as a privilege and a value, is useful and available only to a limited community of scholars. Others, not to be despised, require different civil institutions to prepare them for their humbler lot.

The shift in the educational centre of gravity from schooling to the new vocationalism suggests that this may well be part of the thinking behind the Baker proposals: education for the minority, socialization for the rest. Whereas these conservative positions start from the needs of the society or the health of the culture, alternatives have generally started from the supposed needs and destiny of the individual child – they are often lumped together loosely (too loosely) as 'progressivism'. Although the genealogy of this strand too can be traced back to the nineteenth century, since the 1950s and 1960s it has been most effectively articulated in the area of English by the London Association for the Teaching of English. The 'cultural heritage' approach was rejected in favour of the emphasis on *language*, focusing on its social, context-bound *use* rather than on any normative system of rules. Language should therefore be treated, the argument runs, as an expressive medium which takes many different and equally valid forms. And this equality of esteem should be extended to the already existing culture of working-class children.

From this acknowledgement of linguistic and cultural diversity, two approaches to English emerged.[5] The progressive strand concentrated on the experience, needs, and interests of individual pupils, expressed in the idea of mixed-ability grouping, in the encouragement of autobiographical writing celebrating working-class family and neighbourhood, and in thematic and project work on social issues. A more radical strand was less concerned to idealize working-class culture and individual experience than to develop a critical perspective on their social and economic determinants and to empower people to change them. Looking back on this early 1970s radicalism a decade later, Mike Simons and Mike Raleigh of the ILEA English Centre suggest that its aim had been 'to inject into the English curriculum the kinds of knowledge and experience which would give working class pupils an understanding of inequality and its causes; the emphasis would be on solidarity rather than upward mobility' (Simons and Raleigh 1981:28).

What is now striking about these approaches is less their post-1960s radicalism than their continuity with earlier forms of English teaching. Compare them with the derided Newbolt Report, for example. If you can see past its loopy jingoism, what it actually recommends is a not unfamiliar pedagogy. The task of English is seen as the ethical formation of both students and their teachers. The teacher is to be a moral exemplar. The child is to be encouraged to realize itself as a 'free' agent within an environment which perpetually monitors his or her actions (King 1987). A non-coercive, experiential pedagogy, with forms of assessment and examination based on the pupil's 'self-expression', were therefore deemed more appropriate than rote learning.

This seems to share with the progressive strand a disavowal of the *power* of the normative language and culture. And how different in practice is it from the 1970s radicalism expressed by Chris Searle?

The English teacher in the schools is probably in the best position to give back to the child his own world and identity in

education, to reaffirm it, to share it himself, support it and
strengthen it.

(quoted in Adlam and Salfield 1980: 82)

The same moralizing imperative is there, the same exemplary
role for the teacher, the same demand that the child 'express' the
'experience' founded in his or her cultural origins within a
morally managed environment (Hunter forthcoming). True, it
substitutes class solidarity for national identity as its preferred
imagined community and switches around the positive and
negative poles, but the cultural poles themselves – and thus the
existing hierarchy of cultural dispositions – are left pretty much
in place.

The 1970s were a long time ago, of course, and we have all
learned to be cannier since then. There is also a better case to be
made for teaching people to 'know their place' subversively, to
understand why things are as they are and how they might be
different. Might this not detonate the explosive tensions con-
tained by the cultural distinctions instituted by the schools?
Could it at least teach people *not* to bow down and defer to the
'higher education' of the bourgeoisie? Wouldn't it strengthen
their subordinate positions and identities as points of resistance? Maybe – but at what cost? Of course, the radicals wanted
social change, but they also wanted social solidarity. The
difficulty lay in reconciling the two aspirations – especially if
upwardness, with its connotations of self-seeking and individualism, was seen as the only direction of individual mobility.

Mobility, often made possible by education, has been a
typical and necessary experience in the formation of many
socialist intellectuals. Gramsci's sensitivity to the *power* of language and education, for example, derived largely from personal experience. Being the only Italian speaker in his village in
Sardinia helped him to win a scholarship to Turin University in
1911, where he studied philology.[6] He knew that there are many
possible grammars or dialects – which may in one sense be
equally 'valid' – but he also insisted that the choice between
them was always 'a political act'. And the choice had to be
made. The important problem for him was not how to celebrate
Sardinian peasant culture and dialect, but how to find forms of
language that would contribute to the construction of a national
popular will.

The same priorities are evident in his ideas about education. The starting point here is, to be sure, the culture and experience of the pupil. But, again, the teacher 'must be aware of the contrast between the type of culture and society which he represents and the type of culture and society represented by his pupils, and conscious of his obligation to accelerate and regulate the child's formation in conformity with the former and in conflict with the latter' (Gramsci 1971: 35–6). This did not imply authoritarian learning – Gramsci knew that the active and self-directed engagement of the student with the skills and often arduous disciplines of the school was crucial.

Perhaps it is unfair to conjure up an image of the young Gramsci confronted by a Chris Searle earnestly trying to 'reaffirm and share' his native world and identity. So take another example from closer to home: that of· Raymond Williams. The experience of mobility was central to all his writing, whether fictional, critical, or political. In *The Country and the City*, he acknowledged, again from his own experience, the claims of community or, to use his word, settlement: 'an identification with the people among whom we grew up; an attachment to the place, the landscape, in which we first lived and learned to see.' The value of this first idea of settlement is 'positive and unquestioned'. He didn't need anyone to reaffirm it or idealize it for him, even though he 'had to move out for an education and to go on with a particular kind of work'.

> I know, in just that sense, what neighbourhood means, and what is involved in separation and leaving. But I know, also, why people have had to move, why so many moved in my own family. So that I then see the idealisation of settlement, in its ordinary literary-historical version, as an insolent indifference to most people's needs.
>
> (Williams 1973: 84)

To take 'experience' seriously means not using it as an epistemological category that supposedly guarantees both the authenticity of knowledge and the coherent, self-conscious unity of subjectivity. To celebrate an essentialized working-class or Black or female 'experience' may mean, in practice, reinforcing the scars and hidden injuries of exploitation and oppression: hence Gramsci's insistence on submitting a

student's experiences to critical scrutiny, and setting the perceptions and beliefs they engender in dialogue with different
conceptual frameworks.

The same applies to notions of 'culture' and 'community'.
This is particularly important now in multicultural and anti-
racist strategies. Some multiculturalists, like the old progres-
sives, still see the problem as one of individual or communal
prejudice, a failure to acknowledge the *diversity* of cultures.
'Cultures' figure in such explanations as finite and self-sufficient
bodies of contents, customs, and traditions. Their argument is a
relativist one: *sub specie aeternitatis*, all cultures are equal and so
they *should* be treated as equally valid in the here-and-now. This
disavowal of the structural inequalities of power in practice
allows the potentially subversive difference of subordinated
cultures to be normalized through the practices of the school.
The 'contents' of other cultures are embraced as part of the
narrative of the consensual English culture, but without disturbing the norms which define its categories, its values, and its
patterns of differentiation. Some anti-racists run a similar risk
to 1970s radical English. Just as that sometimes fell into the
populist trap of fetishizing working-class culture, so some forms
of anti-racism can render cultural difference as ethnic absolutism and cultural separatism. Treating culture as the essential
expression of a particular community, they too leave existing
norms and inequalities pretty much as they were.

This paradoxical outcome flows from the premise that the
needs, interests, and aspirations of any group or community are
repressed by culture. If you start from the principle that it is not
communities that produce culture, but culture (understood as a
complex history of symbolic and institutional practices and
relations) that produces and reproduces cultural identities and
cultural differences, then new options are opened up. The
problem, the field of possibilities, then becomes this *productivity*
of culture and of schooling.

Once, in a discussion about literacy during the early days of the
Soviet revolution, Clara Zetkin suggested that, under the old
order, illiteracy might at least have had the advantage of saving
the minds of peasants and workers from being corrupted by

bourgeois ideas. Lenin responded: 'Illiteracy was compatible with the struggle for the seizure of power, with the necessity to destroy the old State apparatus. Illiteracy is incompatible with the tasks of construction' (Hoyles 1977: 20). The distinction is important because it underlines the *limits* of a purely oppositional or reactive stance. 'Anti-racism' and 'anti-sexism' are absolutely necessary as guiding policy orientations. Their perspective can reveal the divisive and exclusionary side of the national consensus that was the original project of English and which is being resuscitated in the proposals for a National Curriculum. They also call into question the celebration of linguistic and cultural diversity as a plausible alternative. But does that mean English teachers should opt for a purely deconstructive programme of 'critical literacy'? Where is the 'pro' side of anti-racism and anti-sexism? What *about* the tasks of construction?

Near the top of my catalogue of 'great political chances missed by the left' would be the failure to think through the cultural implications of the universalizing and then the comprehensivization of secondary education in post-war Britain. The assumption seemed to be that a common institution would be enough to guarantee a new egalitarianism – at least until Harold Wilson came along to declare that comprehensives would provide 'grammar schools for all' and so ensured the continuation of grammar school and secondary modern curricula under one roof. One person who did try to devise a curriculum conducive to the creation of a 'common culture' was Raymond Williams in *The Long Revolution* (1965): 'we cannot in our kind of society call an education system adequate if it leaves any large number of people at a level of general knowledge and culture below that required by a participating democracy and arts dependent on popular support.' Williams therefore attempted to identify 'the essentials of a contemporary general education'. These he saw as an understanding of ourselves and our physical, social, and cultural environments. His broadly multidisciplinary approach drew in discourses from beyond the existing school curriculum – law, political science, psychology, sociology, art history, architecture and landscape, and so forth. Children were to be given extensive practice in both democratic procedures and the critical use of mass media and information networks. These were not Utopian proposals, Williams insisted, but the ones appropriate to 'the real nature of our society' (Williams 1965: 173–6).

There was little immediate take-up of these ideas, not least because Williams had little to say about how, in the face of vested educational interests, they might be implemented either pedagogically or politically. People increasingly turned back to them, however, when they belatedly began to tackle the question of what a properly comprehensive curriculum might look like. What emerged was the proposal for a 'core curriculum' (Hargreaves 1982: 161ff., 213–14).

That is, of course, where I started: with the relationship of the National Curriculum to the core curriculum. Not surprisingly, Williams's conception was more humane and democratic than Mr Baker's could ever be. He presciently warned that the old forms of schooling and privilege might still give way to 'the free play of the market'. He urged that, instead, they should be replaced 'by a public education designed to express and create the values of an educated democracy and a common culture'. This is Williams at his most irresistibly oracular. Solve this riddle, he implies, and it *is* possible to achieve the full development and self-expression of society and culture as 'the way of life as a whole'. This is a problem. Ian Hunter has made a persuasive case against conceiving popular literary education in these terms, which cultural materialists like Williams and Terry Eagleton share with less progressive 'prophets of culture' like Arnold and Leavis (Hunter 1987 and 1988). It may sound less uplifting to define education as a governmental technique for the 'policing' of a population and the ethical formation of subjects but such disenchanted accuracy may allow for more realistic calculations in devising pedagogic strategies. Education does not 'express or create' social relations, it *is* a social relation.

Another problem with Williams's formulation is that his common culture is more common to some people than to others. It embodies a particular tradition and ideal of British radicalism – a very different community from Mr Baker's Englishness, certainly, but still one held together by a normative pole and defined by its own boundaries of representation. Its claim to consensus also, inescapably, defines the terms of its exclusiveness (Gilroy 1987: 49ff.). Williams proposes a different identity and a different culture; he doesn't imagine identity and culture differently.

Is that possible? Surveying the current state of English, Colin MacCabe optimistically asks: 'is it possible to construct a shared culture on differences rather than identities?' (MacCabe 1987: 8). The answer to the question in this form must be *no*, because it is based on a false premise. Culture is *always* constructed on differences. What matters is how those differences are organized around the norms deployed within cultural technologies and institutions. MacCabe cannot have *both* a postmodernist free play of heterogeneity based on the denial of a normative consensus, *and* a consensual, 'shared' culture.

Following through this line of thought does throw up a surprising paradox, however. For, taken at its word, fuddy-duddy old multiculturalism – that is, a culture that was genuinely multiple and heterodox and therefore nonconsensual – would be nothing less than the social analogue of the postmodernist incredulity concerning norms, foundations, and metanarratives! The idea of a world stripped, both experientially and socially, of the centring narratives of identity would be radically alien to the old certainties imagined in the 'cultural heritage' or the 'cultural diversity' or the 'cultural liberation' models of English. Here neither a national community nor a common culture would be a meaningful aspiration. In such a world, what might education's tasks of construction look like? Perhaps (I hope not) Deleuze and Guattari's schizoliberation from the symbolic? Perhaps Habermas's dialogue free from domination? Perhaps Lyotard's agonistic making of connections across heterogeneous language games? Or, even now, Gramsci's project of cultural hegemony reworked to take account of the fragmentation, and the discursive construction, of both subjectivity and the social?

What emerges, in any case, is a shift of emphasis away from the normative or consensual aspects of culture – order, authority, identity – to the dialogic processes out of which these are formed, and which they precariously organize and contain. This means acknowledging that experience is contingent, that subjectivity is fragmented and that there is no automatic correlation between perceptions, needs, and desires and a person's race, sex, and class. It means recognizing that identity is always historically, politically, and culturally constructed – whether the racist ethnicity of English nationalism or the more plural, less coercive identities emerging from the Black experience of diaspora or from feminism and sexual politics. It demands a new cultural and ideological politics, as Stuart Hall has repeatedly argued, based not on the old assumption of common interests between oppressed groups but on a constant negotiation of alliances around provisional identities – not just identities of interest now, but also of aspiration and desire.[7] This is where the dialogic element comes in: in the discursive construction of such alliances.

This is a politics that recognizes that 'there's no there there' in ethnicity. There are no cultures sufficient unto themselves, only cultural relations always in flux, always generating new alliances, new alignments, new boundaries. In this view, *culture* designates the enunciation of systems of identification and of authority. But, according to Homi Bhabha (1988), this process necessarily produces a split. It articulates the demand for law, tradition, community, a stable system of reference – what I have discussed earlier in terms of consensus and norms. At the same time, however, such certitudes are always being undermined by the articulation of new cultural demands, meanings, and strategies. The tension between these two sides of the split is what constitutes political negotiation.

Could these ideas about *negotiation* and *enunciation* offer a way out of some of the old impasses of educational thought? Might they suggest new strategies for schooling's 'tasks of construction' which avoid the constricting assumption that these must aspire to the perfection and expression of either self or society?

I have tried to expose the puny cultural vision encased in the political juggernaut of the National Curriculum. I have also expressed doubts about some of the available alternatives – cultural diversity, cultural liberation, even the common culture. I have suggested that the dialogic aspects of culture might prove a better guide to rethinking educational policies and practices. But I am not putting up 'the dialogic culture' as the latest contender against the exhausted but still effective old bruiser of

'Englishness'. Rather than play that game, I want to find a new one, or at least to rewrite the rules.

The intractable problem with English as a school subject is that, even when it manages to jettison its prehistoric nationalistic traces, it remains trapped within its sense of being called to a social and cultural mission – whether healing the State or empowering people to escape its oppressions. Its underlying ethic continues to be that, if only you can teach people to use language properly and to respond to texts properly (whichever language, whichever texts, whichever 'properly'), then somehow you will produce a particular subjectivity (the deferent worker, the civilized critic, the working-class hero, the radical intellectual) that will in turn lead to your desired social ends (hierarchy, harmony, transformation). It just doesn't work like that. It is not a question of identifying the right content, but of making much more precise and provisional calculations about how to operate within the institutions of education. That means taking acount of the social relations of schooling, its forms of pedagogy and assessment and its deployment of language and texts, the presuppositions that children bring with them, their fantasmatic negotiations of the school experience, and so forth. All of these are too intractably complex to allow for the smooth symbolic engineering the cultural prophets dream of.

Faced with the prescription of content by the National Curriculum and its policing by national testing, the immediate reaction is bound to be defensive. This should not mean a purely negative strategy, though. It demands a self-critical reassessment of which elements in radical English teaching should be defended, and which need to be transcended. Such work is already going on in individual classrooms and schools. The range of activities described in chapter 3 and elsewhere in this volume marks a break from many of the old essentializing radicalisms. What is significant is not the particular *content* of the teaching: that is provisional and always subject to change as circumstances change. What matters is the strategy underlying their choices. They start from theoretical concepts and semiotic skills rather than from the reaffirmation of individual experience or a given literary canon. They treat language as one semiotic process amongst others and, by placing texts in their historical and institutional contexts, they indicate how the production of meaning is linked to the exercise of power. They offer students a critical familiarity with the techniques of different media. They confront them with a variety of intellectual frameworks for making sense of themselves and the social world.[8]

Such work, although – no, *because* – it eschews false prophecies about saving souls or liberating repressed voices, has a broader political significance. It does not fall into the old trap of substituting English teaching for politics. Rather, it indicates a *specific* strategy for English. In place of Mr Baker's 'return to traditional values', it begins to identify what a comprehensive literacy might look like – that is, the competences, attributes, and skills necessary to engage in the dialogic negotiations of an increasingly diverse, 'democratized' civil society. It then attempts to teach them. And that is enough. The political question is how such a strategy might be articulated to other, equally specific, strategies. The possibility of communality lies in the clatter and strife of those negotiations.

Notes

1 The term is Stuart Hall's: see 'Gramsci and us' (June 1987) *Marxism Today*, 17.
2 On my understanding of 'Englishness', see 'How English is it? Popular fiction and national culture' (1988) *New Formations*, no. 6, London: Routledge.
3 Kenneth Baker's Alan Palmer Lecture, 7 November 1986 (mimeo). I am grateful to Jay Snow for this reference, and for his helpful comments on an earlier draft of this article. On the history of 'Conservative nation' rhetoric, see Bill Schwarz (1986) 'Conservatism, nationalism and imperialism', in James Donald and Stuart Hall (eds) *Politics and Ideology*, Milton Keynes: Open University Press, and (1983) 'The language of constitutionalism: Baldwinite Conservatism', in *Formations of Nation and People*, London: Routledge & Kegan Paul.
4 On the relationship of 'academic culture' to 'popular culture', see Pierre Bourdieu (1971) 'Systems of education and systems of thought', in Michael F. D. Young, *Knowledge and Control: New Directions for the Sociology of Education*, London: Collier-Macmillan, 200–1.
5 For a fuller elaboration of these strands and the relationships between them, see Stephen J. Ball (1985) 'English for the English

since 1906', in Ivor Goodson (ed.) *Social Histories of the Secondary Curriculum: Subjects for Study*, London: The Falmer Press and (1987) 'English teaching, the state and forms of literacy', in Sjaak Kroon and Jan Sturm (eds) *Research on Mother Tongue Education in an International Perspective*, Enschede, Netherlands: International Mother Tongue Education Network.

6   See Jonathan Steinberg (1987) 'The historian and the *questione della lingua*', in Peter Burke and Roy Porter (eds) *The Social History of Language*, Cambridge: Cambridge University Press, 205.

7   Stuart Hall, talk at the '*Black film/British cinema*' conference, Institute of Contemporary Arts, London, 6 February 1988. See also his 'Thatcher's lessons' (March 1988) *Marxism Today*.

8   On the importance of starting with concepts, skills, and competences in multicultural and anti-racist teaching, rather than with content, see Keith Kimberley (1986) 'The school curriculum', in Jagdish Gundara, Crispin Jones, and Keith Kimberley (eds) *Racism, Diversity and Education*, London: Hodder & Stoughton, 104.

Two cheers for liberal education

Alison Light

> My experience of Utopia has convinced me that in taking
> thought for the education of the young it is impossible to
> be too idealistic, and that the more 'commonsensical' and
> 'utilitarian' one's philosophy of education, the shallower and
> falser it will prove to be.
>
> (Holmes: 1911: 177)

Imagine twenty adults sitting around a room trying to think of a
name for a multidisciplinary degree: 'Critical Studies?' – 'too
vague'. 'Urban Studies?' – 'too specific'. 'Combined Studies?' –
'too traditional'. 'BA Humanities?' – 'too dodgy'. After much
deliberation, and precious few jokes, they come up with a
suitably euphemistic and (they hope) temporary title for the
course: 'Integrated Studies'. That, it is felt, is surely an inoffen-
sive appellation. It has the virtue of sounding impressive whilst
giving very little away. With any luck, if they can look incon-
spicuous, people might not notice what it is they actually
do (teach some version, however transformed, of history,
philosophy, English, and geography). Most importantly of all
they might make it into the 1990s.

Such a scene is by no means a caricature of the scramble for
survival which has been taking place in many polytechnic
departments around the country over the last four or five years.
One thing is for sure: 'Humanities' is a dirty word these days.

This kind of institutional hysteria has to be understood, however, in a wider context than the more obvious one of cuts. It is an
atmosphere created by the quite paradoxical nature of the educational policies of Mrs Thatcher's government. Advocating

on the one hand an apparent return to the liberal economics of *laissez faire*, the government has urged that education open itself up to the 'free market'; on the other, it has introduced a much more interventionist style of running the system. Schools and colleges have become subject to endless 'costing' exercises, haggling over every penny, but also to rigorous 'strategic planning' in a series of sweeping directives from above. The debates over tenure, the granting of corporate status to polytechnics, dissevering them from LEAs and turning them into privately operated enterprises, the appearance of 'performance indicators', setting the agenda for the redistribution of funds as well as intending to keep an eye on staff 'efficiency' – all have been elements in this new 'rationalization'. Monitoring and evaluation are the new buzz-words of this pedagogic accountancy. The humanities, like everything else, must either sink or swim with the cash-flow. The frugal balancing of the books, whereby resources are to be magically multiplied by cutting out the 'dead wood', has gone hand in hand with a more global restructuring of educational institutions and the recasting of educational philosophy itself.

Mr Baker's new dispensation combines educational thrift with market segmentation; all the proposals in the Education Bill of 1988 work toward a multi-partitioning of education. Above all, they call in question a moral economy which has underpinned educational reform since the 1944 Act: the establishing of universal provision. The belief in education as a social good and as an opportunity for all reached its climax of hope in the two reports of 1963 – Newsome for secondary and Robbins for higher education. Both envisaged further educational expansion and greater social mobility in a more equal and open society. It is this principle which is being undermined by a return to a 'payment by results' mentality: a cruder and more extensive version of that Revised Code which so riddled nineteenth-century education and against which the early National Union of Teachers fought. Universalism is – in this philosophy – sheer waste. Why bother teaching everyone French or Art when only a few will 'use' it? If you're going to be plumber or a systems analyst (so the argument runs) – you don't need to read poetry or know about Picasso so why waste valuable time learning about them? Time is money, after all.

The educational cloth must be trimmed and stretched; most customers must content themselves with standard fittings. 'Why not try this little number on for size? It's a bit thin round the arts subjects but don't let that worry you. It's not as though you need to have more than one change of clothes. In any case; can't you make do?'

This kind of cut-price tailoring leaves in shreds a whole fabric of idealism. For over a hundred years the foundation of educational values, especially within sixth forms and colleges, has rested on the idea of a 'liberal education'. Liberal education saw itself as being about the formation of character, the learning of values – moral, ethical, aesthetic – 'the inner being' as much as the outer. It believed that education could only be called such when it engaged and involved the full range of human activities and potentialities. Ultimately education was for nothing less than to help us learn how to live and what to live for. Culturally and socially it had a limited sense of what such a 'civilized' life might be, but at its best liberal education had a boundless faith in individual capability, and it allowed for the insight that teaching and learning are cultural processes. Within them all human beings are able to develop and change. Such a language now seems archaic. Yet it was not so long ago that it was possible to argue that the needs of education should transcend the imperatives of the market-place. Such a philosophy has a long and respectable tradition in many cultures, and nowhere more so than in Britain where it has been crucial to the idea of the university since the 1850s.

In fact when the demand for more science and industry-oriented graduates began first to be heard in the early 1960s, the 'white hot heat of technology' produced not a curtailing of the arts but a deliberate and careful supplementing of all 'training' courses with 'Liberal Studies'. Liberal Studies was introduced precisely to counter any fears for what might seem like in-strumentalist leanings – fitting students too closely to precon-ceived notions of their job capacities – in HND, diploma, and vocational courses in the technical colleges, colleges of edu-cation and further education, and later the new 'poly'technics. The vision of the student was a democratic one: ideally all could benefit from both the skills-based learning of more 'technical' subjects, and from exploring other, more discursive and critical modes of inquiry. The creation of 'humanities' departments (as the name implies) institutionalized this resistance to any notion of differential curricula: neither the arts nor the sciences were to be monopolized by any one social group, or any one kind of educational establishment. Where the humanities and Liberal Studies sought to complement the more technological bias of some polytechnic courses, some of the new universities, like Sussex and Keele, taught science students arts subjects in broad foundation years.

The Liberal Studies charter for expansion embodied an expansive view of human potential. It is this generous conception of education which is now being stigmatized as 'wasteful' and dismissed as 'outdated'. For whatever was wrong with the gentle paternalism of its 'pastoral care', liberal education did at least recognize that learning is more than the process of swallowing facts, teaching more than the inculcation of skills. 'Education' must always be in excess of 'training': it is about a critical, dynamic creation of knowledge, not an instrumental measuring of information. Good teaching is more even than good dialogue: it is a dialectical exchange – a two-way process in which adapting to the needs and skills of particular learners is different every time, and produces quite different kinds of knowledge. The passing on of information is actually often the easiest part of the job, one that can take the minimum amount of professional commitment. It may bear very little relationship to real learning, neither does it have much to do with what people value when they look back on their education.

There are no short cuts in education. No amount of managerial wizardry is going to make it a nice little earner. Neither student enthusiasm nor staff commitment can be costed any more than they can be made to measure. Unlike industrial modes of production, education *ought* to be labour-intensive; no one really learns anything in a hurry. Allowing yourself to be waylaid by students in the corridor or even outside the building has rightly been part of the job; knowing more about them than their first names shouldn't be a luxurious extra. Teaching necessarily means having time for different sensibilities, for constant exceptions to the rule. In any case, equality of respect assumes that education is a process of 'bringing people out' and of encouraging them to speak up for themselves. The whole point of education is to change people. The last thing teachers should be doing is keeping them in their place.

Not surprisingly the government's moves are a recipe for the further demoralization of the teaching profession. A whole edifice of commitment to what used to be thought of as vocation is being hammered in to the ground. With the government's 'priorities' teachers become liabilities rather than assets; an embarrassing problem to be managed rather than a resource to be respected. We will inevitably find ourselves de-skilled as the new hierarchies allow for 'performance pay' and the 'incentivizing' of top management (imported from outside); devalued as our range of contributions to the job is judged in purely pecuniary terms. One of the government's most brilliant successes has certainly been to make whole populations of teachers feel guilty about themselves and their activities. Many of us already slink about the place worrying whether the desire to teach Kant or Renaissance painting isn't really a mask for base self-indulgence. Much departmental planning seems to consist in wondering what you can get away with. You might smuggle in a bit of philosophy if you can call it a 'transferable skill'. *Middlemarch* will soon have to be read under brown paper covers.

And there is little sign that the Labour Party is speaking a different language or offering a different vision. It too invokes the 'economic performance' of Japan and West Germany as the models for our education systems of the future; it too assumes that competition, training, and market-orientation is the name of the game: prosperity is the core of the curriculum.[1] When in the past many of us were understandably impatient with the sonorous pieties of liberal education, we argued for modernization and relevance. The chances are that to do so now, is not to find ourselves attacking the complacency of the scholar-gentleman so much as echoing a management theory of education which sees us as either its new technocrats or its docile monitors.

A recall to the values of liberal education is certainly as likely to produce a queasy feeling amongst radicals and teachers on the left as it is amongst conservatives. Liberal education has been the favoured target of a whole generation of teachers and theorists since the late 1960s. Nowhere has that attack been more central than in the pages of the New Accents series. Inspired by a heady mix of Althusserian Marxism, French psychoanalytic rereadings of Freud, and post-Saussurean linguistics, many of us teaching in the humanities have – for over ten years – lambasted the assumptions of liberal education and especially the edifice of English, exposing both as the purveyors of the comfortable social and ideological universe of the English middle classes. Through the attack particularly upon 'Leavisism' (the influence of the work of F. R. Leavis in colleges and schools), the notion of reading as an intrinsically valuable, morally and personally fulfilling task has received a severe pasting. Instead of aiming at the encouragement of 'maturity', recent literary theory has skirted the problematic question of value, textual, educational, or personal, focusing rather upon pluralities of interpretation, the historical context, and the social determinations which limit writers' and readers' understanding.

With the democratic intention of widening the analysis of our culture and our past, we have waged an unstinting assault upon liberal education as backward looking, exclusive, and individualist. Our own projects have indeed seen themselves as new accents; as reforming and modernizing the curriculum, pioneering new areas of study (women's writing, black studies), and dismantling the theocracy of the classics. In the name of the historically specific and the socially shared, collective rather than individual experience, this new wave has asked for studies in the humanities to be accessible to and respectful of different cultural groups; their emphases have fallen upon methodological learning skills, the relevant and the applicable, rather than upon what is argued to be an antiquated set of mandarin sentiments, cut off from 'the real world'.

It is painful for us now to consider how far, in our accusations of liberal education's lack of intellectual rigour, and weak sentimentality, we may have been preparing the ground for a right-wing appropriation of that agenda, setting up the terms in which Tory radicals can begin their own disciplinary procedures. Have the new realists in Mr Baker's think-tank found some of their justificatory arguments in our own earlier proselytization? That the left's zealous attack has had quite different ends in mind does not lessen the difficulty now of our complicity with a reading of educational idealism as a kind of moral and national overspending. Relevance and accountability are key words for all who share some sympathy with the notion that the needs of education are ultimately determined by those of the economy. Not all of the government's policies are ignoble in intention.

If only because we are in danger of mimicking our master's voices we should reconsider the unspoken premises of the relationship between socialist thinking and liberal ideals. If the strongest point of difference from liberal political thinking has been that it ultimately advances individualist notions of people and society, our aim is surely not to deny the claims of human beings to live with a strong sense of their own inner realities – with what has been called a 'soul' in a religious outlook, or more secularly, a 'self', and in another twentieth-century usage, a 'psyche'. Each of these terms, within very different epistemologies, has tried to resist a narrowly empiricist account of the human in which external reality is the sum of existence. Socialism's leading category of 'the social' has frequently dwindled in practice into an unhappy recourse to a collectively ordained 'realism' and one which relegates as in every sense immaterial all those other vocabularies. Yet it can be argued that a species of humanism, even the most idealistic, galvanized many thinkers and activists in the socialist tradition, including Marx himself. Simply to replace the schismatic 'individual and society' with an all pervasive set of social determinations is to leave us not just without a concept of historical agency, but also without an acknowledgement of subjectivity, without ways of theorizing and discussing the inward life of thought and feeling. Any educational policy which does not allow for the autonomy of its human subjects is woefully inadequate. And for the left to leave that linguistic space open, and to evacuate from its own educational accounts a language in which it is proper to talk generously and compassionately about teachers and students as people driven and deceived by all kinds of fancies, is to make room for those wishes to be fulfilled by the kind of dreams which more conservative aspirations have to offer.

The rhetoric of educational monetization will continue to seem realistic to those on the left who never really felt at ease with any kind of attention to 'the private sphere' and whose understanding of liberalism dismisses such concerns as 'bourgeois' distractions, not properly part of a public politics. Collapsing all liberal thought into its tendency towards a

possessive individualism, means that *any* discussion of the
interior world of a human being – needs, fears, hopes, and
dreams – becomes immediately suspect. Many who have been
ill at ease, for example, with some feminists' insistence upon the
'personal' can now breathe a sigh of relief and get back to the
good old 'economic realities'. Yet we are in a better position to
recognize now just how much the individualism of liberal
education helped create the conditions of our own existence as
teachers, as educationists, and the very institutions of the
post-war world which gave birth to such a generation of rebel-
lious progeny. The post-1968 generation have been neither
heroes nor villains but they certainly haven't escaped being
shaped by the conflictual legacy of knowing only the special
years of educational boom. Such particular experience may go
some way to explain the enormous demoralization felt by that
generation teaching in higher education, as well as the painful
migration of many to the more progressive liberal institutions of
the United States.

In our onslaughts upon liberal education we have actually
had very little to say about its missionaries and its pioneering
spirits who set about building a public education system in this
country. We might begin to look more closely at the complexities of liberal thought – which can range from the worst kinds of
nationalistic pieties to the democratic initiatives of those who
argued, much as we are having to do, for the principles of an
egalitarian state education system, and against the mentality of
'payment by results'. For the notion of liberal education is
precisely as old as the notion of a public education system itself
and has gone through many and various forms. Arguments
which attack the 'mistaken idealism' of the educational expansion of the sixties have also to take into account the very effective
idealism of whole generations of primary school teachers, adult
educationists, trade unionists, as well as civil servants and
politicians who couched their campaigns for extending educational opportunity in similar terms. What is so extraordinary
about the 1980s is that it is the first ever period of educational
decline – education has *always* been expanding; indeed this has
been part of its rationale as a state system.

Once we begin to press upon the notion of 'liberal education'
its coherence falls apart in our hands. The strangest of alliances

and cross-fertilizing of interests can be discovered in the arguments for 'humane' education from the 1870s onwards. Many of the university gentlemen and clerics did indeed resist the extension of education 'to the masses', maintaining that man's spiritual well-being depended on education being more than a training for specialized work and was best left in the hands of the cultured few. Equally, however, their arguments – the arguments for a more liberal education – were used by public educators trying to prevent universal education being channelled into pre-industrial instruction. And those progressive teachers who later entered the elementary and grammar schools tried to appeal to many of these ideals in order to infuse the minimalist notion of curriculum with just this liberality of conception (Williams 1961: 125–55).

What about one Edmond Holmes, for example, an inspector (and eventually Chief Inspector of Elementary Schools) from 1875 to 1910, who was also a poet, a Christian, a champion of Walt Whitman, writing love-sonnets and introducing Eastern philosophy in his studies of Buddhism and mysticism. How is he to be neatly characterized? For over thirty years he argued furiously against the payment by results mentality in schools, roundly condemning its 'externalism', the forcing of children onto 'the path of mechanical obedience'. In *What Is and What Might Be* he places his ideal school quite unashamedly in the village of Utopia, and it is 'imaginative sympathy', 'a wide and free outlook', 'self-forgetfulness', 'joy of heart', inquisitiveness, as well as constructiveness which he values in children. The relationship he sees between the State, the teacher, and the child, is as pertinent now as it was in 1911:

> The teacher who is the slave of another's will cannot carry out his instructions except by making his pupils the slaves of his own will. The teacher who has been deprived by his superiors of freedom, initiative, and responsibility, cannot carry out his instructions except by depriving his pupils of the same vital qualities.
>
> (Holmes 1911: 104)

Holmes is speaking as a liberal but these ideals of autonomy, tolerance, and cooperation have been the bedrock of all progressive, including more overtly socialist, educational philosophy.

Ever since the Second World War, the insistence upon personal feeling, response, and sensibility has taken many forms, from the emphasis upon practical criticism within English, to the new designing of infant and primary classrooms as open-plan learning, from the student-centred pedagogies of liberal arts and adult education, to more libertarian demands for deschooling. All have been touched in some way by a faith in 'the individual', all are essentially idealist in conception and humanist in persuasion, refusing to see any human life as cheap, and insisting rather that human potential is always in excess of social and economic determinations. This humanism fuelled generations of teachers, administrators, and educators, from the elementary school to the university system. I wouldn't be writing this now if it hadn't been for the rampant idealism of many of my own teachers in infant and junior school at Penhale Road in Portsmouth, where working-class children were encouraged to develop 'as individuals'. The point is that these teachers believed we were worth encouraging: their language of 'self-fulfilment' did at least acknowledge my existence, assuming that I had a right to express myself and to feel a sense of self-worth. This may indeed be part of a process of 'embourgeoisement', but it helped create for many the possibility of self-respect without which collective politics can be fruitless. Only those who have never known what it is to be relegated to the ranks of the ignorant and the inferior – and to believe yourself to be just that – can afford to sneer at the language of liberal humanism.

As Raymond Williams begins to map in *Keywords*, the idea of the liberal arts emerges with the very notion of a secular education for the free man in feudal society. The word 'liberal' itself carries many connotations before it narrows into the more political meanings of the word in the nineteenth century and certainly before it takes on pejorative overtones for some socialists. Within liberal education there is typically an emphasis upon personal freedom, but equally crucially a stress upon the autonomy of the educational process, its necessary freedom from more direct forms of State or local control. Within this more libertarian conception education can encompass the free-thinking, even the antinomian and the anti-authoritarian. But more importantly its province is the ultimately unaccountable.

The new accents of education in the 1980s leave no space for what in different historical vocabularies has gone under the headings of the moral and ethical, the sentimental and the imaginative, the emotive and the expressive. It cannot deal with education as 'lived relations' except in the most public senses of the structures and demands of the market-place. The expressive arts and the humanities are being squeezed out but with them too an entire language which respected and nurtured the idea of the learner as someone whose inward processes of development we precisely could not account for and certainly not control – that too is vanishing. Not surprisingly, the educational documents of the past decade must be numbered amongst some of the dullest and most inert in history. They demonstrate just how much these other registers are needed in order to communicate, let alone engage or inspire. Such linguistic deadness continues all the way down the line. It already paralyses many new curricula with whole tracks of barren jargon. Without a leavening of those other accents, nothing ferments, nothing can grow – and, as those who like power know only too well, nothing can get out of hand.

There is a sense in which education as an activity may not be about the real world at all, but about past and future worlds, the dreams, fantasies, and imaginings of human beings – about their capacity not simply to live in the real world but to imagine new and better and different ones. If education keeps alive the human freedom to think differently, then in this sense the seventeenth or the twelfth or the fifth century BC are as 'relevant' as the twentieth. For education to be educational, as many have claimed in many different times and cultures, it should deal not with the immediate and the applicable but with the curious and the gratuitous, the random and the heterodox, the perverse and the apparently useless. In fact there is precisely no way of knowing what might be the most useful: Tories should surely appreciate that the makers of the British Empire took their models from the classics not from the nineteenth century. We might want to argue that any education worth its name (and often despite itself) fosters the unpredictable, the wayward not the familiar, the untethered not the bound. Perhaps the better educated are still the most unworldly of people. Hitching our curricular wagon to the star of 'contemporaneity' we are inevitably chasing an illusion. There is not an undisputed real world which we (like so many sorcerer's apprentices) fit people to – they already are in the real world and they already are fitting it for themselves.

Certainly we should be wary of those – whatever their political persuasion – whose watch-word is accountability to 'reality'. Reality has an obstinate tendency to refuse to obey orders without a certain amount of indelicate persuasion. Already we've seen that the appetite for proscription and sacking within education can be whetted right across the political board. 'Rationalization' tempts left-wing machiavels too; here's a chance at last to get rid of (in the words of one of my own colleagues) the 'morons' and the 'cretins' – namely, those with a background in teacher-training – who have 'obstructed' higher education for so long. Those who favour the hard line will no doubt be at home in their managerial niche, vociferously opposing government policies whilst exhibiting in departmental meetings distinctly Bonapartist tendencies. The hard line isn't any less inhumane for being ours, though it may be a ready and reassuring way of feeling that we're getting something done. As a reaction to authority it is necessarily authoritarian.[2]

Finally, one irony is worth pondering further: what should we make of the fact that as the glorious opportunities for business studies, industrial training, and vocationalisms increase, so too does the demand for all those other disappearing 'expressive' subjects. It seems that thousands of sixth formers want nothing better than to read novels and listen to music. For those of us carrying on in 'State' education, this is at once a heartening and a disturbing omen. What, I wonder, will they have in mind when they say to their own children – 'I want you to have an education'?

Notes

1   See, for example, the tenor of the discussions of 'oppositional' educational policy in the *New Statesman* series which began in September 1987.

2   For a moving fictional account of (amongst many, many other things) the experience of *realpolitik* in school teaching, read Graham Swift's novel (1983) *Waterland*, London: Picador.

3

But is it English . . . ?
the National Curriculum and
progressive English teaching

Sabrina Broadbent and Ros Moger

During the past forty years the London Association for the Teaching of English (LATE) has been an active participant in the debate over secondary school English. The work of Jimmy Britton, a founding member of LATE in 1947, and other LATE colleagues, Douglas Barnes, John Dixon, Nancy Martin, and Harold Rosen offered a challenging alternative to the 'cultural heritage' model of English teaching. The confident emphasis on the role of language in learning and the constant encouragement given to children's talk and writing helped to redefine English as a school subject in comprehensive schools of the 1960s and 1970s and continues to influence the practice of English teachers today.

Sometimes characterized as the promoter of a London-based 'new orthodoxy', LATE has attempted to focus on theoretical and practical issues which spring directly from the experience of teachers working with London children. The list of LATE conference titles over the last decade runs from *Exams* (1978), through *Race, Society and School* (1980), *Language and Continuity* (1981), *Through Women's Eyes* (1983), *Race, Class and Language* (1984), *Schools-English-Sexuality* (1986), and *Popular Culture* (1987) to *English after 16* (1987). In amongst these we have spent a good deal of time on the 'staples' of English teaching: talk, writing, and reading, with increasing attention paid to the practical applications of literary theory.

Examinations and assessment have occupied much conference and working party time. It is in this area that LATE has been able to exercise some corporate influence by providing a voice for English teachers who wished to ensure that the new GCSE syllabuses reflected their classroom practice and acknowledged their expertise as assessors. This expertise has been gained over the last decade of painstaking negotiation with local London CSE examination boards to establish the validity of coursework assessment. By 1983 the principle and practice of assessment through a folder of writing rather than a final examination had been established sufficiently to enable a consortium of schools to operate a 100 per cent coursework CSE syllabus which had been written and submitted by three classroom teachers. This syllabus allowed students to include for assessment a wide range of language activities from literature-based work, through work generated by study of the mass media, to the study of language itself. The syllabus immediately attracted interest and support from many schools because it provided a way of validating the regular activities of English classrooms across London. It also enabled departments already using the 100 per cent coursework JMB (Joint Matriculation Board) O level syllabus to teach mixed ability fourth and fifth year groups, deferring as late as possible the invidious decision about CSE and O level entry.

Against the background of this development, the introduction of a joint 16-plus examination, in the form of the GCSE, seemed for many English teachers to be a very positive step. With much practical experience of syllabus design, revision, and coursework assessment behind us, it looked as if we might finally have the opportunity to harmonize classroom practice and assessment through an examination which would give every student, of whatever ability, the chance to have their work assessed on a common scale. As English teachers across the country grapple with the realities of trial marking meetings and the demands of the examination boards the full implications of coursework assessment become clearer. Not only is it hard work and a nerve-racking responsibility, it exposes much more of the student and the teacher for evaluation than ever before.

These issues will require serious consideration in the future, but we also need to hang on to a sense of the distance we have travelled, for at the beginning of the last round of the GCSE debate, London English teachers found themselves negotiating with a university examining board which was far from convinced about the appropriateness of coursework assessment. To persuade it to drop its much vaunted multiple choice O level format took several years of discussion and lobbying, and in this LATE played a major part by organizing conferences for teachers to discuss the draft stages of the syllabus and by compiling comments and responses to be passed back to the Board.

In the current climate it is likely that LATE's lobbying function will become increasingly important, although it was with dismay that we witnessed the setting up of a national enquiry into English teaching in January 1987 without representatives from LATE or the national association, NATE. This committee of enquiry was established to recommend

> a model of the English language, whether spoken or written which would;
> (i) serve as the basis of how teachers are trained to understand how the English language works;
> (ii) inform professional discussion of all aspects of English teaching.
> — the principles which should guide teachers on how far and in what ways the model should be made explicit to pupils, to make them conscious of how language is used in a range of contexts.
> — what, in general terms, pupils need to know about how the English language works and in consequence what they should have been taught and be expected to understand on this score at age 7, 11 and 16.
>
> (DES 16 January 1987)

In announcing the appointment of Sir John Kingman as chair of this committee, Mr Baker said:

> I am working towards national agreement on the aims and objectives of English teaching in schools in order to improve standards. But I have been struck by a particular gap. Pupils need to know about the workings of the English language if

they are to use it effectively. Most schools no longer teach old-fashioned grammar.

But little has been put in its place. There is no common ground on teaching about the structure and workings of the language, about the way it is used to convey meaning and other effects. We need to equip teachers with a proper model of the language to help improve their teaching.

I am setting up this high-powered committee to advise me on this. It will start work shortly and report to me within a year. The members will be announced shortly and will be drawn from some leading exponents of the English language, including poets and authors, as well as linguistic experts, teachers and others.

(DES 16 January 1987)

A full page in the *Daily Telegraph* of 13 May 1987 was devoted to the Kingman Committee's progress so far. Some committee members felt free to talk to the press well before the final submission of the report. Not surprisingly, their comments reinforced our fears that the whole exercise would be backward looking, narrow, and ill-informed. A teacher's failure to correct a pupil's grammar when talking to one of the committee in a city school 'full of ethnic minority children' was thought, for example, to be 'very dangerous because it could create a sort of underclass': a view demonstrating an alarming ignorance of the recent wide debate about language, class, and power.

In the event, the Kingman report attempted to discover a middle way between two supposed extremes of English teaching: 'old-fashioned grammar teaching and learning by rote' and teaching which assumes that any 'notion of correct or incorrect use of language is an affront to personal liberty'. The result is a muddled and confused document, open to many different readings. Mr Baker's preferred reading is that it is 'an interesting report which will contribute to discussion about the teaching of the English language and about the importance of the grammatical structure of the language and of the correct [sic] use of the spoken word' (DES 29 April 1988). In his brief to the working group on English chaired by Professor Brian Cox he wilfully rewrites Kingman, instructing the group to 'build on' the recommendations for attainment targets at 7, 11, and 16 with the emphasis on 'the grammatical structure of the English language' (DES, Terms of Reference 29 April 1988). There is a desperation in the tone here as Baker struggles to restate the terms of reference in order to bring about the educational programme which Mrs Thatcher has had in mind since she came to power.

It seems unlikely that either report will be adopted in detail. What, even so, Kingman failed to describe and Baker ignores in his instructions to Cox, is an account of the English curriculum as it is experienced now, in many schools, on any given day. A first-year class for instance, might be discussing cultural assumptions and narrative forms through the reading of folk-tales and fairy stories, using simple deconstruction strategies. A second-year class might be considering the publicity and marketing of a class reader or its adaptation for television while a third-year group plan and draft pieces for a poetry anthology to be used in primary schools. In the fourth year, language itself might be under discussion with pupils exploring regional and historical shifts in dialect. Fifth years might be involved in Literature Open Studies; exploring the genre of crime fiction or comparing a Hardy novel to a work of contemporary popular fiction. In the sixth form GCSE mature students might be analysing the representation of children in television advertise-ments. CPVE (Certificate in Pre-Vocational Education) stu-dents might be writing an account of their work experience. An A level class might be reading a Hemingway short story from the perspective of a number of critical stances; Leavisite, post-structuralist, feminist, or psychoanalytical. None of this is spectacularly radical, but these and many other approaches contribute to an English curriculum which, at its best, is both rigorous and flexible, challenging and responsive to the needs of its students.

It is with this kind of curriculum in mind that we turn to Mr Baker's suggestions. The consultation document allows for 10 per cent of the school timetable to be given to English. This represents four 35-minute lessons. On a purely practical level it would be extremely difficult to maintain the wide variety of activities encouraged by good English teachers within this time allowance and quite impossible to offer the chance to obtain the three separate certificates currently offered in most schools:

English, Oral Communication, and English Literature. This neat arithmetical division of the school week; 10 per cent for Maths, 10 per cent for English, and 20 per cent for Science is symptomatic of the whole document but the allowance for English does suggest either complete ignorance of the scope of current English teaching or a more sinister intention to confine English teaching and force literature out to the optional edges of the curriculum where it would have to compete with all the rest of Mr Baker's marginalized subjects. The upshot of this is quite obvious: English Literature would become again the choice for a small minority.

Ignorance flavoured with political determinism characterizes the curriculum discussion document. Even as we write, the terms of the debate are shifting almost daily because whoever speaks on it seems to give some new interpretation, adding or denying various details. It is tempting to think that the rules are being made up as they go along and that there is no coherent plan except the dismantling of state education. As it stands in its consultative form, arts subjects are marginalized by allocating them only 10 per cent of the school week. Thus Art, Music, Drama, and Design would be forced to compete for the same space on the timetable. Totally absent are: Media Studies, Peace Studies, Social Studies, Economics, Political Studies, and anything else that might cross traditional subject boundaries.

Baker's plans for the National Curriculum appear to be motivated by a nostalgia for an education system that dealt with discrete subjects. Encapsulated within this rigid and limited diet is a utilitarian view of the whole learning process which dismisses much of the educational thinking of at least the last fifteen years and, more specifically, some of the findings and recommendations of the DES 5–16 Report of 1984. In this document, schools are encouraged to redefine the traditional basic subjects so that children are given the opportunity to experiment, design, invent, enquire, select, and evaluate evidence and draw conclusions. In contrast to this, the National Curriculum speaks of 'programmes of study which include the key content, skills and processes which (children) need to learn' and 'to secure for all pupils in maintained schools [sic] a curriculum which equips them with the knowledge, skills and

understanding that they need for adult life and employment'
(DES, *The National Curriculum 5-16*, 1987: 3).

What concerns us as socialist teachers is the nature of this
adult life envisaged by Baker and his colleagues. It is no
accident that the 'studies' subjects are absent from Baker's
curriculum and that the areas of curriculum development
which have taken teachers and students across subject boundaries are not acknowledged at all, for it is precisely in these areas
that real enquiry and open-ended learning is made possible.
Similarly, it is often within those areas of the curriculum which
fall under the 'studies' heading that real critical analysis of our
society takes place. Baker's document is obviously interested in
creating a depoliticized, 'neutral' curriculum and in view of
Clause 28 in the Local Government Bill concerning materials
promoting homosexuality, it seems possible that teachers' freedom to discuss difficult human issues relating to gender may be
curtailed. Baker's recognition that education is indeed a potent,
political force which must be curbed and directed leads us to
wonder how long it will be before similar sanctions are applied
to the areas of class and race in schools. In the back of many
teachers' minds is the growing fear that we are approaching an
era of book burning. Over the last few years it has been possible
to encourage an enthusiasm and independence in reading by
introducing a wide range of texts reflecting the cultural diversity
of our classrooms. Have we got to defend, all over again, the
place of books which raise questions and allow discussion about
gender, race, and class? Or worse, will the atmosphere of
distrust and fear promote an internalized self-censorship?

The proposed National Curriculum offers a blueprint for an
education system that can be delivered, policed, and made safe
for all but those who can afford to buy themselves out of it. Mr
Baker is proposing a political curriculum which has grown out
of the hysteria over 'loony left' local authorities; a hysteria that
has been heightened and orchestrated largely by the press. We
find ourselves in a climate where progressive, imaginative, and
effective teaching has become the scapegoat for all that is wrong
with education and the world, while boring, uninspired, and
irrelevant teaching, though thoroughly documented by Her
Majesty's Inspectorate, attracts no political comment. The
teaching profession's own fight to professionalize and maintain

standards has similarly been presented by the government and press as further evidence of irresponsible left-wing behaviour which must be eradicated. Allowing boroughs to opt out will create a dangerous vacuum of expertise and experience which the government has no plans to fill. Its reasons are themselves political. Behind the deceptively harmless appeals to parental choice and local democracy lie motives of political revenge and class advantage.

The consultative document acknowledges that 'There must be space to accommodate the enterprise of teachers, offering them sufficient flexibility in the choice of content and to adapt what they teach to the needs of the individual pupil, to try out and develop new approaches, and to develop in pupils those personal qualities which cannot be written into the programme of study or attainment target' (DES 1987: 11). That unfortunate phrase 'accommodate the enterprise of teachers' belies the lack of appreciation of the way the curriculum has developed over the last twenty years. Most of the exciting innovations at classroom level have of course been generated by teachers collaborating with other teachers, often supported by the Schools Curriculum Development Council or Grant Related In-Service Training. There is something insulting about the suggestion that such enterprise has to be 'accommodated' but we should not be surprised when the whole document is based on the premise that curriculum innovation can be imposed from the top through legislation. Should there be any doubt about it, the 'delivery' of the National Curriculum is to be policed by a cumbersome system of assessment which will give the government a set of statistics, educationally facile though they may be, which can then be used against local authorities, schools, and even individual teachers.

The assessment plans themselves rest upon two assumptions, neither of which has any solid evidence to support it. Firstly, it is claimed that the introduction of regular and externally set tests provides a 'proven and essential way towards raising standards of achievement' (10). The English teaching profession can only conjecture as to the origins of these claims, but we are aware of much evidence to the contrary. The saying that babies do not get heavier by being weighed was coined some years ago in a different political climate but it remains just as pertinent.

Everyday classroom experience confirms that regular testing is more likely to reinforce failure than encourage improvement. Those of us who came through the 11-plus selection procedure know very well the effect that failure had on us and our peers and we know as teachers that children thrive on the recognition of their achievements. The second assumption is that universally standardized tests are feasible. If children learned in a linear, age-related fashion, and brought with them similar cultural experience and expectations, then it might just be possible to provide some kind of common test. Even then, all one is likely to discover is which children are good at taking tests. Most English teachers working with mixed ability, banded or streamed groups, have found that development is often unrelated to age. Attempts to work out hierarchies of skills in English have proved extraordinarily difficult, often involving rather absurd but revealing squabbles over lower and higher order of skills. For example, the Draft Grade Criteria for English published by the Secondary Examinations Council in September 1985 identify a C/D grade in terms of a candidate being able to 'give a coherent account of both actual and imagined experience'. A grade A/B candidate would be expected to 'give a coherent and perceptive account of both actual and imagined experience'. The implicit subjectivity in the word 'perceptive' illustrates the problem.

Without some knowledge of the kind of testing the assessment group has in mind it is pointless to conjure up the spectre of 'basic skills' testing, though the curriculum document certainly implies an acquisition model of learning and we suspect that it is really only 'basic skills' which could be assessed in any unified form. Interestingly and encouragingly, the first report from the Task Group on Assessment and Testing set up by Baker in 1987 and chaired by Professor Paul Black, seems to reflect the same anxiety. Published at the time of writing, the report appears to endorse the belief that good assessment should be formative, providing information to help the pupil to improve, rather than a purely summative statement at the end of the course. It also argues that assessment should be 'the servant, not the master of the curriculum, an integral part of the educational process' (*TES* 15 January 1988:6). The writers of the report recognize the need to move away from the notion of a test as 'an externally-prescribed paper and pencil test, formal and unimaginative in scope, to be attempted in a set time on a formal occasion and marked according to set rules' (ibid.). This at least sounds as if Professor Black and his team have been talking to teachers. The report is also aware of the need to recognize and support pupils' achievement and is informed by a wider understanding of the learning process and children than the curriculum document. There are already signs that Baker, and more importantly, Mrs Thatcher find these considerations unacceptable but even if this more enlightened tone is incorporated into the final system, teachers will still need to be concerned about the sheer weight of preparing and administering a continuous national assessment system, and about its effects on the curriculum and students.

What teachers fear most is the move towards a test-directed, test-orientated curriculum. The implications of this for pupils have not been thought through sufficiently. First to be penalized would be all those children with special educational needs. If they are to be exempted from the demands of the curriculum then their 'specialness' will be confirmed for ever. If they are not then they are likely to face the negative effects of early and repeated failure. The whole movement towards the integration of children with learning difficulties, tied as it is to the effort of making the curriculum more accessible to all pupils, is likely to be undermined by the introduction of Baker's national assessment procedures. Children with learning difficulties are not the only ones likely to be affected by the changes for there are very serious implications for all those children for whom English is a second language. For them, age-related tests may be discouraging at key points in their linguistic development. Other children likely to be at a disadvantage are those whose culture is neither reflected nor valued in the test itself. There is also the gritty problem of sex differentiation in school achievement. Gender differences in achievements in maths and sciences are well known but gender differences in English achievement are not so commonly debated in public. As Margaret Sandra reports:

> Whilst girls, on the basis of examination results, are judged to do badly on the maths/science area, little attention seems to have been paid to the excellent results achieved by girls in English. Over 45,000 more girls than boys passed English

Language 'O' level in 1979 and repeated this success in Literature 'O' level by just under 40% extra passes. This was on an entry percentage difference of approximately 9% in both examinations.

In CSE the results are even more compelling:

Entry girls	279,550	Grade 1	51,280
Entry boys	281,706	Grade 1	30,949
			(Sandra, 1981: 8)

It is one of the murkier details of both the old 11-plus scoring system and the ILEA's banding system that the verbal reasoning scores of boys were statistically compensated to ensure a balanced entry at 11 because boys score less well than girls. Only relatively recently has the ILEA dropped this procedure. It is significant that the Task Group 'recommends steps for dealing with gender and ethnic bias in assessment' (*Education and Science News*, 1988). Without resorting to statistical compensation, Mr Baker might find himself saddled with some awkward scores. Of course, it is high time that the underachievement of boys was exposed and discussed, but this needs a more constructive context than is available at present.

The final insult to all teachers is that the government's proposals imply that we simply have not been assessing children's progress all these years. Within a school context there are several reasons for needing clear assessment procedures:

to diagnose pupils' understanding and competences in ways which can inform teaching and encourage learning.

to describe the achievements of individual pupils to parents.

to provide summative information at the end of compulsory education.

English teachers already assess all aspects of reading, writing, listening, and talking during a pupil's five years in secondary school. In the best of English classrooms there is a regular dialogue between teacher and pupil and a growing awareness of the importance of self-assessment in the learning process.

The question of what should be taught in our schools has been made a political issue by the National Curriculum document. It is now important for us to keep open the debate about curriculum content and to extend that debate to include questions of pedagogy. We must keep on the agenda the discussion about the kind of classroom practice most appropriate to a democracy, and be prepared to explain and promote our philosophy and practice. All our pupils should have access to a curriculum which enables and empowers, and which has English at its core because English can be critical, reflective, and responsive to the diverse needs of the children in our classrooms. Such a curriculum must be enacted through classroom practice which does more than transmit skills and knowledge; it must give all pupils the opportunity to be active participants in the learning process. The Conservative government's attack on state education means that LATE and NATE will have to play a more overtly political role in asserting the achievements of pupils and teachers over the last forty years.

4
Future imperfect? English and the new vocationalism

Jenny and Phil Rice

A few years ago it was common to read of 'the crisis in English Studies'. Today it could be argued that the critical theories which largely engendered that crisis have become an established part of the landscape. But while the map of English Studies is being redrawn to incorporate theory, another crisis lies on the horizon; one that is set to revolutionize the subject far more radically. Government initiatives that are already affecting secondary and further education will soon be applied to the higher education sector and departments of English Studies will not be exempted. We would argue that lecturers in higher education need to open up a dialogue with those in further education who have already faced the new initiatives. They have responded by developing progressive modes of teaching from which much can be learnt.

Initiatives such as TVEI (Technical and Vocational Education Initiative), CPVE (Certificate in Pre-Vocational Education), and GCSE are currently transforming teaching in further education and in schools and are rapidly assuming the status of a new orthodoxy, the 'new vocationalism'. That orthodoxy is now to be extended into higher education through, on the one hand, government legislation and on the other, a multiple funding policy. The Government White Paper 'Higher education: meeting the challenge' (HMSO 1987) makes it clear that the rationale for higher education will be driven largely by the needs of the economy and the ideology of enterprise culture. It is explicit about the 'aims and purposes' of higher education; it should 'serve the economy more effectively', 'pursue basic scientific research and scholarship in the arts and humanities', and 'have closer links with industry and commerce, and promote enterprise' (iv). With regard to the arts and humanities, it 'fully recognizes the value of those areas of learning and scholarship which have at most an indirect relationship to the world of work' (1). Such statements seem to be anticipating a need for reassurance rather than signalling any tangible financial commitment; the main thrust of the paper is obvious, 'above all there is an urgent need for higher education to take increasing account of the economic requirements of the country' (2).

Since 1981, as we know, there have been extensive cuts in budgets, and contractions in levels of staffing. Government is looking more and more for contributions from industry and commerce. But it is also changing the basis of funding in a way that will give them much more control over what is resourced. As well as transferring polytechnics and colleges away from local government, making them corporate bodies which will 'permit greater responsiveness to economic needs' (2), the University Grants Committee has been reconstituted as the University Funding Council, membership of which 'will include a strong element of people from outside the academic world' (2). Additionally, more directed methods of funding according to Government imperatives come in such forms as MSC (Manpower Services Commission) money; and that money is closely tied into the educational initiatives that have already set the agenda for teaching in the further education sector:

> The new MSC Enterprise Programme announced last week, under which universities, polys, and colleges will be offered up to £1million each to establish the provision of management and business learning for all their students, was described by Mr Holland [the then director of the Manpower Services Commission] as 'taking the example of TVEI into higher education'.
>
> (*TES* 30 October 1987: 10)

These £1 million inducements to make teaching more relevant to commercial needs and responsive toward enterprise skills are conceived in relation to the new initiatives; the funding aspect ensures that response is made in terms of constructing the right course emphases. In the face of this, departments in higher education will be expected to put together packages which look like they address the new educational imperatives of enterprise, business skills, and links with industry as well as the educational rationale of schemes like TVEI. But how will English manage, given its present curriculum?

In further education English is already in the process of transforming to respond to the new initiatives and their stress on 'relevance'. Not the relevance to 'life', as we might have seen in the 1960s, but relevance with its 1980s connotations, as in 'relevance in meeting the demands of the modern world' (as the Government Green Paper 'Better schools' describes it) – that is, relevance to the demands of the market and enterprise. The imperatives have had the effect of relocating teachers with an English base into new courses, where they teach 'core skills'. English as a subject is transformed into English as a functional skill with the stress laid on communicative competence. Literature with a capital 'L' hardly figures in this future.

English Studies in higher education cannot realistically hope to escape the imperatives embedded in the new initiatives. If they make little or no response then the future they can look forward to will be one of increasing contraction to the point where a few courses, run in a few of the 'better' universities, can fulfil the limited functional role of guardians of 'the best that has been thought and said', given the task of dusting down our national literary heritage in a concession to civilized and cultural values. If English is to avoid such a future then how is it to respond? Can it adapt its curriculum to address the new initiatives? The problem for English Literary Studies is that, in the final instance, it is an 'object knowledge', the object of its knowledge being the literary text (or, in some revised versions, the cultural text/cultural artifact). The new initiatives are new because of the emphasis they place on process skills rather than object knowledge, that is to say they deal in the skills and competences that enable the production of knowledge, amongst other equally important things such as competence in communicating; the objects of knowledge are secondary. In the new vocationalism, process is at the centre; it is process that is the object sought, teaching students not knowledge about, but how, amongst other things, to get knowledge. If English Studies in higher education is to survive at its current level than it will need to adopt strategies that will address this difference and to quite radically redirect a significant portion of its teaching and its rationale.

Of course, it could be argued that this is all a result of Thatcherite and New Right policy, and if we just play a game of resistance where possible and sit it out till a more sensible government gets into power, then a more reasonable educational rationale will prevail. This is not a viable response, firstly because current projections suggest a Tory majority that will last until the next century, and more importantly, because it misrecognizes the basis on which change is being forged. It is too easy to blame the situation on Thatcherite ideology and Tory government policy; the impulses behind the educational initiatives that seem to be introduced by and for Thatcherism extend beyond Thatcher, beyond party politics, indeed beyond the parochial, national terms within which much of the debate has been framed. These changes are related to a series of shifts in the order of things in the contemporary world. Recognition of a new order is signalled by the mythic weight carried by such key phrases as 'postmodernism', 'the third wave' (Toffler 1980), 'the new world information and communications order' (Mattelart, Delcourt, and Mattelart 1984), and 'postindustrialism'. The world is changing along the lines of a Foucauldian discontinuity; we are witnessing a shift in the episteme, and education has to re-evaluate itself to meet the new conditions.

These changes might have been given a particular inflection by Thatcherism which we find unwholesome but it is an inflection, not the sole determinant of the changes. The new vocationalism has been couched in the Thatcherite rhetoric of enterprise culture, with its objectives set around self-interest and self-motivation and an emphasis on self-achievement and self-reliance, but the situation that the new vocationalism confronts and attempts to deal with is a situation in which the workforce increasingly requires flexible and transferable skills in order to operate in the employment market-place. Initiative, setting one's own objectives, flexibility, positive attitudes, and self-presentational skills are, at one and the same time, the skills needed in the market-place and an expression of the ideology pertinent to that situation. The agenda is being set not by the needs of young people, nor by the needs of the workforce, but by capital and by a market-place that will increasingly be divided into periphery and core workers:

> A guaranteed job for life is and will increasingly become a thing of the past. Instead what we will increasingly see is the development of the core worker/periphery worker dichotomy. The core workers will be multi-skilled, flexible, and have firm specific knowledge. They will be valued for their functional flexibility particularly in regard to changing technology. The peripheral workers on the other hand will be fairly homogeneous with low skill levels who will be required to provide numerical flexibility in the face of fluctuations in production or demand.
>
> (Hamil and O'Neill 1986: 320)

Both sectors of the workforce will need, then, flexible and transferable skills at some level; core workers as an integral part of their jobs, peripheral workers to enable them to move between different jobs. The new vocationalism attempts to address this situation. Whether we find this acceptable or not simply isn't at issue; we will all be forced to confront it. While much of the Thatcherite inflection can be noted in the rhetoric in which such initiatives are couched, and indeed in some of the effects generated by such rhetoric, it has to be recognized that new modes and directions in training and education did not simply arrive on the scene in 1979.

The introduction of the new form of vocational education into this context is complex and cannot be seen only in the framework of party politics. To begin with it was a Labour government which introduced YOPS (Youth Opportunity Scheme) after the Holland Report suggested that 'all young people should have access to some form of post-school education and/or training' (Munby 1978: 185); and Len Murray later backed TVEI with the reported comment that 'the education system did not need one short, sharp shock but several' (Owen 1984: 11). The development of vocational education has had much cross-party backing but that is not to say that such initiatives were not recognized as ideologically suitable to Thatcherism; rather, elements of them were found to suit varying political persuasions. Not only the government, but others, including educationists, have helped lay the foundations of the new vocationalism.

It had been recognized some time before the 1980s that types of vocational education would have to be introduced to encourage the group of non-academic 16–19 year olds to gain some form of skilling and training. It was also recognized that it was no longer suitable to 'apprentice' somebody with the view to doing the same job for life, firstly because there were fewer jobs and secondly because it was unlikely that occupations would remain static. What was needed was an approach to vocationalism concentrating on breadth – one that recognized that it was important to train people to take up wider opportunities and be able to move from one area to another, as and when work became available. Skills that had once been learned exclusively in order to practise one occupation were now seen as unproductive for a workforce that needed to extend over a wide range of occupations. Thus 'skills teaching' had to be reassessed, with the result that the skill itself, and the object knowledge that went with it, lost some of its importance in favour of teaching how skills could be made transferable across the job market. The emphasis now in any skills curriculum is placed on 'transferable' skills; and with the boundary between skills and knowledge breaking down, the concept of transferable skills is beginning to be considered in the more academic courses, such as English. This has not been a sudden development but can be traced through a number of educational initiatives.

The area of education that has offered most to this development has been what is commonly called pre-vocational education. This has its roots in a host of pre-employment courses, but it came to fruition in the common objectives proposed by the Mansell Report to the Further Education Unit (FEU) in 1979 and published as *A Basis for Choice* (ABC). These courses would attempt to meet the lack of provision for a section of the 16–19 year olds who were neither concerned to follow an academic career nor had decided on a particular vocation. This was built on by the DES who, in October 1980, published a consultative document *Examinations '16–18'*. This proposed that there should be an examination for the 17-plus group who were not catered for at the time. It would concentrate on helping students in the transition from school to work and be vocationally orientated. It considered that *ABC* would provide the most favourable foundation for the development of pre-vocational courses. The suggestions of *ABC* were incorporated in some pilot schemes and their success was reported in *ABC in Action* in which these courses were said 'to motivate young people who have been "turned off" by conventional academic courses' (FEU 1981: para. 26).

Meanwhile the MSC were themselves developing schemes which emphasized similar proposals. They had already looked at the idea of transferable skills (*Grouping of Skills* 1975) to promote 'occupational mobility in order to remain competitive in a rapidly changing world' (FEU 1981: para. 55). By 1981 the FEU had published *Vocational Preparation* which drew together the work of both pre-vocational courses and MSC-led schemes and suggested that they could both use the proposals of *ABC* for the common core. Furthermore when MSC presented its 'Task report' to the government in April 1982 it was clear that it wanted schools to concentrate on vocational preparation in the pupil's last years; education and training – though not for the first time since 1944 – were being pulled together.

The government meanwhile were working on the ideas in the paper *Examinations '16–19'* and in 1982 published their proposals for the new qualification in *17+ A New Qualification*. It reiterated their earlier promise to provide further education for those 16–19 year olds who had no definite academic or vocational plans. This they named the Certificate in Pre-Vocational Education, and it would they believed give 'more effective preparation for working and adult life [and] . . . help more young people to find a suitable job when they leave full-time education and improve their performance in employment' (DES 1982: 2). It recognized that there would be common elements in CPVE and YTS training programmes. To add to the development of prevocational courses, the government rather abruptly announced TVEI to the House of Commons in November 1982. TVEI is funded by MSC and so with TVEI we have the link between training and education, which existed more tenuously between CPVE and YTS, made explicit. TVEI has now almost come to the end of its pilot phase and is being extended into the 1990s. All 14–18 year olds, in certain authorities, will have the opportunity for an education based to a large extent on the proposals of *ABC* with an added emphasis on new technology and links with industry. These links are also being encouraged between teaching staff and the business world. In 1982 PICKUP was announced to make 'lecturers and teachers familiar with the need for better links between education, training and work' (Owen 1984: 2).

These, then, are some of the educational initiatives that have recently taken place especially in courses set up for 'low achievers'. They are now beginning to filter into the more traditional academic areas of education including English. Before looking at the effects on English and its staff, we will outline the teaching strategies present in these courses since they are fundamental in reshaping the study of any subject.

The overall aim is to give students more responsibility for their own learning. If students are part of the learning process rather than passive receivers of lecturer's notes they will respond better, gain more knowledge, and be able to transfer both the knowledge and the skills that they have employed in this method of learning to other environments and situations. The learning process itself is seen as the most important element: 'the process by which things are learned, and the skills and concepts underlying them, will often be more important than the information involved' (FEU 1982: 21).

By concentrating on the processes of learning rather than the knowledge gained, students are more aware that they are learning 'transferable' skills more suited to today's occupational mobility. Also, so that students have more control over their learning, they are encouraged to negotiate learning objectives and evaluate their own learning programmes. This means using process skills such as problem solving, decision making, and self-evaluation. Much of this takes place in 'real-life' contexts, such as work experience, residentials, and enterprise education (e.g. running a business), when students participate in activities which are not simulations, but are 'real' in an economic or social sense. This reinforces the students' greater responsibility for their own and their fellow students' learning. As *Active Learning – A Guide* suggests, this greater responsibility is gained first 'through making decisions affecting others – including the group within whom they may be working', second, 'through being accountable for their actions', and third, 'through experiencing the consequences of their actions, including failure' (FEU 1979: 5).

Real-life contexts offer the experience that students need to develop skills, but they also need to reflect upon such experiences in order that they can learn from them and plan new learning objectives. This relationship is endorsed by the FEU in *Experience Reflection Learning* as a useful learning model, in which the student characteristically moves through the pattern: experience = existing and extending; reflection = guided by the tutor to consolidate, interpret, develop concepts and theories, and look at attitudes and values; learning = usually skills or knowledge. The emphasis of real-life learning depends on expanding the boundaries of the teaching environment: 'The classroom cannot be separated from the environment of which it is an important part. Teaching is a process, not simply a training of students, but of "the formation of the proper social life"' (Curzon 1985: 56).

These teaching strategies are now affecting staff and students in English Departments. English lecturers have been asked to contribute to these courses as 'core tutors', possibly because 'Communication' is one of the core areas; and furthermore, the educational philosophy that these new initiatives share is now seen as valuable for a wider range of courses, one of which is GCSE English.

To take the first point: English lecturers in further education have for a long time taught Communication as well as English language and Literature O and A level. Communication has been a component of, for example, business study courses and City and Guild courses. This was often used to teach business English (letters, reports, etc.) and was seen as merely teaching a different syllabus rather than using a different teaching style from 'academic' English. When the syllabuses of the new courses were devised one of the core objectives was Communication and it was natural to ask English lecturers to teach on the courses. However Communication was now to be integrated with other objectives wherever possible and the role of the English lecturer changed. As a core tutor, she or he had to work as part of a team. This might involve writing integrated course material with other, non-English based, members of the team and team teaching with them in the classroom. It also meant working within a new philosophy where the lecturer became a 'facilitator' and 'structurer' of learning experiences.

It seems useful to give an example of these new teaching strategies that an English lecturer, participating in a new vocational course might adopt. The CPVE course offers a range of vocational options for students to choose from. The students may during the year study in two or more vocational areas, such as Business and Administration or Services to People. For each vocational area there is a team made up of a vocational tutor (someone with knowledge and skills applicable to this vocation, e.g., a business studies lecturer) and a core tutor (someone with knowledge and skills applicable to the core competences, e.g., communication, numeracy, life and social skills lecturer). The student is assessed on the basis of achievements in core competences which include communication, numeracy, problem solving, and personal and career development. As the student participates (usually in groups) in learning about a particular vocation, for example, running a business which might include selling, buying, accounts, and marketing, they are aware of the processes that they use and the core competences that these relate to. So that marketing, dealing with customers, and dealing with suppliers all use communication competences. Planning the venture, booking a classroom, and knowing how much stock to order demand the use of problem-solving competences. These competences obviously overlap so that booking a classroom uses both communication and problem-solving competences. The student can thus become aware of the value of being able to transfer these skills. The strategies that are employed throughout this type of learning, and which complement the process skills, include first, student-centred learning, since the students plan, organize, and run their own business; second, active learning in that students make decisions and self-evaluations; and third, experiential and real-life learning, gained from running a real business and taking responsibility for its success or failure.

What is the English lecturer's role in all this? Obviously their knowledge of communication skills is valued enormously as communication competences are present in probably all or most activities. They are expected to be able to give students the opportunity to recognize and develop their communication skills; which also means helping the vocational tutor to recognize the importance of communication in his or her vocation. For example, successfully dealing with a customer requires not only knowledge of the product being sold (the vocational input) but also the ability to communicate this to the customer in an effective way (the core input). However, the English lecturer's role is much broader than this. Because communication can easily be analysed in terms of process skills, English lecturers are seen as having the ability to work over the range of core competences. Haven't they always encouraged students to analyse, project, and evaluate? They are therefore in demand and often make up part of the central team which co-ordinates the vocational areas through core skills which are transferable across the vocations.

The further point we raised was that such teaching strategies are being incorporated in the practices of GCSE English. Experiential learning is recognized as providing a good basis for the project work that now forms a central feature of GCSE English teaching. The aim in project work should be that the *student* gathers his or her own material, usually working in groups: this may be through conducting surveys, questionnaires, making links with local businesses, or visiting institutions. Wherever possible the students negotiate the projects they want to work on. The emphasis is on student-centred research rather than teacher-centred dissemination and therefore personal experience is thought more relevant than second-hand experience. This is not self-indulgence however. The lecturer should subsequently structure class time so that the students are able to reflect on their experiences in order to develop clearly considered concepts and theories, become aware of attitudes and values, and then articulate and express how they feel about their experiences. Through this process they will learn skills such as aural/oral competences, transactional writing (for example, letter writing), report writing, creative, discursive, and descriptive writing.

With the extension of TVEI even GCSE courses will be encouraged to make closer links with industry, possibly as some English pupils already do when they 'work shadow' as part of their projects for their English assessment. They will be encouraged to use new technology such as word processing and language software packages wherever possible and 'residentials' will also be encouraged to expand on students' experiential learning opportunities.

Lecturers in further education can be seen to be developing strategies which take account of the imperatives imposed by central government while at the same time moving out of the restrictive modes of teaching that are still dominant in other sectors of education. Rather than seeing these shifts as negative, the teaching modes and strategies developed in response to the new initiatives should be viewed as positive advances over traditional teacher-centred practices in a number of ways. They can produce students who are more competent and confident in finding their way around the contemporary social and cultural formation; 'flexible and transferable skills' provide students with the means by which they might produce knowledge for themselves, and through which they might think more analytically about their own lives and the social organizations into which they fit. With an emphasis on group work (alongside the more individualist self-motivational ideologies) an attitude to working as a collective can be developed. Put together, these features can result in motivated, self-directed action. For the English-based lecturer there are more opportunities to engage with a wider range of students from various courses. Contact with students is no longer centred around the dissemination of 'truth' delivered in a lecture situation, discussed and responded to in seminars/tutorials, then re-presented, sufficiently modified so as to appear new, in essays. While relations of power and authority are still in place, the particular configurations of power and knowledge inscribed in the lecture situation have been significantly altered; the lecturer no longer stands as the source of wisdom and knowledge, but as the facilitator; the subject at the centre is no longer the subject of power but the facilitator of what is often a group-oriented process. While this does not wholly break down power relations it does tend to put them on a different basis, as students look to lecturers for advice and for particular knowledge rather than for the authoritative word on the subject or topic. So while English in further education has responded to modern conditions it has done so in a way that enables it to present strategies which are not simply fulfilling the needs of capital and business; skills application is not party political specific.

Meanwhile English in higher education has changed little in terms of its subject area or its teaching mode. Some tinkering around the margins with the non-literary text and some inclusion of theory has done little to get beyond the outmoded lecture/seminar/essay/exam format based on object knowledge. Where the range and corpus has been extended to include discourses and subjects other than Literature, these are generally treated as texts, to be picked over, subjected to a controlling and surveying gaze, and domesticated through the production of knowledge about and around the text. This seems to be the fate of such subjects as film, the media, and popular cultural forms when included in what are basically Literary Studies syllabuses. Radical literary and critical theories which are supposedly teaching students to question all authorities, from the author to the text to the reader, are delivered from the front of the class; peddled via a form that contradicts the content. Extending the curriculum to cover such areas as Media Studies might produce a more 'relevant' course; incorporating critical theory might open the discipline to a degree of process orientation; but while the teaching and learning structure remains in place neither of these are going to sufficiently address the issue.

English has always been teacher-centred in its delivery through lectures and tutorials and this has helped to encourage an individualistic approach to learning that is perhaps more insidious than the up-front self-motivation enshrined in the new initiatives. Traditional Literary Studies courses produce specific kinds of subjectivity through their emphasis on the individual response and through the individualistic mode of working inscribed in their practices. Students work alone, engaging the text and knowledge; when they do work together in small informal groups this is more of an oppositional practice contradicting the normative expectations inscribed in the discipline. And where the course invites them to participate in group situations, such as the seminar, students are expected to bring with them their responses and knowledge or to be ready to receive knowledge from the lecturer. All work and processing emanates from and has its density in the individual; it does not see the group as primary. Groups are constituted as a series of individuals each with their knowledge and responses to contribute – the group discussion is the end-point of the knowledge process, the point where knowledge is delivered and a new topic assigned. Group work in the new modes of teaching encourages student-centred learning and gives primacy to the group as a group rather than as a collection of discrete individual talents. It is the point at which the process starts rather than ends.

Group project work and student-centred learning are two of the strategies that need to be introduced into English Studies. But at the centre of any strategies would be the core element of skilling, with its emphasis on process. Of course, it could be argued that Literary Studies does already teach process skills – that there is a hidden agenda to the discipline where it is not the surveying knowledge of the field of literary texts that counts, but the ability to process that knowledge in certain ways. On this hidden agenda are the skills of discourse analysis, language manipulation, and rhetoric as well as presentational skills in writing and speaking. While such skills are seen as necessary they are treated as secondary, the acquired but not explicitly taught aspect of the discipline. To address the current imperatives, the hidden agenda is going to have to be made explicit and placed at the forefront of the curriculum. Though this does not entirely meet the demands of the new educational imperatives in that it does not forge links with industry and business, it does, nevertheless, deal with the kind of flexible and transferable skills that the market will require of its core workers.

To talk in terms of skilling students for the market-place may, of course, be anathema to some. Throughout its history Literary Studies has nurtured a suspicious attitude to commerce. The opposition between culture and commerce is present not only in Arnold and Leavis, but also in the more radical positions embedded in recent literary theory and in the cultural politics of left teachers. While this may present no apparent contradiction for those permanently working on Literary Studies courses, for the majority of students who have finished their degree the contradiction has to be lived and negotiated in a very concrete way. Ideological purity is often a luxury that has to be forgone and a cultural politics that does not confront this issue is doomed to an ideal realm in the face of pragmatic and contingent demands. English lecturers have to find ways of negotiating this if they want to produce an effective cultural politics that students can identify with and that will retain some relevance to students who face an increasingly competitive workplace. In any event, the purity of cultural forms, as well as being compromised by recent critical theory, is increasingly subjected to the rationale of the market-place where the 'cultural industries' are foregrounding the fact that culture is just another commodity produced for consumption. There's very little ideological purity left to the subject. The old form of cultural politics will soon be appearing in the new heritage theme parks that are springing up everywhere and which are already commodifying the culture of working-class struggle in the Victorian era.

Presumably those teaching in higher education who read a book such as this are interested in changing the subject. The crisis that is currently looming will produce the conditions which will make radical transformation not only possible but necessary; for, like it or not, the kind of rationale and the imperatives and initiatives that have confronted the further education sector are set to move in on the higher education sector. The forces impelling change might not accord with those our ideologically sound theoretical excursions have suggested are the desired ones, but at least the opportunity for change is presenting itself. English lecturers in higher education need to be devising strategies that will meet the challenge and make use of it.

PART II
Theories, Pedagogies, Initiatives

5
Refunctioning theory:
'at most pedagogics'

Peter Brooker

In the year 1986–7 I taught a new course in Modern Literary Theory. In the same year the hostility towards 'Theory' which had been so evident in the 1970s appeared to get its second wind – and to have shifted its course, since it blew fiercely now less from conservative than from liberal and progressive humanist positions (see Bergonzi 1986, Parrinder 1987, Tallis 1987, and Weissman 1987). A catalogue of faults and failings was laid especially at the doors of Catherine Belsey and Terry Eagleton, or rather Belsey's *Critical Practice* (1980) and Eagleton's *Literary Theory. An Introduction* (1983). These texts have been attacked, I believe, for what they are not. They are polemical introductions rather than first-order theory, but they do not represent 'Theory' (there is no such homogeneous thing) or 'deconstruction', nor do they have genocidal designs upon Literature. The fact that they were singled out, however, does suggest how literary theory has assumed a certain cultural profile; one in which these texts, and others from alerted publishing houses, have sold well, and in which their arguments have taken effect in reshaping the curriculum and therefore student knowledge and performance in colleges and schools. Literary theory has penetrated to the nitty-gritty of syllabuses, essays, and exam papers. Hence I believe the new source of attack, and its animus.

This is not a question of black and white success or failure,

however, even if we understand the deconstructive and politi-
cizing aims of recent theory correctly. Modern theory has
reached deeper into the system of literary education over the
last half dozen years, but it has not transformed it, and it would
be a mistake (though publishers' lists and booksellers' windows
suggest otherwise) to picture its massed ranks advancing upon a
thin line of humanist defence when the numbers are the other
way around, and when there is more manoeuvring and compromise than undiluted ideological combat. The course I
taught was evidence of these mixed and uneven effects. Students
responded with indifference, incomprehension, belligerent
common sense, informed interest, and hungry enthusiasm. It
became clear also that what were welcome new concepts and
approaches for some students had no explicit presence on other
courses and that these students had therefore to retreat or force
an entry with them. I do not mean to complain about this state
of affairs, nor draw up a blueprint for the unimpaired transmission and integration of a new model 'English'. I want to say
that in this process of cultural dissemination, the popularization
of theory has both provoked and enabled dissent, largely within
existing structures; that it has gained a contested place (a place
of contestation), where the ideological content of English and
Literature may be overhauled, but that, and crucially in my
view, it has not addressed the routine structures of teaching and
learning in which this is practised. In short, though in its own
terms the political criticism of a reconstituted literary or cultural studies would be concerned centrally with the production of
human subjectivities, this very aspect of a literary education
and of its own supposed counter-influence has been ignored. In
this respect it has so far failed.

Many teachers will have recognized this gap between theory
and pedagogy and it is likely that there has been a more
common awareness of it in further education and in schools
than in higher education since progressivist assumptions, traditions of child- and student-centred learning, and practical or
creative work have been much stronger there. It often seems in
fact that innovative pedagogic practice has proceeded in one
area while theory has advanced in the other, and that the
solution therefore is to bring the two together. I believe it is
necessary to stress continuities and exchanges across these

'levels' but that new theoretically-informed pedagogic practices will be differently inflected across different sectors and objectives. My own thoughts in what follows are addressed chiefly to the orthodoxies of higher education as I have experienced and perceived them in universities and polytechnics. I want, however, to respond to the standardized forms developed in this intellectual culture in other than empirical or experiential terms; not certainly so as to theorize a perfect model since there can never be one, but so as to swivel theory around and explore its potential for altered, more democratized pedagogic forms. I can perhaps best suggest this potential by the names Bakhtin, Brecht, and Gramsci. Though in themselves these three are neither an exclusive, nor as figures in a male Marxist tradition, a sufficient theoretical or political source,[1] they have appeared in a steady series of citations, and in different alliances with deconstructive and feminist traditions, as influences on the work of Eagleton, Belsey, Bennett, and Raymond Williams, all highly visible in the popular profile of modern theory in Britain. These writers have in turn of course been influential on other critics, teachers, and students. The names Bakhtin, Brecht, and Gramsci therefore – as Eagleton says of Brecht in relation to his own work (Eagleton 1986: 7) – condense many of the motifs of recent theory and critical and cultural politics.[2]

Brecht and Gramsci offer firstly I believe two equivalent sets of ideas which summarize the aims of radical criticism, and apply beyond this both to the professional and political position of left teachers and critics, and to pedagogic forms. These are in Brecht the concept of 'complex seeing', the ability to 'think above the stream' and 'in the stream' (though the first 'is perhaps more important' (Brecht 1964: 44)). In this and allied statements Brecht describes the dialectical perspective necessary to the estrangement of habits of perception and understanding, the production of an ensuing 'critical awareness', and a readiness to act upon this in the world. This is compatible I think with Gramsci's description of the 'strangely composite' personality of 'collective man' (containing 'Stone Age elements and the principles of a more advanced science') and the tasks allotted to a 'philosophy of praxis' (Gramsci 1971: 324). This, says Gramsci,

must be a criticism of 'common sense', basing itself initially,
however, on common sense in order to demonstrate that
'everyone' is a philosopher and that it is not a question of
introducing from scratch a scientific form of thought . . . but
of renovating and making 'critical' an already existing
activity.

(Gramsci 1971: 330–1)

Brecht and Gramsci here describe the common position and
endeavour of those writers, critics, and teachers who seek to
intervene in and so change the world of common sense from a
position in and above the stream, of shifting consent and dissent
in relation to the hegemonic order.[3] Virginia Woolf I think
discovers this in *A Room of One's Own* in her relation to Oxbridge
and in the 'splitting off of consciousness' which occurs for a
woman walking down Whitehall 'when from being the natural
inheritor of that civilisation, she becomes on the contrary,
outside of it, alien and critical' (Woolf 1929, 1977: 146). Terry
Eagleton's relation to Oxford and Raymond Williams's to
Cambridge and more broadly, in Eagleton's account, to public
and counter-public spheres in the post-war period would be
further instances of this double consciousness (Eagleton 1984:
108–15). In other examples, Peter Widdowson, from a base in
the polytechnic sector, has set out a range of proposals for
radical criticism which 'would operate *within* an educational
structure . . . hostile to them' (Widdowson 1980: 147), and Nick
Peim writes in this volume and elsewhere of new ways of
teaching A level against the grain of theoretical and pedagogic
orthodoxies (Peim 1986: 10–17).

What this means is that left writers, critics, teachers, and
students enter or pass through the specific discourses of
'English' as already 'decentred subjects', already experiencing
a series of tensions and contradictions of generation, gender,
class position, and political attitude, which are then deepened
and made more 'strangely composite' by the jostle of traditional
and more progressive ideas and approaches. Terry Eagleton
has suggested that what is taught and learned in 'Literature' is
less a body of knowledge than a discourse, a 'moral technology'
producing 'an historically peculiar form of human subject who
is sensitive, receptive, imaginative, etc. *about nothing in particular*'

and that it is in the acquisition of this 'humanity' that students are then accredited (Eagleton 1985: 5). I think we need to add that although there may be a desire and a will in orthodox forms of English to produce clones of the one discourse, there are other discourses in the life surrounding accreditation which aid and abet or contest it. Students, that is to say, enter and continue in higher education with all manner of discourses to hand, from the progressivist or vocational ethos of school or college, to the discourses of peer groups, family, and work, and the idioms of different social and political ideologies. These then join in consensual or conflictual relations with 'Literature', or with parts of it; from 'stone age' positions – of the 'analysis destroys pleasure' type, to the compacted submissiveness and subversion of 'I've never liked poetry', to 'advanced' calls for an across the board treatment of questions of race and gender. Teachers also, even within institutions, employ different discourses, formal and informal, with colleagues and students; not least in the important extra-curricular niches and by-ways which supplement and exceed the system, even as they are produced by it. I do not think it is useful to view these as accents in the same unitary and 'humanizing' discourse or 'moral economy'; nor even that the most common modes of the lecture and seminar necessarily have the same pedagogic and ideological effect.

It is the generally conventional uses of these forms and their possible transformation that I wish to consider. In a quite unique discussion of the discourse of the lecture, Roland Barthes describes the 'gloomy' choice before the teacher of choosing the dominant 'lawful' mode of 'conscientious functionary' or the role of the 'free artist' (Barthes 1977: 191–2). In the second option the lecturer attempts to 'get round', to skirt the expected official discourse, but only, says Barthes, to receive back the reflected image of the 'imperfect orator' and 'liberal'. This is grim and painful enough; though it is at least something to receive a reflected image, for most often, Barthes writes, 'the mirror is empty'. The teacher speaking to a silent student body is

> the person who says *I* (the detours of *one*, *we* or impersonal sentence make no difference), I am the person who, under cover of *setting out* a body of knowledge, *puts out* a discourse,

never knowing how that discourse is being received and thus forever forbidden the reassurance of a definitive image – even if offensive – which would constitute me.

(Barthes 1977: 194)

And yet the teacher is 'exposed'; much like the TV newsreader, he or she puts out a 'personality' over and above the facts or content being imparted, or communicates a position, a stance towards a standard theme, or in the very choice of theme, which shadows the rhetorics of disinterestedness or ironic distance. For Barthes 'every teacher occupies the position of the person in analysis', 'the Other is always there *puncturing* his discourse', for though silent 'the student audience . . . *has an air* of not speaking – and thus, from the bosom of its flatness, speaks in you so much the louder' (Barthes 1977: 195).

To lecture or not to lecture when the positive choices are equally 'professional' and, Barthes says, 'equally repressive'? An alternative he suggests, evoking Brecht, is to speak as the 'representative' or 'oblate' of the proletariat, interpreting the meanings of culture – 'an interpretation of Zola, Poussin, pop music, the Sunday sports paper or the latest news item' – on its behalf (Barthes 1977: 210). A position similar to this emerges in a discussion of pedagogy and television studies in articles by Manuel Alvarado and Bob Ferguson. Alvarado argues, against conventional progressivist wisdom, for the role of 'direct teaching', that is, 'those situations where a teacher talks/ dictates/reads to a silent class' on the grounds that authoritarian methods need to be distinguished from the authority of the teacher, and that '*all* modes of address need to be deployed and exploited' in restructuring the educational process of the classroom (Alvarado 1981: 64). Alvarado's underlying political project appears in a later article with Bob Ferguson (headnoted with a statement by Brecht on realism adapted to the conditions of pedagogy). Thus it is said the teacher can modify her or his power relationship with students in a 'greatly democratised system of education' but not eliminate it. Neither 'wise companion' nor 'dictatorial pedant', the teacher requires 'the will to work towards the possession of power as a goal of education'. Whereas the private sector perpetuates 'the power relationship of the capitalist class to the working class. State education will be concerned to pass power to the proletariat.' They conclude that 'The terrain upon which education is conducted must become an intellectual battlefield rather than a consensual swamp' (Alvarado and Ferguson 1983: 64).

We are presented then with a choice (the immediate reference here is media education in schools) between progressivist orthodoxy and a discourse of Leninist instruction and intellectual struggle (see also Connell 1983 and Lusted 1986a: 2–4). Though Barthes introduces the idea of this second form of political education, the problems he identifies with it are very telling ones. Thus the 'oblates' devoted to the proletarian interpretation of cultural facts are removed from the proletariat and the sphere of production, the objects of study are bourgeois, and the intellectual methods of study 'bourgeoisified' (211). It will be noted too that the politics attributed to the intellectual/teacher/student in these accounts are traditional class politics and that its participants are either undifferentiated or designated as male. Many radical critics and teachers will nevertheless feel the force of Barthes's remarks in relation to the rereading of canonized authors and texts and the study of popular forms. Moreover, his point would remain if his discussion were advanced into the 1980s and revised to take account of deconstruction and feminism. For the struggle for ideas in education is neither the centre, nor by any means the only site of political struggle, and these critical methods, like Marxism, are also prone to 'bourgeoisification'.

The implication is that teachers *cannot* assume the role of political 'representatives' and that the strategy which substitutes a vision of the revolutionary class-war, or any other teleology, for the politics and pedagogy of the classroom is a mistaken one. Or rather the mistake is to substitute strategy for tactics, the long-term perspective of metanarrative for the complex vision which can change focus. The lecturer, this is to say, who speaks in the name of the proletariat or women's movement is in danger of ballooning, or 'overlooking' the power–knowledge relationships which *are* active in education. I would be deluded if I thought that in teaching *The Ragged Trousered Philanthropists* I was passing power to the proletariat, even though I count myself a socialist, and I could not possibly premise a lecture on texts by Alice Walker or Toni Morrison on the thought that I was serving the cause of Black American women, even though I am committed to sexual equality and anti-racism. What I may be doing in these cases is intervening in the world of cultural meanings, but if, as I believe, the object of this activity is the production of 'useful knowledge', it can only effectively be judged by those directly engaged in its production. It may be heartening to think that I have said or done the right thing politically, but the beneficiaries of the lecture or direct teaching (though the point applies more broadly than these forms) cannot be thought of as outside or ahead of that discourse. The winners and losers are the self and 'Other', the students whose silence and assumed prejudice, common sense, and sexuality, whose class or feminist or Black consciousness help constitute that discourse and the teacher as subject.

How is one to negotiate this inside and outside of political teaching and conviction? In asking how culture is to be evaluated Barthes proposes 'dialectics', which 'Although bourgeois . . . does contain progressive elements', only then to ask 'but what at the level of discourse, distinguishes dialectics from compromise?' In other words what distinguishes a socialist-feminist from a liberal-humanist pedagogy? Not I think commitment and single mindedness, nor being in two minds, but the flexible, transformative 'critical' practice founded on the estranged consciousness of the 'alien inheritor'. Barthes's own answer affirms this dialectical mode:

> cultural criticism proceeds *successively, diversely and simultaneously* by opposing the Old with the New, historicism with sociologism, formalism with economism, psychoanalysis with logico-positivism, and then again, *by a further turn*, empirical sociology with monumental history, the New with the strange (the foreign), historicism with formalism, scientism with psychoanalysis, and so on. Applied to culture, critical discourse can only be a silk shot through with tactics, a tissue of elements now past, now circumstantial (linked to the contingencies of fashion), now finally and frankly utopian.
>
> (Barthes 1977: 211)

We come, along these same lines, closer to a model for pedagogy once more in Brecht, though less in his credentials as a representative of the proletariat than in the dialecticizing techniques of his artistic practice. As early as 1930 in the period of his 'didactic' plays, Brecht distinguished his work from propaganda and agit-prop. 'This isn't', he said, 'the same thing as committed art. At most pedagogics' (Brecht 1964: 67). It was as is well known a theatre of estrangement, employing, as a matter of tactics we might say, innovative means of artistic representation (in lighting, music, song, screens, etc.) and different modes, both old and new, to stimulate indignation at inhuman conditions – 'by direct description . . . stories and parables, by jokes, by over and understatement' – for the strategic end of putting 'living reality in the hands of living people in such a way that it can be mastered' (Brecht 1964: 110, 109). Brecht did not seek disciples or 'oblates' or to unify his audience but to divide it and provoke active critical thinking. The chief device of this theatre was 'gestic acting' which aimed to demonstrate or 'quote' a character or event in the third person (so far the technique of liberal disinterestedness) but in so doing to 'historicize' it and reveal its contradictory and therefore alterable nature (the technique of dialectical materialism). Brecht described this as 'fixing the "not . . . but"' (Brecht 1964: 137), a reply once again to the liberal triuism that there are two sides to every question; replacing its partial even-handedness with the fuller truth of difference, contradiction, and change.

Although, therefore, I have queried Alvarado and Ferguson's statement of the political aims of radical pedagogy, I do not disagree with their adoption of an adapted Brecht. Their headnote ends:

> he [Brecht] tried to develop a pedagogy (art) on the basis of a montage of discourses dealing separately and in different manners with different areas and levels of reality. He also believed that the task of changing the structures of ideology (and society) was a common task, to be finished together by teacher (artist) and learner (spectator). He therefore preferred open to closed education (works). He believed that popular forms and conceptions should be used but also suspected.
> (Alvarado and Ferguson 1983: 20)

If this mixed mode and purpose cannot be applied in the 'performance' of the lecture (the short talks by two or more

speakers with following discussion which is increasingly common in conference workshops move, I think, in this direction)
then the options for this form will remain 'lawful', or 'liberal', or
'committed' in the adamantine or propagandist mode discussed
above.[4]

Many of course would abandon the lecture in favour of the
seminar where students are less a 'silent body' than a participating company of minds and bodies. My own argument has
suggested that the lecture be devolved into a 'montage of
discourses' but this does not mean that as a form of presentation
it should not contrast with other forms or have a different
source, or sources, from them. The seminar or seminar series
needs to become in reality the form of collaborative work it is
usually at best in name only, and there are models in theatre
(including the Berliner Ensemble), in community groups, and
in political traditions, as well as project-oriented work in
schools which could be drawn on for inspiration and encouragement here.
   An obvious theoretical source for this development lies in the
writings of Mikhail Bakhtin and the 'Bakhtin School' (including P. N. Medvedev and V. N. Voloshinov who are often
thought of as pseudonyms for Bakhtin). 'Discourse lives', writes
Bakhtin, 'on the boundary between its own context and
another, alien, context' (Bakhtin 1981: 284). Speech is always in
reality in dialogue, shadowed by other framing and opposed
utterances in a verbal and ideological system which works to
disguise its relativism and internal contradictions. Bakhtin saw
the novel especially, in a much extended history, as revealing
and revelling in this interaction and double life of contending
discourses, calling up the other, a word or utterance's rejoinder
and rebuttal through parody and satire. By thus 'de-alienating',
by giving combative voice to unofficial, subordinated vernacular or folk languages the novel in its dialogic activity embar-
rasses or subverts the pull towards a unitary, official language
and meaning in society. This anti-authoritarian and centrifugal
impulse then culminates in the 'carnivalesque', a celebratory
up-ending of social and linguistic convention for which
Bakhtin's major example is Rabelais. He finds precedents for

this in the serio-comic genres of the Menippean satire and the ancient pedagogic form of the Socratic dialogue in which Socratic irony plays upon popular opinion and speech so as to familiarize and degrade the contemporary world, thus bringing it closer for free investigation.

Much of this might be cross-referenced in Brecht's political aesthetic. What is more, is not the Socratic dialogue a precedent for the interrogative style of deconstruction and for the more materialist play of Gramsci's philosophy of praxis upon common sense in a world (and classroom) where everyone is a philosopher? This is not to say of course that these theories have a direct application to classroom pedagogy. Brecht offers in the first instance a theory of artistic production, and Bakhtin a theory of literature as dialogic practice and a mode of critical analysis. Just as Brecht's theory needs then to be translated into a theory of the production of knowledge (which can seek to employ artistic means in an aesthetic political pedagogy), so Bakhtin's needs to be transposed and enlarged if it is to apply to the social and linguistic forms of the seminar. For although Bakhtin talks of the destabilizing of language and ideology as 'an activity that goes on both within the limits of the literary dialect itself and outside it' (1981: 371), he tends to confine the dialogic function to the literary form of the novel, and does not explicitly include the critic (i.e., the teacher/student) as an agency or voice in this activity as any dialogic model of the seminar/workshop must. All the same the 'novel' is a broad and transferable category in Bakhtin's thinking and there may be some point in thinking of the seminar as a lived form of this 'genre', a method in Bakhtin's description of genre, for 'seeing and conceptualising reality' (Bakhtin 1973: 134). If we can, as it were, 'socialize' the theory in this self-reflexive way, then the dispersal of the unifying voice of an originating author of the kind Bakhtin identifies (Dostoyevsky's characters, he writes, 'are capable of standing beside their creator, of disagreeing with him, and even of rebelling against him' (Bakhtin 1973: 4)) could serve, by example, to open the seminar as it opens the text to marginalized and unheard voices in both classroom and society.

In general terms, the relevance of the Bakhtin School lies in its broad underlying theory of language as a shifting multi-accented heteroglossia, deeply inscribed in ideology and material conditions. In its recognition of the unequal distribution of power across discourse, dialogics enables us also to supersede the common-sense humanist axioms that 'everyone is entitled to their opinion' or of 'agreeing to differ' which administer to liberal dialogue and pedagogy. The whole thrust of dialogics is to dismantle fixed hierarchies, to make them wobble in the presence of the alien and low, to prod and poke them with subtle ironies and bring them down with the belly laughs of vulgar ribaldry. English teaching can certainly attempt to dialogize its standard forms; it can make room for irony (some would say there has been room for nothing else) and seek to employ the serio-comic investigative rhetorics of imitation, parody, and satire. There are moments too when it is right to pull a face and scoff and grin and laugh. A Rabelesian raspberry is sometimes needed to bring even literary theory down to earth, and we can all, if pressed, spot the ridiculous in 'epiphany', or 'objective correlative', or 'verfremdungseffect', or 'writing with the body', or 'heteroglossia'. We might, who knows, occasionally find a place for the 'carnivalesque' without making a song and dance about it.

These ideas clearly raise the issue of authority in teaching relationships and the feasibility of democratizing these. Is the couple teacher/pupil to be dehierarchized in the manner of the deconstruction of nature/culture, speech/writing, man/woman, white/black? Does the death of the teacher succeed the death of the author and of Literature? There is a difference of course between authoritarianism, being an authority, and being in authority. Teachers can avoid the first, they will very often be positioned as the second, and may rightly be regarded this way – though this does not imply that their role is to transmit a finished body of knowledge – but they cannot avoid the last. I am therefore personally held back from an act of attempted self-cancellation because I think it patronizes students and cheapens the notion of equality to suggest that differences of sex, age, colour, remuneration, and qualifications count for nothing. They count for power, in education as elsewhere. The progress-ive teacher in seminars is in the position I described earlier, in this world but agitating for a better: trying most probably, in terms of the analogy with Bakhtin, to resist the pull of habit and expectations towards monologism and a monopolized power over knowledge. As much as anything then, his or her task is to demonstrate the very features of this situation; to show the process with all its punctuating tensions, settled convictions, and rough ends, by which his or her own ways of thinking and reading have been arrived at. The deconstructive act would of course be less an act of suicide than of simultaneous self-cancellation and reinscription, but I prefer, borrowing again from Brecht, to think of this 'gest' as an act of self-estrangement which 'historicizes' the present structures of power in the interests of change.

On this issue, Roland Barthes in the essay 'Writers, intellectuals, teachers' distinguishes between 'social "roles"' and 'the regions of speech'. 'The problem', he writes, 'is not to abolish the distinction in functions (*teacher/student* . . .) but to protect the instability, and as it were the giddying whirl of the positions of speech' (Barthes 1977: 205–6). He seeks the floating position of no '*final place*', since for everyone to be in their place would be a reason for giving up teaching. In the 'peaceable speech' which obtains in the discussion group he describes, Barthes would therefore wish 'to suspend or at least to delay the roles of speech – so that listening, speaking, replying, I never be the actor of a judgement, a subjection, an intimidation, the advocate of a Cause' (Barthes 1977: 214). The politicized pedagogy I have outlined does not depend for its credentials on the advocacy of a Cause, but would not suspend or efface the teacher's discourse or separate this from his or her social role in the way Barthes suggests. The teacher would exercise authority by explaining (rather than suspending or proseletizing for) a political or theoretical position or critical reading, and by instigating an enabling discourse which would allow for support, development, disagreement, and contestation. It would also be important for this activity, necessarily again at the teacher's instigation, though better as a structured requirement and habit, to go discursively and literally beyond the seminar room and the teacher's domain. Barthes's seminar is a separate space for 'free speech' with no apparent end or anchor, but it does nevertheless assume a decided form, divested of aggression and conflict, and does arrive at an effect: week after week brings 'a certain dispropriation of speech . . . *a certain generalisation of the subject'* (Barthes 1977: 214). The reconstruction of the subject I have in mind amounts not to this laid-back feeling of oneness (Barthes refers to a similarity with 'certain experiences with drugs' and is plainly loath for his 'floating signifier' to come down), but to a recognition of equality in difference, a montaged human collectivity. To paste together phrases on Brecht and *via* Gramsci (whose words instructively bear the imprint of earlier bricolaged authorities and the seeds of later discoveries) this subject will be reconstructed in 'social solidarity' and will come to 'know the/thyself' ('The starting-point of critical elaboration', wrote Gramsci, 'is "knowing thyself" as a product of the historical process to date which has deposited in you an infinity of traces, without leaving an inventory' (1971: 324)).

Much of this will seem airily Utopian and abstract (though not I hope as Utopian as Barthes's 'no place'). I want lastly, however, even if it is to aggravate this reaction, to offer a frankly speculative hope on a further aspect of the issue of authority, to point to a concrete example of the pedagogy I am imagining in action and to two problems this illustration raises.

I listed above the role of assessor as one of the roles of the teacher in authority. The moment of assessment is the moment of truth for good democratic intentions, and the moment of examinations, particularly, where the teacher is abruptly silent examiner and no longer dialogizing guide, their ruination. At this point there can be no more 'floating'; the idea of 'collaborative work' comes to sound like 'cheating', and 'intertextual discursive practices' like old-fashioned plagiarism. There are many questions and opinions on examinations which I cannot consider here. It is obvious, however, that the traditional three-hour exam, whatever its variations, employed to finally discipline, punish, and reward undergraduates, is incompatible with the pedagogy I am proposing. In its place I suggest a process of assessment continuous with the dialectic of support and critique outlined as the discourse of the seminar above and a more generous notion of the work which can be submitted for accreditation. To go no further than written work, this could include criticism, theoretical essays, case studies, interviews, reportage, autobiography, or the use of literary forms; a variety, in short, equal to the range of discursive forms English under its newer dispensations aims to study.

The practical example I have in mind is the Marxist–Feminist Literature Collective, a group of feminist students and teachers who met over a period of years in the late 1970s to read theoretical texts in Marxism, feminism, and psychoanalysis, and who then collectively worked towards the presentation of a paper on women's writings in 1848 (published in Barker *et al.* 1978), ten women reading parts of the paper from the platform. Cora Kaplan who was a member of this group emphasizes the importance of its collective experience but warns too of reifying a moment or style of cultural intervention when the political situation for the women's movement and more generally has changed. The critic–tutor, she argues, must respond to changed circumstances and to the changed needs and political consciousness of new generations of students: 'It is no use trying to create an ideal model of cultural intervention out of a social movement whose character has changed with the changing times' (Kaplan 1986: 66). This is a warning in a sense against 'formalism' of the kind Brecht, arguing for a historically responsive conception of realism, saw in Georg Lukács, and expresses a further form of the complex seeing, here switching between past and present political moments, which left teachers are called upon to exercise. A second problem is that though I have cited this example it is not mine to claim. If, as a male critic–tutor I avoid idealizing the achievements and strategies of the women's movement, I remain in Cora Kaplan's description an example of 'recent Marxist criticism "friendly" to feminism' (Kaplan 1986: 64). The term ' "friendly" ' implies hypocrisy on one side and suspicion on the other, while 'friend' describes an admirable personal and political relationship between allies. Here for male Marxists finally is the acutest form of split consciousness: 'alien and critical' of capitalist civilization in their own eyes, they are nevertheless alienated and the object of criticism as its 'natural inheritors' from a feminist point of view. Other essays in this volume, and elsewhere, discuss this problem more directly and fully. My own clipped judgement as a last word here would have to be that it is one thing to remove inverted commas in writing and another to remove them in the world, and that the solution to the problems these small marks indicate lies in the end in the second, where men (sic) must live and work with and against them.

Notes

1   Other sources in poststructuralism, though not obviously aligned with Marxism or feminism, are also relevant to education and pedagogy. See, for example, Michel Foucault (1970) *The Order of Things*, London: Tavistock, ch. 10, and the essays (1977) 'History of systems of thought' and 'Intellectuals and power' in *Language, Counter-Memory, Practice*, ed. Donald F. Bouchard, trans. Donald F. Bouchard and Sherry Simon, Oxford: Blackwell.

2   I have tried to explore the relevance of Brecht to changes in English Studies in (1987) 'Why Brecht, or, is there English after Cultural Studies?', in *Broadening the Context*, ed. Michael Green, London: John Murray.

3   I do not mean to suggest that this is 'everyone's' position, nor that it is not marked by further considerations of race and gender, nor to imply that those in these occupations are *centrally* placed within the culture, though opposed to it. I agree with Toril Moi's response to Julia Kristeva's estimation of rebels, psychoanalysts, the *avant-garde*, and women and workers as equally dissident groups. She writes:

> The paradox of the position of women and the working class is that they are at one and the same time central and marginal-(ized). In the case of the intelligentsia, whether *avant-garde* artists or psychoanalysts, it may well be the case that their role under late capitalism is truly peripheral in the sense that they have no crucial function in the economic order.
>
> (Moi 1985: 171–2)

Both Jacques Derrida and Edward Said have recently described the paradox of affirmation and critique in their situations and responsibilities as teachers. Thus Derrida,

> You have to train people to become doctors or engineers or professors, and at the same time to train them in questioning all that – not only in a critical way, but in a deconstructive way. This is a double responsibility: two responsibilities which sometimes are not compatible. In my own teaching, in my own responsi-bilities, I think I have to make two gestures simultaneously: to train people, to teach them, to give them a profession; and at the same time to make them as conscious as possible of the problems of professionalization.

Edward Said, though he feels 'The late-1960s notion of the pol-
iticization of pedagogical discourse has spent itself' comments
similarly and in ways which are relevant to the general discussion
here:

> if one is working with the texts of English Literature, then one
> feels a great constraint. The problem there is that you have a
> responsibility to the material which is a real one; but the main
> goal is to create in your students a critical consciousness. The last
> thing I'm interested in is disciples. Any kind of overt com-
> munication of a message or method is the last thing I want to do.
> In that respect, it's very difficult to be a teacher, because in a
> certain sense you ought always to be undercutting yourself.
> You're teaching, performing, doing the kinds of things that
> students can learn from, but at the same time cutting them off
> and saying 'Don't try to do this.' You're telling them to do it, and
> not to do it.
>
> (Imre Salusinsky (ed.) (1987) *Criticism in Society*, London:
> Methuen, pp. 17–18, 146)

4   I realize I am in danger of ascribing intrinsic features and unalter-
able effects to these forms when my argument is that they are
conventional, and therefore subject to change. Cora Kaplan writes
of the importance in her own experience of speaking out and of the
use of the public lecture in bringing together ethical and political
imperatives with personal need and desire (Kaplan 1986: 219–22).
Tactically, it might therefore be in certain conditions subversive or
empowering for more women, or students, to lecture more. However, this does come to seem rather like the argument that it's a
good thing for more women to enter the House of Commons as
elected MPs. Yes, of course; but as Tory MPs? See also Jan
Montefiore's view in this volume on the teacher's responsibility to
lecture.

6

Never mind English: this is theory in the secondary school

Paul Moran and Nick Peim

> 'Why are we doing this, Mr Moran?' asks a 14 year old.
> 'Well, we're doing this because . . .'
> 'My mum says that phenomenology isn't English.'
> 'Perhaps it isn't.'
> 'Why are we doing it then?'
> 'We're doing phenomenology now because later on it will help you with some work that we're going to do on the material production of the meaning of texts.'

The 14 year old wasn't convinced. For that matter, neither were her parents. Phenomenology, as far as all of them were concerned, was clearly not English. Its relevance to the subject was, to their very best knowledge, arbitrary and superficial. Why, then, was Patricia being made to do phenomenology, particularly when her own English teacher seemed uncertain about whether or not this obscure branch of speculative knowledge fell within the arena of either English Language or English Literature?

These questions, which we were faced with in the Spring term of 1987, are all important. Unfortunately, in what later became known as 'the phenomenology scare' in the school, a number of parents sought to remove their daughters and sons from the groups in which this kind of activity was taking place: our answers obviously proved to be insufficient to allay their anxieties about what was being taught. Assurances that any writing produced on phenomenology would be legitimate material to submit for their coursework folders – the form of their final assessments at GCSE – were not entirely settling. We have since had the 'structuralism scare', the more general 'poststructuralism scare', the 'feminist textual politics scare' and others, none of which, thankfully, ever reached the intensity of the original phenomenological crisis. But what, precisely, was the nature of this parental, student, and later on, institutional anxiety?

The concern of all these bodies was not that phenomenology was being taught incorrectly, or that, for example, Husserl was being preferenced above Hegel. The general approach that was taken towards phenomenology during the classes was one that emphasized subject/object relations, examined their possible dichotomy, and looked at the formulation of a perceived objective or external reality. No books or extracts from books on phenomenology were actually read; neither was this objected to. Students were given diagrams of sides of houses and other two-dimensional representations of single planes or three-dimensional objects, and were then asked to describe what they 'perceived to be'. We looked up the words 'perceive' and 'being', and discussed whether 'being' was the same as 'to be'; of course, different people came to different conclusions, but that hardly mattered since it was not our aim to teach Husserl or Merleau-Ponty or anyone else in an explicit and prescriptive manner. We were concerned that students should raise for themselves, as far as possible, themes and questions that phenomenology expresses. This was the position that we tried to maintain throughout the two weeks that we spent on this topic. During the initial period short pieces of writing, in response to a series of questions, were set, completed and discussed by the class as a whole. Questions such as:

'How do you know what you are looking at?'

'Can you tell what you are looking at is?'

'If you looked at something differently, would it change?'

'Is it entirely up to you how you look at things?'

'Is the world as we know it made up of the description of how things look?'

'Is how things look how things are?'

Texts, physical objects, general notions of culture and the self were all used in different ways to confront and discuss these questions. Again, though we constantly made suggestions about how ideas might be examined or developed from different perspectives, we made no attempt to suggest that any ideas were right or wrong: we were keen to encourage students to extrapolate the implications of their own ideas to their fullest extent.

It was the implication of this last point, it seems, that was partly responsible for the collective phenomenological angst. In conjunction with the general bemusement as to why English teachers were inflicting arcane philosophy on their classes, there were complaints that little or no direction was being given as to whether a student's ideas were correct or otherwise; that pieces of work were steadfastly ungraded, despite the fact that the GCSE Literature and Language courses were entirely examined on a selection of two years' coursework; that comments which had been written on returned 'essays' offered no corrective guidance as to how the topic might be done properly; and that a number of 'essays' had been produced by student collaboration. All of the allegations, which were quite justifiable, implied the relinquishment of some kind of authority. But what, then, was this authority, we asked? How could it be identified, and was its relinquishment, perhaps more imaginary than real? We also suggested that students might like to include a discussion of this matter – of authority and the subject of English – in their own writing, and possibly explain how it might be linked to them doing phenomenology in the fourth year. There was a general reluctance to take up this suggestion because of the very grounds on which it was offered. It would clearly be impossible to grade such a piece of work, since grading, according to all of the antagonistic bodies, implied some kind of objective assessment. It would obviously not be possible to apply, in any meaningful way, objective assessment criteria to a piece of work whose significance was essentially its self-analytical quality. And anyway, it was argued, phenomenology, particularly with this additional discussion of teaching and learning practices in which the division between the two would tend to become indeterminate, was most definitely not English. Disaffected students and parents were especially anxious to make this point by alluding to cases where the subject appeared to be clearly identifiable; and it was the authority of this identity, which was also the authority of English – including teaching practices and the application of an external and objective grading procedure – that was most important.

This point in the crisis illuminated most clearly the various positions which had been taken up. The greatest outrage that had been committed against the integrity of the subject during the entire phenomenological crisis, an outrage which launched some of the protagonists into a veritable apoplexy of existential bad faith, was our expression that, if students felt the need for grades to be awarded in respect to their pieces of work then this could be done by the students themselves, perhaps working with each other in groups. Written explanations would have to be provided about how and why students awarded grades as they did, as well as including in their own writing some description of whether or not there could be any justification for imposing their own self-determined grades on others who were perhaps unwilling to participate in, or disagreed with their established criteria. What we are interested in, we made obvious, is what a grade and a system of grading means in relation to the production and identity of any piece of work and, as a result of this, the meaning, position, and identity of the student in relation to the subject. Outright opposition followed (by some), and it was even suggested that a few students, in accordance with their own and their parents' wishes, be removed from the groups concerned.

When later ourselves and some of the classes that we taught became engaged in a piece of work about the determination of meaning in relation to the power of institutional structures, the kinds of questions that we were left with were as follows:

'What, now, as a result of this piece of work, is the subject?'

'Have we changed, through our discussion and our collective practices, what English means?'

'Is what we are doing still English, and if it isn't, to what extent does it still depend upon the notion of English and the practice of English in other places?'

These questions, however, did not arise out of a collective certainty that what we were doing was correct: even after the threatened exodus of some students, there remained some uncertainty about the way that the subject was being treated, particularly in respect to the absence of grades. The issue of marking and grading and the authority which this seemed to express about the subject became a focal point for anxiety. Much of the work that followed was an attempt to analyse the meaning of English in this respect. In general terms, our intention was to make the subject of English the subject of analysis in order to reveal how its assumed integrity was 'made up' and held in place.

The work through which these questions evolved was relatively simple. We wanted to emphasize the importance of the reader in the production of textual meaning; we also wanted to demonstrate how an array of seemingly extra-textual forces intervened in this process, and also how these forces were dealt with and expressed by English in its institutional context. Everyone had to produce a piece of writing about a short story called 'The Rose'. It didn't matter how long or short their own piece of writing was, but it was important that they should think seriously about the short story and not be afraid to write down what they really thought. It was important, for our purposes, to prefigure in this process the eminence of the individual via the sovereignty of their genuine opinions, feelings, and experiences, since it was this very eminence, as we hoped to demonstrate in their own work, that was problematized by the material conditions of its production and was denied by the operations of the subject of English.

At first, writing paper and nothing else was handed out to the class. Students were asked to consider what would happen if we asked them to get on with the task of producing their own work about 'The Rose' which was to reflect, we emphasized, their most sincere thoughts and feelings about the short story, without them being given the chance to read it. A productive confusion followed: how would it be possible to produce a piece of writing which reflected the essential individuality of a reader's experience of a text if the text itself couldn't be read? What if, we asked, we allowed a few people to read the short story and then allowed these people to relay their reading of the text to the rest of the class. Would that be a satisfactory way of producing the requisite piece of work? Again, there was a degree of confusion and ambiguity about what was occurring: the whole point of the exercise was to produce a piece of work which reflected their genuine feelings and ideas about 'The Rose'. The authenticity of these feelings and ideas as their own true reflections on the story was deeply jeopardized by the mediation of an other (or others). Despite the initial uncertainties and the simplicity of the language which was being used, a series of complex and cogent philosophical themes were clearly starting to emerge from the ensuing debate. Firstly, the necessity of the activity of reading for the production of textual meaning, and the problem of the identity of the individual in relation to this activity; and secondly, the notion of the individual or pure self – in this case, as a reader – being impeded in its expression by that which is other to itself. During the very early stages of this work the class as a whole was generally very ardent in its contention that the entities of self and other-than-self were quite distinct. The fervency with which this point was made, that the difference between self and other-than-self should be maintained in order to preserve the authenticity of their own work as a reflection of their seemingly intact individual selves, suggested that we were dealing with urgent moral matters rather than abstract or philosophical issues. 'I might not agree with what they think the story is about'; 'They might have got it wrong'; 'But it won't be my feelings if someone else does it' were opinions which were commonly and forcefully expressed. In these circumstances, it was fairly easy to introduce and demonstrate the terms 'self' and 'other-than-self', which quickly became 'other'. And, if future work was to be done on post-structuralist themes, it was important that this should be so.

'The Rose' – a very simple and perhaps bizarre short story that we had devised produced a variety of different reactions.

The Rose

The old woman looked at the road which had been built across what used to be part of her garden. The enormous house where she used to live had also gone, and in its place stood the grim factory. She stood and watched in the cold of the morning as men and women marched along the road and in through the factory gates. 'I remember', she thought to herself, as she turned away from what used to be her home, 'that which used to be.'

Since we had taken pains beforehand to emphasize the importance of the carefully considered frankness of each student's response to the story, it was perhaps unsurprising that among the
relatively detailed critical appraisals of 'The Rose' there were a
number of pieces of work which were notable for their brief but
nevertheless complete condemnation of the anonymous story as
well as some that expressed a thorough indifference to it. Because of this degree of variation in response to the story, students,
working in groups, found it exceptionally difficult to determine
grades and criteria by which these responses might be objectively
applied to their work. An expression of the difficulty of this task
developed on the grounds that even though some pieces of work
appeared to be more sophisticated, all of the work which had
been produced was correct because it reflected the genuine belief of the person who expressed it. But how, we asked, was it
possible to determine whether or not genuine beliefs were
being reflected in any given piece of writing, regardless of
how sophisticated this work might appear to be? Did this also
mean that a text had a variety of meanings, all of which were
equally correct? And where did all these meanings come from?

The main response to these questions were the assertions that
the meaning of 'The Rose' was produced by the reader of 'The
Rose'; the true meaning of 'The Rose' was lost forever since it
only existed to the creator of the text – though it was difficult to
determine who the creator of the text was – perhaps it was the
reader, especially when it was remembered that originally no
work could be produced since the text was not available to read;
it was also asserted that the meaning of the short story could not
be criticized by anyone other than the creator of the meaning.
The manner of the expression of this last point especially
seemed again to suggest that an urgent moral problem was
being discussed rather than an abstruse and insignificant point
of philosophy or literary theory.

Students were able to articulate their responses, particularly
in relation to the last point about the creator of the meaning, by
making use of the notions of self and other which had only
recently been discussed. The moral vehemence with which they
now defended the integrity of their expressions of self through
their work about 'The Rose' against the incursion of the other
was intensified when the cover sheets for their English Litera-

ture and English Language coursework folders were handed out, and the implications of the boxes on the cover sheets entitled 'Teacher's Grade', 'Sub-group Moderation Grade', and 'Final Grade' were explained to them. It became increasingly obvious that the other, which was now clearly represented by the intractable power of the institution of the schoci and the examination structure, would intrude very significantly upon anything in English which represented their individual self integrity. Was this, in effect, what English was – the intrusion of the other in the form of an examination structure and a set of grading criteria which were supported by a variety of institutional powers? It was with this discussion and students' own written work about what had taken place during these lessons that the questions we started with emerged.

In some subsequent lessons the issue about whether or not the self was autonomously constituted reappeared. While a significant proportion of students believed in the autonomy of the self, alternative arguments were developed and admitted by students which expressed the dialectic of self and other in the formation of the identity of any subject.

The explicitness with which the teaching described above confronts the subject of English is difficult to sustain. There are other activities which throw into question assumptions about the subject's integrity. This can equally be done by looking at some of its more commonly agreed – and less controversial – contents, by using the insights of the students while introducing some fresh terminology and ideas. In preparation for the students' so-called 'extended studies' – a compulsory component for their English Literature coursework folders which must be organized individually – we decided to attempt to produce a collective taxonomy of fiction. Fiction was to be the object of study for this work. Fifth-year students were invited to produce a 'taxonomy' of fiction and a list was written, compiled from their suggestions, on the board. As the list lengthened, the viability of organizing discrete and definite categories became increasingly tenuous. Types of fiction included a thematic breakdown: war fiction, romantic fiction, science fiction; or fiction designed for particular audiences: children's fiction, women's fiction, men's fiction; as well as other, less easily identifiable forms of difference: realistic fiction and fantasy fiction, or popular fiction and classical fiction, fiction in written narrative form and TV fiction. Questions emerged: what did these differences mean and how were they held in place? How is it decided that some fiction is popular and some is classical? What is fiction, anyway? Is fiction simply not true? In what senses could fiction be true, or taken for truth? Is all writing which is not fiction simply true? Producing and confronting these questions and many others, students very quickly raised points that relate reading practices to social conventions, that recognize the arbitrariness of some of the distinctions made, that understand the constructedness of the category Literature and that identify the problem in maintaining a strict division between what is taken for truth and what is taken for fiction in a more general sense. If fiction is one of the objects of study in English, what becomes of English when the object proves so difficult to define?

Tackling the theme of the deconstructed subject of English, we have at times also attempted to involve classes as much as possible in discovering for themselves some of the themes which, for example, Derrida's work deals with: especially ways of looking at the ontology of meaning. We've tended to do this by asking questions in relation to specific (textual) examples, setting up practical activities about where meaning comes from, how it can or can't be decided, about where it varies, the extent to which it can vary, and so on. At times, terms such as '*différance*' or '*supplement*' have been introduced – terms certainly no more baffling than students are likely to encounter in maths or science lessons. Students at 15 can quite easily understand the kinds of questions which Derrida's work so very often deals with: What is textuality? What is a textual event? From where does textual meaning emanate? The variety of answers which often follow these kinds of questions can themselves be used to invite classes to think about and discuss the assumed unity of texts – and of the subject – they are examining. The implications of deconstructive thought about textual unities and integrities can then contribute towards, say, doing some theoretical work about the productions of meanings of texts in relation to culture, society, institutions, language.

An important element in work which is focused on how meanings operate, can be tackled, for instance, by an examination of ideas which tend to be called Lacanian but which are not necessarily dependent on Lacan's knottily obscure texts for their introduction. So, with simple diagrammatic representations the idea of the divided subject can be introduced. The difference between conscious and unconscious can be explored. The importance of repression, the operations of memory and censorship can be dealt with as part of a topic which is dealing with the theory of the subject according to Lacanian psychoanalysis, though it won't necessarily announce itself as that. The role of language in the splitting of the subject and the 'sliding of the signified under the signifier' can be introduced, too, so that the whole issue of meanings in relation to the individual and to culture can be understood in a more far-reaching and critical fashion. Simple word games, or very direct and simple explanations conducted in dialogue with the class can be used to convey these conventionally difficult points, to the extent that mixed-ability classes of 15 and 16 year olds can begin to use with confidence arcane terms such as 'imaginary', 'symbolic', and 'real'.

Despite phenomenology, despite the almost anti-textual work with texts, and a further year and a half of exploring English in relation to a wide variety of essentially poststructuralist themes, the original questions remain disturbingly unanswered for both ourselves and our students: what now, as a result of this work, is the subject? Have we changed, through our discussions and our collective practices, what English means? Is what we are doing still English, and if it isn't, to what extent does it still depend on the notion of English and the practice of English in other places? In the end, of course, teachers' grades, moderators' grades, and final grades, in the name of the subject, will be awarded, and on this basis subject positions will inevitably be effectively prescribed. It would, however, be too easy, and perhaps also self-indulgently nihilistic, to suggest that ultimately, for all concerned, our work must come to nothing in the face of the enormously powerful institutional, and other, structures which support the subject. What the questions require is at least some further consideration of some of the issues they involve.

If, according to Gramsci, 'everyone is a philosopher', not everyone enjoys the status of a philosopher nor equal opportunity to practice philosophy or theory. In the school context it is perfectly possible to accord Sanjay Patel (a student engaged in GCSE English and English Literature courses) the right to appropriate the privileged discourse of, say, deconstruction. And this need not simply be a matter of handing on Derrida's formulations, remade for accessibility, to the vacuum of Sanjay's imagined ignorance of these things, but can also be a matter of enabling Sanjay's own deconstructive drives a place in the formulation of teaching and learning. But the pedagogic practice which unorthodoxly grants this right of access to Sanjay and his contemporaries without distinction or exclusion remains embedded in the institutional functions that serve, quite crudely, to award grades, to establish distinctions, to define positively and negatively, opportunities as widely differentiated as YTS or Oxbridge. The principle of difference could hardly be more clearly illustrated. There is no immediately available position for the English teacher in the secondary comprehensive school which could dissolve the contradiction of this position. Any pedagogy, though, which doesn't in some critical way explicitly address the punitive element in the function of the reward system – and the ideology that disguises and 'naturalizes' it – is in danger of being politically impotent and gestural. For English teachers in schools, particularly, attempting to engage in alternative, politicized pedagogies, this must remain a difficult issue, because the subject is not compatible with its theorization. Any approach to this difficulty must – in the context of the comprehensive school, the very site of social reproduction – be related to ways in which teachers negotiate their own status as authorized purveyors of knowledge in institutions which, more blatantly than many others in state education, display the equation of knowledge with power. At the moment we are faced with English: realistically, we have to accommodate theory alongside/within/against English.

But what is the subject, English? – the question raised for us during the minor drama of the phenomenological crisis. A perplexed head struggled to understand the issues which were involved. Clearly the notion of an established English was being alluded to by parents and students who worried for the sake of the subject's integrity. An earnest desire was expressed in letters to the perplexed head that the English offered by the institution should be 'based on our cultural heritage' and that a traditional English course with set texts reflecting 'the English literary cultural heritage' would be preferred to what was described as 'interesting and innovative efforts'. The traditional English that was being alluded to was conceived of as being a cohesive and uniform subject. Its existence in this sense was undoubted. Other than being a powerful allusion, however, the existence of this English is much more doubtful.

In secondary schools throughout the country there are many Englishes. It requires no detailed or extensive empirical research to verify this fact. Indeed, the history of English is undisputably a history of changes. Even within a single institution the subject can be fractured into different levels – GCSE and A level, for instance. Across institutional boundaries, syllabus requirements, and pedagogical practices, English is discontinuous to say the least.

Where, then, does the notion of a cohesive English come from, and how is it sustained? As the above comments from parents would seem to indicate, the subject of English pre-exists any analysis of what that subject might be. Its security is founded upon unchallenged notions of a common 'cultural heritage'. Any analysis of what this common cultural heritage is and how it is sustained through the teaching practices of English runs the risk of undermining the subject's integrity.

One way of examining how this subject is held in place is to consider some points about the production of the English teacher. Teacher-training courses, whether they are the Postgraduate Certificate of Education or the Bachelor of Education in English, seem, in our view, to have relatively little to do with the formulation of the English teacher's subject position; they are more likely, from our experiences as teacher tutors of student teachers, to be about modifying the prospective English teacher's subject position in relation to the new context involved in becoming a teacher. The PGCE (Postgraduate Certificate of Education) lasts for only one academic year, during which there is an approximately fourteen-week contact period with schools.

Whilst the B.Ed. takes four academic years to complete and a
considerably longer time is spent actually teaching, the nature
and length of the course, like the PGCE, is not to displace the
already established subject within the institution of the school.
The common feature of all PGCE and B.Ed. courses is that they
approach English on the assumption that it is already there:
whilst different strategies are adopted by different courses about
how to gain proximity to the subject most effectively, it remains
true that the teaching practices themselves are not seen as
actually determining what the subject is. Indeed, the PGCE
and the B.Ed. in English depend for their existence upon the
identity of a subject that precedes its own formulation.

Again, from our own experience of PGCE students, teaching
courses seem to be obsessively concerned with discussions
about the accessibility of texts and ideas. The force of already
existing assumptions about what is teachable and what it is
desirable to teach inevitably constrains choices available to
student teachers, whatever position they may be starting from.
English – and in this case specifically English in schools – has
already been written before the education student embarks
upon the PGCE; since, while this course supports the subject in
its a priori contingency of existence, the English of the PGCE is
only meaningful in relation to the English of the institution of
the school. The content of English must be redefined for a
different audience. The teacher thus becomes an agent in the
selection of what are deemed to be appropriate activities, topics,
texts: the various aspects that constitute the specific kinds of
learning their students will have access to. Even where PGCE
courses enable theoretical or deconstructive approaches, student teachers meet, on teaching practice and during the probationary year, the institutional forces that place them, and the
ideas about English teaching they may arrive with, in subordinate roles within a very hierarchical establishment. A process
of integration occurs: the student or probationary teacher will
be expected, in varying degrees, to endorse whatever values
and ethos pertain within the school. Within departments the
student's and probationary teacher's working horizons will be
determined not only by their own already established subject
position, but also by what texts are available, what practices are
maintained, what exam syllabuses are followed, what reading

and writing practices prevail, what kind of student–teacher relationships are in order, and so on. These will, in one way or another, contextualize their efforts as teachers of English in production.

The importance of teaching courses, and of the probationary year, lies in the fact that they are processes by which the certification, that is to say the professionalization, of the English teacher is achieved. The ontological status of English is expressed by the existence and practices of a professional class. To interfere with that status is potentially, at least, to molest a professional class position – as one aspect of the phenomenological crisis demonstrated to us. One of the teachers involved critically in that crisis was, in fact, working through the probationary year. The situation was institutionally made more manageable by the fact that the other teacher involved was invested with the grander role of Head of Faculty. The professional and institutional investment in the bearer of the latter position was an important factor that enabled the crisis to be ridden. To promote a deconstructed English, it is important that institutional features – including, for example, exam syllabuses – are utilized opportunistically.

Mode 3 GCSE schemes can in effect offer limitless possibilities to put theory to work in the cooperative production of 'useful knowledges' for the subjects of certification. They cannot, of course, undo the grading system. That would require much greater general political will and initiative, and would constitute a much more revolutionary situation within the whole field of education that can at present be imagined. Nevertheless, the points of intervention have to be realistically identified and utilized. What we offer in our description is not an account of a course, still less an exemplary model or paradigm, but it does, we believe, go some way towards defining the possibilities of change in the nature of the subject. Pedagogical relations in the theorized classroom of 'English' must be founded on the notion of empowerment. The position of the teacher still depends more than in some liberal progressive practices on the urge to make the conditions for learning possible – that is, on the position of authority. To 'deconstruct' is not to get rid of. But this authority is one which is founded upon the consciousness of what it means to be in control of a discourse; it sets the limits, defines the terms, enables or disables lines of pursuit – directs enquiry here or there. The very authority which has this function of control and surveillance can be used itself to enable examination of its own discursive inheritance, its own institutional position.

Also, and perhaps more significantly, the authority of the teacher is that which allows the unities of the discourse – in this case English – to be actively deconstructed – explicitly, in the very form and content of its practice. A substantial spate of work, for instance, on gender, beginning with an elementary introduction to Saussurian linguistics and semiotics, and going on to apply techniques to critical readings of various cultural forms and products – TV ads, soaps, magazines, children's stories, and canonical texts – which may not appear especially radical or innovative, may actually make clear the decentring potential of this kind of analysis and may extend 'beyond the text'(ual) to explore the relations between the textual and the forms of subjectivity being experienced by students. This may, for example, be explicitly related to the specificities of dialogue in 'daily' social discourse and its many, various contexts – a field not much examined by textualists and textualisms.

This kind of deconstruction is practical: it equates – by treating with equal seriousness or irreverence – TV ads with D. H. Lawrence, Dickens with Janet and John; gives credibility to – while questioning – the pleasures of texts as various as the 'Swan' kitchen appliance advert, *Jackie* magazine stories, and Chekhov stories. One of the major effects of working with gender in this intertextual way is to deconstruct canons, assumptions, and orders – practically, involving the active participation of the students in the whole process, not just in dialogic interchange, but also in the work of analysis and reconstruction of meanings and positions – in short, in textual relations.

The same kind of deconstructive effect is possible working within the field of so-called multiculturalism – where the unities of the discourse are differently undone. If the text in question is a product of Black South African theatre, or the Bengali novel, 'English' (its 'Englishness') is immediately, if not necessarily explicitly, called into question. The same kind of decentring moves can be made with student's writings. The invitation, 'Compare your story with Chekhov's and with a friend's' can have the same kind of effect. This kind of offer can take many forms: 'Compare your representation of female identities with Lawrence's: which do you prefer and why?', and so on.

In the classroom it has been traditional that the teacher exerts some kind of control over the texts that are under scrutiny: whether the texts are *Jackie* magazines, classic realist novels, poems, or TV programmes, it is most often the teacher who authorizes them as appropriate objects for study, the teacher who claims to command the various strategies for reading them. One way of deconstructing this aspect of teacher authority and control in order to adjust the weighting of dialogic exchange (the dialogue always remaining, of course, within the institutional structuring of 'English') is to allow students to choose their own texts in free reading time, and for the teacher and student to keep reading records. The teacher in this way is not in control of the knowledge. The teacher in dialogue with the student thus enjoys a more genuine hermeneutic relationship while the student enjoys possession of the texts which come in time to constitute a personal reading biography. This biography, itself a flexible text, is available for exchange with other students, and this, too, can open possibilities for exchange and control.

We have argued that English is very firmly in place, ideologically and institutionally, and have attempted to describe some of the processes and forces that keep it so. We've also tried to describe some elements of a practice which utilizes institutional gaps in order to deconstruct, at the discursive level, what English is in its fundamental 'subject being'. We've attempted to utilize the very forms and contents of English itself, in conjunction with the kind of consciousness that theory has afforded us, in order to work both within and without English: to expose English and its complicity in the cultural and institutional powers that have sustained it. It is in this ceaseless interplay between what English is and is not – the dialectic between its self and its other, to put it phenomenologically – that we see the main thrust of our work.

7
Teaching difference/
teaching differently

Peter Humm

I thought briefly of calling this chapter, which describes the experience of teaching a course on Gender and Society, 'Teaching like a man'. The trouble with that title, as second thoughts sensibly suggested, is that what was intended to echo recent theoretical work on gendered reading sounded more like a mock country and western ballad or a track from Lenny Henry's tribute to soul. However, I still want to use that discarded opening to introduce some of the questions that worried me as I thought about the course and how to write about it in this book.

Why begin with a joke, albeit a modest joke, a joke about modesty? Why open with worries? Who was I trying to disarm apart from myself? Elaine Showalter has described the importance for feminist critics of the 'anxiety of authorship' and it is that useful insecurity in writing about gender, getting it right, that I want to take on (Showalter 1987: 130). For just as feminist critics have to cope with the spectre of the 'humourless feminist', so male teachers and critics interested in learning from feminist theory have to deal with the imaginary imposition of the 'right-on man', who can be trusted to tread the correct path, one of the righteous brothers to the women's movement. That is not how I see my role on a course that I teach with three feminist colleagues – Alison Assiter, Angela John, and Joan

Ryan – to around thirty second-year students, nearly all of whom are women. The structure of the course will be described later but first, something more on the serious implications of that thrown-away title – what does it mean, what should it mean to teach as or like a man?

The phrase was suggested by the essays by Stephen Heath and Robert Scholes collected in the recent and very helpful anthology *Men in Feminism* (1987), which imagine what it might mean to read as a man. Their enquiry echoes Jonathan Culler's section in his book *On Deconstruction* called 'Reading as a woman'. Culler in turn is responding to the work of those feminist critics such as Luce Irigaray who have described *l'écriture féminine* and suggested ways in which it needs be read. Pausing this critical loop at Elaine Showalter's essay from the same collection, 'Critical cross-dressing: male feminists and the woman of the year' enables me to move from questions of reading strategy to the conjunction of theory and pedagogy which is the subject of this chapter and this book. Showalter suggests that 'the way into feminist criticism for the male theorist must involve a confrontation with what might be implied by reading as a man and with a questioning or a surrender of paternal privileges' (Showalter 1987: 126–7). That first critical project is now under way, producing individual readings of texts from an announced male perspective. What interests me in this chapter is how male teachers and their students can benefit from this feminist questioning of paternal or patriarchal authority.

Collected accounts of feminist pedagogy emphasize the interactive, cooperative styles which women's studies has learned from the women's movement. That tradition can be connected to the radicalizing effect of poststructuralist theory in breaking open canonical traditions of authority and hierarchy. Feminism has been the most effective critical approach in forcing the recognition of the 'folly of thinking about reading in terms of a transcendental subject: the ideal reader reading a text that is the same for all' (Scholes 1987: 206). Robert Scholes's description of the encounter between texts and readers can be applied to the seminar, for just as readers are constituted differently, so are teachers and their students: 'both texts and readers are already written when they meet, but both may emerge from the encounter altered in some crucial respect' (Scholes 1987: 206). So teaching or studying like a man would involve recognizing as feminist critics, teachers, and students have done that a neutral reading of any text denies both subjectivity and history. Male students and teachers can learn what their female colleagues have never been able to ignore – the difference their gender has made and continues to make in their experience of education.

Accepting the feminist invitation to confront the meanings of masculinity is certainly important for men but within a degree such as the Thames BA in Humanities, which always attracts as many if not more women as men, both sexes need to benefit from that analysis. This will mean moving the discussion of difference from the high ground of theory to the immediate practicalities of how a course on gender and society is designed and structured. We may not get it right, the course will change and take on new directions but that uncertainty remains an important principle. As Stephen Heath has argued, 'correctness is not the point: being properly correct is purely theoretical, pure theory; the reality is different, is unceasing, difficult, heterogeneous, impossible, everyday' (Heath 1987: 44–5). The reality of Gender and Society is that it is also the course I have most enjoyed teaching and have learned the most from.

Gender and Society is designated in the Thames code as an 'ID' course, meaning simply that it is taught by staff from different disciplines/divisions within the School: Alison comes from the Philosophy division, Angie and Joan are historians, and I am a member of the English division. But ID conventionally has another meaning, and it's this question of *identity* that I want to include within my account of how such an interdisciplinary structure works in practice. We begin the course with a six-week series of lectures and seminars designed to raise the question of how gender can be used as a problematic. We talk about theories of gender identity, the notion of difference, the development of feminist theory and scholarship; seminar texts range from Sheila Rowbotham's *Hidden from History* (1973) to the Pluto anthology on *The Sexuality of Men* (Metcalfe and Humphries 1985) to the students' own short written accounts of how they want to make use of the course. The students then choose between two historical case studies on either 'Women and work in the twentieth century' or 'Protective legislation', followed nine weeks later by either a study of feminist theory focused on the work of Simone de Beauvoir or the section I take on the representation of gender. The year ends with another series of general seminars using texts such as Lynne Segal's *Is the Future Female?* (1987), and Anne Phillips's *Divided Loyalties* (1987), which keep the debate over the significance of gender open and the course itself open-ended.

The interdisciplinary contrast that is first apparent is between areas of study recognizably placed within feminist history and philosophy and my own reconstruction of 'English' as a more restless movement between distinct discourses and cultural practices. There does seem to be a need, as other essays in this book attest, for those inverted commas which can signal the useful uncertainty over the present identity of English. It is my reworking of the subject of English as much as my gender that gives me an edgy position on this course.

I was going to ascribe a kind of double marginality to this redefinition of my discipline base and my rarity as one of the few men on the Gender and Society course. But that would be to evoke a plaintive distinction that I do not feel. Just as I greatly approve and enjoy the broadening of English into cultural studies so I value the different context, the context of difference provided by the gender course. I want to consider how difference can be used both as an issue for discussion and as a method of enquiry – difference as theory and in practice.

The question of difference is certainly controversial. When, in one of the introductory seminars, we asked students to decide whether anonymous passages from autobiographical essays were written by a man or a woman, one person explained with great conviction just how uncomfortable such an exercise made her feel – she did not want to separate and label people in this way. Earlier, the same woman had commented that she was pleased to find a seminar on male sexuality included because that had never been a significant issue in her enjoyable woman-centred life and now might be a good time to find out something more. So it is never possible to predict any pattern of responses to the questions raised on and by this course; it is this uncertainty which accounts for the nervous confidence with which I approach my lectures on the theoretical debate within feminism over the meaning and value of difference. The nervousness comes from my recognition of the ironies surrounding a male lecturer quoting the work of Luce Irigaray and other celebrants of *l'écriture féminine* or in my mentioning Gayatri Chakrovorty Spivak's suggestion that women today may have to take 'the risk of essence' in order to think really differently. The confidence comes – and it came more slowly – from the realization that students are deeply interested in these questions and do not much mind who introduces them as long as he or she does it well. Besides, I am not sure that the paradox is so much greater than the one inscribed in my perennial role as someone lecturing on the need for more democratic and open ways of learning. I do know that to ignore such arguments and contradictions in my teaching on the representation of gender would be to bleach out much of the most exciting and valuable work done by feminist theorists and by those men who have tried to present their own response.

The presence in the seminar room of two or three men places difference on the agenda of the Gender and Society course in a more immediate fashion than may be found in the separate sphere of women's studies. The practical decision of my feminist colleagues at Thames to develop a joint course on gender rather than to move apart into women's studies touches upon some of the most charged political and theoretical arguments in feminism. That debate I must leave to them but there are complementary issues that I and other male teachers working within coeducational systems need to address.

Several of the essays collected in *Men in Feminism* approach this polarized ground with a careful attentiveness that is worth following. Stephen Heath in 'Male feminism' argues that

> men should take seriously at last the 'hetero' in heterosexuality which means the heterogeneity in us, on us, through us, and also take seriously the 'sexuality' which means, I think, giving up precisely heterosexuality, that oppressive representation of the sexual as act, complementarity, two sexes, coupling.

(Heath 1987: 22)

Elizabeth Weed in 'A man's place' attaches Heath's argument to the 'utopian vision so necessary as the always receding horizon of any political project . . . the realizing of *real* difference, of real heterosexuality and not the imaginary, constructed, determining two sexes with which we live' (Weed 1987: 75). Naomi Schor in 'Dreaming dissymmetry' discusses the seductive dangers of Roland Barthes's 'discourse of indifferentiation [whereby] denied sexual difference shades into sexual indifference and . . . into a paradoxical reinscription of the very differences the strategy was designed to denaturalise' (Schor 1987: 100).

What I find valuable in these arguments is more than the validation of a male presence on the course as the most visible marker of difference. Being the true male grit in the feminine oyster – father of pearl – may be a necessary but is hardly a comfortable role. The move from heterosexuality to heterosexualities provides more than a subject for discussion in lectures and seminars; it suggests ways of teaching and learning that can make a significant break from the old authorized patterns. The multiple advantage of hetereogeneity is particularly important in such an interdisciplinary course attended by the ever-available stereotype which sets the feminine seductions of English against the hard case studies of History. Before I describe in more detail the section of the course I am responsible for, I want to say something about the pedagogy which influenced its design and which has in turn been shaped by the way in which students made the course work.

In her essay 'Keeping the color in *The Color Purple*', Cora Kaplan suggests that Alice Walker's 'parable of the history of Black female subjectivity' needs to be read and taught in a 'three dimensional, diachronic and dialectical manner' (Kaplan 1986: 187). Elsewhere in *Sea Changes*, Kaplan invokes a fourth 'D' in referring to Bakhtin's concept of the dialogic imagination. This stream of double-consciousness has been an important resource in feminist criticism and there is a tradition which sees, as Alice Jardine puts it, that 'doubleness . . . has some fundamental, historically specific but fundamental libidinal connection to women and the way they experience the world' (Jardine and Smith 1987: 250). I can recognize the ground of that claim but at the same time I want to discover how men can learn from and contribute to that liberating notion of a full heterogeneity. This means something more difficult than the careful study of feminist reading lists even if they do include Bakhtin and Barthes and Foucault in the canon of critics useful to feminism. It means recognizing that my own experience of feminism has been a criss-cross of theoretical reading and teaching practice and intense, at times tensed, discussions, arguments, and misunderstandings with those feminists who have become part of my unsingular life.

I do not have the space here or the confidence in relating the personal to the political to extend this further into autobiography. But I do believe that any account of teaching gender cannot and should not avoid the material, social, institutional, domestic context in which the ideas that inform this course have been worked out. For that movement between a debate in the seminar room and the varied, often contradictory knowledges and experiences that we all carry into our education is what I am trying to encourage in those taking the course, and that must include myself. That is not a call for a series of self-regarding conversion narratives – 'How I discovered the Smirnoff effect of feminism' – but it does mean that male teachers need to learn the arguments around experience that have been so important a part of the interchange between women's studies, feminist theory, and the women's movement. Recognizing the tensions within feminism over the value to be placed upon experience can provide suspiciously neat separations between theory and practice, abstraction and confession, the historical and the autobiographical to which it is all too easy to ascribe gender stereotypes. And yet, as Michèle Barrett has pointed out, 'the early women's liberation practice of consciousness-raising was based on a recognition of the fact that each woman's experience needed to be made collective in order to be understood; that is, it needed to be theorized' (Barrett 1987: 32). Similarly, Teresa de Lauretis has argued the need for women to 'theorize experience on our way to theorizing and textualizing the female subject' (de Lauretis 1984: 197).

I can refer students to these articles and debates but I can also try to provide a context in which such a collective theorizing of experience can take place. It is here that recent accounts of the 'dynamics of feminist teaching' do provide a valuable shock of recognition. Many of the reports collected in *Gendered Subjects* or in the recent overview of the 'dynamics of the Women's Studies classroom' in *Women's Studies International Forum* emphasize the need to ensure a sense of security and confidence which can be shared by those discovering the difficulty and excitement of moving between the personal and the politically charged. It is the practical details of how to encourage such a way of working that proves the value of what is so seldom discussed in most British higher education – how effective are the teaching methods that remain hidden within the sanctuary of the seminar and lecture room. At Thames, as at other universities and colleges where I have worked, such discussions of pedagogy are confined to the occasional case-conference on why a particular group is not going very well; modestly, we keep the successes to ourselves. I want now to describe briefly some of the successful work that was produced by a group of students who chose last year to study the representation of gender.

I had decided on this title and this general area of study because it immediately moved me off base in a way in which a course such as Women and Literature or even Gender and Writing would not have done. Using films, television shows, and the minidrama of advertising narratives, paintings, and music videos as well as fiction both popular and canonical made it harder for me to settle into the role of expert reader which seems to hover over my shoulder as I confront a literary text before an awed or bored or anyway fairly silent audience in an English seminar. There is then a double sense in which the term representation of gender signals a political commitment to a more cooperative and open style of learning. First, it acknowledges the feminist argument that questions of the representation of women and men, sexual difference, and gender relations have always been political questions; representation has its effects. The other advantage is that watching slides or video tapes focuses attention not on some mysterious deeper meaning discernible only to the trained eye of the professional but non-Machereyan reader (although she or he is not going to reveal it until everybody in the seminar has been coaxed into having a try) but on what can be seen illuminated on the screen.

Close reading of a Georgia O'Keeffe painting or a careful comparison between the appearance of Madonna in a triptych and in an MTV video works in a way that the textual criticism of a literary text finds difficult in the unnatural setting of a seminar – people can see immediately what somebody else in the room has found in a scene. This has a particular advantage in a course dealing with issues of sexuality which are difficult to discuss in the best of circumstances. As Nancy K. Miller reported on her own use of paintings in a course called 'Studies in French eighteenth-century fiction and painting: ideologies of representation':

> showing slides and 'reading' paintings . . . brought woman's body . . . physically into the classroom . . . [as] a consequence . . . it identified all of us in the room as gendered and sexual beings . . . It was a kind of enactment of the inescapable relations between bodies and theories, the intersection of the personal and political.
>
> (Miller 1985: 197)

What I would add is the need to ensure that this responsibility is not borne only by the female body: it is important to reproduce slides from Margaret Walter's *The Nude Male* as well as from Roszika Parker and Griselda Pollock's *Old Mistresses*. This year I have used Rosemary Betterton's *Looking On* as the core text but there is still a case for supplementing the book's subtitled concentration on *Images of Femininity in the Visual Arts and the Mass Media* with, to take past examples, advertisements of Nick Kamen or Ron Peck's wry short film on the vulnerabilities of male desire – *What Can I Do with a Male Nude*. This risks parodying as some kind of equal visual opportunities policy but, in a coeducational course on gender, there is a serious need to consider the consequences of always depicting woman as the sole, gazed-upon object of desire.

These questions of pleasure are caught up in other issues of power and authority in education. For as David Lusted points out in 'Why pedagogy?', there has long been 'an implicit assertion that a revised subject constitutes in itself a radical intervention in education, somehow shifting the social relations of the class-room in more democratic directions, providing a site for dramatic changes of consciousness in and by itself' (Lusted

1986a: 8). So simply switching channels from a Reithian syllabus to a determined attention to the popular taste of ITV does not in itself guarantee a radical teaching practice. What is needed instead is precisely the variety and complexity of discourse available to any viewer with a facility for switching from one channel to another and back again. Translating difference not as either/or but as both/and is both a theoretical position and a pedagogic one: part of the process of questioning the binary schemes of intellectual tradition is a means for students to ask their own questions, to become creators and constructors, as well as learners of knowledge.

The most persuasive example of the theory and practice informing this course comes then from the work created by the students. I had early on suggested to those choosing 'Representation of gender' that the essay requirement might be met by a piece of short fiction or other forms of what we have still to call 'creative writing'. Despite earlier experience, both in America and at Thames, of including such alternatives to the essay in coursework, I was still unsure how this would be received by those concerned about the formality of examinations. I therefore advised those who chose to write a story or a passage of autobiography to preface the piece with a more theoretical account of the issues it allowed them to consider. Nobody would be left to face the finals without the protection of an essay: the story-plus-essay became belt-plus-braces designed to keep up standards.

Not everybody accepted this back-tracking invitation; I received a good number of essays written in conventional style if not on conventional English subjects. But there were also an impressive number of packages putting together, for example, a video compilation of television advertising with a detailed analysis and survey of viewer responses, a tape of music videos and a witty account of heavy metal masculinity. Others wrote about the conflict between theory and practice in their own lives so that a question on gender sterotypes was answered by a dual account of the confused models of female identity provided by *Cagney and Lacey* and by women in manual trades; another double essay used Nancy Chodorow's work to theorize the experience of becoming a stepmother. One final example is of someone using John Berger's *Ways of Seeing* and other theories of the gaze to write a short story on how a woman is 'almost continually accompanied by her own image of herself' which went along with a sharp account of the way in which women singers such as Mel and Kim play to their audience.[1]

Switching in this way between the familiar icons of popular culture and the difficult discovery of the uses of theory gives a greater confidence to humanities students facing the conservative complaint over the easy luxury of their chosen course. By drawing on students' own experience and expertise in decoding the visual narratives so dominant in our cultural understanding of sexual difference, 'Representation of gender' became a more democratic and individually useful course. The women who read John Berger or Laura Mulvey or Luce Irigaray's critique of the 'scopic economy' could also place that theory alongside their daily knowledge of what it means to be the surveyed. The men on the course could hear very directly of the anger and hurt caused by the incessant, inescapable depiction of women as commodity. The short stories, autobiographies, video presentations that resulted from this doubled knowledge are the best evidence of the advantages of heterogeneity.

What these doubled essays proved is both the skill with which people can move from one discourse to another and also the pressing links between those forms of writing and experience outside the seminar room. The issues raised in this course matter a great deal to the students who take it: there is an urgency in the discussion of the family wage or the stereotyping of motherhood that is not often found in our seminars. It is in that sense that a course on gender and society can take on what Alice Jardine describes as the necessary characteristic of 'a feminist text – whether written by a man or a woman . . . the *inscription* of struggle' (Jardine and Smith 1987: 58). But that struggle needs to be part of a process that will encourage and empower those trying to make sense of what they learn from their reading and from their knowledge of the world.

The theorizing of experience needs then to have effect outside the seminar room if courses such as Gender and Society are to realize their full educational value. It is this political purpose that can make the study of difference really different from an abstracted theoreticism or an inward-looking exchange of experience. 'Difference, to be operative, has to be acted ON and acted OUT, collectively, in the *here and now* of our common world' (Braidotti 1987: 241). The need for collective action in the common world of the polytechnic is apparent whenever we consider questions of access to our courses or equal opportunities within them. The problem still is that such urgent educational issues are marginalized in exactly the same way as the study of gender is separated out from the 'male stream' of academic enquiry. Every term, we have meetings between staff and students to discuss the implementation of Thames's equal opportunities policy; it is no surprise that the most conscientious and helpful contributions come most frequently from those students who have taken the Gender and Society course. Meanwhile, many of the others whose programme in Part Two includes no systematic study of gender (and this goes for the majority of our male students) continue to remain apart from the collective discussion of how to improve child-care facilities or make our patterns of teaching more sensitive to the patterns of our students' lives. On a degree where over one-third of the students do not enter directly from school, such issues cannot remain separated. It is important, to give some obvious but easily unregarded examples, that a seminar on gender and education is not offered only at three in the afternoon when parents have to leave in order to collect children from school, or that a reading week designed to allow space for individual study does not coincide with the school half-term holiday, which immediately invades that space.

Making these connections between the living room and the seminar room is one of the ways in which the course Gender and Society can generate the useful knowledge that can effect change as well as talking about it. It is important to be clear and realistic about what kind of changes I have in mind. Accounts of life in American classrooms can be as cheering as the actual enthusiastic presence of American students. And yet, despite my frequent nostalgia for the energy of the students I taught in Massachusetts and California, I retain a modest English scepticism about the claim implicit in such anthologies as *Gendered Subjects* – 'this course changes lives'. Nevertheless, there are, as the testimony of the students who have contributed to this book makes clear, secure autobiographical grounds for sharing that unEnglish ambition: people do think differently after three years on a degree and that difference does effect change. Many of those changes take place in the public sector to which large numbers of our students remain so stubbornly committed, but there are other changes in people's career and personal direction that cannot be so clearly traced. What a course such as Gender and Society within an area such as Humanities can provide is a space in which these connections between the public and the private are taken seriously. This might mean inviting former students to come back and talk about their current work in providing wider training opportunities for women and ethnic minorities; it must mean considering carefully the opportunities we provide for all the different communities who take our degree. For if teaching Gender and Society has any point, then the society we analyse and challenge must include the one we work in.

Note

1 I have referred directly here to the work of Jane Pond, Sue Lubowitz, Mitzi Weighell, Libby Agate, and Tracey Poole. I would like to thank them, Marcella Marshall, and the others who made this course such an encouraging experience. Helen Taylor and Alison Light read earlier versions of this essay and I have greatly appreciated their advice.

8
Notes in the margin:
teaching women's writing

Jan Montefiore

My teaching at the University of Kent includes two feminist courses: a postgraduate course, 'The feminist aesthetic', an option taught by Dr Kate McLuskie and myself in alternate years for the MA degree in Women's Studies offered by the Faculty of Social Sciences, and 'Women and poetry', a two-term course offered as an option to students doing a BA degree in English and American Literature. In this chapter, I intend to discuss the main problems – and rewards – of relating feminist theory to teaching practice.

The fact that the University of Kent has had from the outset an intellectual and institutional commitment to interdisciplinary teaching and learning, and a pluralist openness to experiment, and has moreover pioneered the first MA degree in Women's Studies offered by any British university, might all suggest that this is an ideally enlightened centre for feminist teaching and research to flourish. It is quite true that feminist academics have here a degree of freedom to pursue teaching and research in the area of their interest. But this freedom is neither unconstrained nor uncontested. Although there is, for example, knowledge of and interest in feminist criticism and theory among some members of the English Board, there are also less positive responses, varying from unenthusiastic tolerance through indifference to hostility. It is only during the last three years that teaching 'The feminist aesthetic' has been formally recognized by the English Board to the extent of allotting teaching credit:

previous to this, the two-hour weekly seminar had to be taught in our own time as it didn't officially count as part of our teaching. The course 'Women and poetry', which I am responsible for constructing and teaching, and which was new in the academic year (1987–8) is the first woman-centred course ever offered to undergraduates by the English Board.

The structure of the English BA at Kent includes 'options': relatively specialized areas (e.g., Irish writing, American writing in the 1920s, melodrama), of which students choose one each year in addition to their 'basic' courses, which cover the main map of English Literature in a fairly conventional way. Those options allow staff to connect teaching with research and to teach in their particular areas of interest. This meant that it was easy to propose the 'Women and poetry' option. But getting this approved at a Board meeting turned out to be difficult. Decisions taken at Board meetings are generally reached by consensus. This one was put to the vote and passed by a two-thirds majority, not without much argument and against some strong opposition. Meanwhile, although space is made in most of our 'basic' courses for at least one lecture outlining a feminist critique or approach, their content and structure remain on the whole unaffected by feminist (and other) critiques of the construction of the canon of English Literature. For example, the 'basic' course 'Eighteenth-Century Studies',[1] on which I taught for a short time, includes as key texts Pope's *Rape of the Lock*, Defoe's *Roxana* and *Moll Flanders*, and Richardson's *Clarissa*; Fielding's *Tom Jones* and Swift's misogynist poems are also taught, the latter as a version of pastoral and anti-pastoral. No woman's writing is studied at all. In other words, nearly half of the texts on this course are dominated by masculine representations of women, defining them (us?) in terms of a sexuality which is either an object of male appetite (or distaste), or a problem in representation, or both. The lecturers who planned and taught the course were all men except for me (but I came in for one year only when the course was long established). None of them found it odd or questionable that they as men should be teaching a clutch of texts so obsessively concerned, mostly in very demeaning ways, with female sexuality, to classes consisting mainly of young women. The presence of a woman teacher plus the addition of, perhaps, a feminist lecture on *Clarissa*, can't make much difference to a syllabus whose implicit assumptions are that intellectual discourse, including that Reason which was so important to eighteenth-century thought, belongs to men, and that women are unimportant except in terms of their sexuality and its arousal of masculine desire, fear, disgust, or pleasure.[2]

In this context, feminist criticism certainly has a presence, but only as a marginal practice: without much political clout, it is felt to constitute a threat to the authority of established practice, not least by its uppity claim that women's writing is *important* enough to study and teach. So the first problem that a feminist course raises, even before you begin to teach it, is how to transform its marginal existence into an effective challenge to the blind spots and inadequacies of conventional literary-critical practice. This task is much easier in constructing and teaching 'The feminist aesthetic', because the context of an interdisciplinary MA in Women's Studies enables students and teachers both to begin from the assumption that women's writing – and experience – are important and interesting, and to draw on varieties of discourse, such as political theory or psychology, other than literary criticism. In this context, studying feminist theory together with women's writing doesn't feel like a marginal practice. Yet even here, the problem of self-definition recurs in seminars. We cannot as feminists just wish away the literary-critical traditions which we engage with and oppose: we then have the problem of defining our relation to them[3] – a relation which appears however misleadingly, to be marginal.

Their marginal status affects the teaching of feminist courses at Kent in good and bad ways. They are enjoyable and interesting to teach and students bring to them much enthusiasm and a sense of intellectual adventure. Feminist students and teachers feel part of a much wider feminist intellectual and political life. The large-scale and still increasing publication of women's writing by feminist publishing houses; the challenging scholarship and theory produced by feminist academics; the establishment of journals like *Signs* and *Feminist Review*; the profusion of conferences, day schools, and public lectures on feminist issues and women's writing (as well as debates around sexuality, gay writing, black, and post-colonial literature and politics) – all these are manifestations of a flourishing international feminist community. But we still have a problem, both theoretical and pedagogic, with our relation – or lack of one – to 'mainstream' English studies. This problem is not of course unique to ourselves. (It is interesting in this context to compare our experience as feminist academics to that of colleagues in the USA, where Women's Studies has become much more firmly established than in Britain.) Both Margo Culley and Barbara Hillyer Davis write, in the anthology *Gendered Subjects* (1985) that Women's Studies is now academically respectable and being taught to large numbers of students, and their problem as teachers lies in preventing their classes from becoming tributaries to the mainstream of conventional thinking (Culley and Portuges 1985: 245, 252, 209–17). It is not, then, that feminists at the University of Kent are in an intellectual backwater or even a dull canal: the ghettoization which Julia Casterton (1979: 95–8) prophesied ten years ago as the likely future of Women's Studies has not happened. Yet our connection with the wider community of feminist thought and action doesn't of itself solve the difficulty of establishing and defining our relationship to English Literature. This problem directly affects both the undergraduate 'Women and poetry' and the postgraduate 'The feminist aesthetic', since the object of both courses is to introduce students to women's writing and feminist theory without disconnecting those from the rest of their knowledge and studies in literature: a difficult exercise, since disconnection is already implied by most literature syllabuses.

'The feminist aesthetic' is the more ambitious of the two courses, and so far the more successful. Its aim is, by looking closely at a careful selection of women's writing and feminist theory, to introduce students to key areas of feminist criticism and debates about language and identity. It is not planned as a survey of female/feminist classics, though I do try to stick to writing that the students and I will both admire and enjoy. The texts are chosen for their relevance to the theoretical problems and resolutions which the course covers; questions about what-might-constitute-a-feminist-canon-according-to-which-criterion seem to me to lead up an intellectual blind alley. So we study one or two obvious classics like *Jane Eyre*, less well-known texts like Jean Rhys's *The Wide Sargasso Sea* and H. D.'s *Trilogy*, working-class writing, and Black writing (Maya Angelou and Toni Morrison). Much of the prose material studied is auto-biographical: this is planned as a possible solution to a problem in the course which is both pedagogic and political, and which is central to feminist theory; namely, how to understand the relation between women's writing, language, and experience.

This problem often surfaces in the form of a disagreement between teacher and students about how far texts can or should be read primarily as representing their authors' lives and experiences as women. Women students who read a master's degree in Women's Studies generally share a strong feminist consciousness, and usually have a productive history of interrogating their own lives as women; they very often want to read a literary text as a way of getting access to other women's experience, and can be very resistant to what they see as the unnecessary abstraction entailed in a more theoretical approach. Students, particularly if they are influenced by Adrienne Rich, are often enthralled by the idea of a women's tradition which will connect contemporary feminism with a newly-excavated history of writing by women through a trans-historical network of female identity and experience; and they get understandably frustrated if I attack these exciting ideas as 'monolithic essentialism' and want to replace them with a more rigorously theoretical and culturally specific approach.[4] My own approach to women's writing as teacher and critic is opposed to any insistence on the unity of female experience. I agree with Joan Cocks who argues in 'Suspicious pleasures' (Culley and Portuges 1985: esp. 177–82) that when feminists insist on conscious experience as the be-all and end-all of thought and writing, we disable ourselves politically as well as intellectually. Although I agree with radical feminists that the articulation of personal experience is of crucial importance for feminists, that this is an aspect of women's writing which no feminist critic can afford to ignore (see Montefiore 1987: ch. 1, and Scheman 1980), nevertheless it is context, not separateness, that needs stressing, and difference, not identity – in particular, the difference between the woman writer and the traditions she engages with or opposes. Criticism needs to understand women not only as writing their selves but as engaged with the dominant masculine discourses which have claimed to define both femininity and writing, and to identify the particular discourses which the women writers are engaged in transforming or inventing. (Cora Kaplan's work is exemplary here, and I use the essays in her *Sea Changes* on both post-graduate and undergraduate courses.) This culturally specific approach means reading, say, *Aurora Leigh* not for the way it gives access to women's experience but for the way it represents that experience, including Barrett Browning's investment in the Romantic ideal of the poet as a person of supreme imaginative awareness, at once speaking for and transcending her community; her relation to such figures as Wordsworth; and the ways in which Romantic inspiration defines, limits, and energizes her writing. Once the promise is shifted from 'writing gives access to experience' to 'writing represents experience – how?' feminist readers can be free of literal interpretations and essentialist assumptions of the universal identity of all women; and the argument leads on to wider feminist debates about the relation of women to language, the notion of the woman reader, feminism and deconstruction.

This may be a good model for literary criticism – I think it is; but as the basis for a teaching programme it raises major problems, which look political and partly are. It is not that to read texts in a more complex way than taking them as records of experience is in itself unpolitical: obviously not. But in order to talk about the transformation of a tradition or discourse, you need to know the tradition which is being transformed, and students do not necessarily come already equipped with this knowledge. Because the Women's Studies MA is an interdisciplinary degree, students will have done their BA degrees in a wide variety of subjects, so that one complication of seminars is that participants often have very different levels of literary knowledge and sophistication. The problem I've outlined arises most acutely when a majority of students taking 'The feminist aesthetic' don't already have degrees in literature. It would clearly be absurd to make historians and sociologists spend all their reading time in acquainting themselves with the same patriarchal monuments that they are probably trying to get away from in taking an MA in Women's Studies. However important it may be in the long run to assess and appropriate those monuments, one can't, as a socialist feminist friend once ruefully observed, make an entire politics of teaching out of constantly saying 'But it's more complicated than that.' And the main theoretical issues which the course covers are actually based on the notion of the specificity of women's writing. Summarized briefly, they are: the feminist debate about experience and essentialism, focusing on Adrienne Rich as representative of the authority of experience and Cora Kaplan and others for the opposing view; working-class writing and the political role of the articulation of experience, including the work of Carolyn Steedman; black writing and the feminist response to cultural difference and racism, including essays by Gayatri Spivak; French feminism and the theorizing of sexual difference (Toril Moi's *Sexual/Textual Politics* (1985) is valuable here as an introduction to the debate, as reference point, and finally as a seminar text); the question of female language, including Hélène Cixous and Luce Irigaray; and the relation of the woman writer to tradition, using my own book *Feminism and Poetry* (1987). And to have a good discussion of these debates we need to know the texts which the theoreticians argue over. We cannot effectively argue through the pros and cons of 'experientially based' feminist criticism based on readings of nineteenth-century realist classics versus Kristevan subtleties about the play of language in modernist texts without a shared knowledge of, say, *Middlemarch* and *To the Lighthouse*. An acquaintance with Colin MacCabe's theory of the hierarchy of discourses in George Eliot's prose, or even with the elegant summaries in Catherine Belsey's *Critical Practice*, won't work as a substitute. The solution to these problems seems to be, first, to make discussions of theory keep coming back to close reference to the chosen literary texts, and second, to concentrate study on autobiographical texts, but ones which don't purport to record experience straightforwardly; or if they do, have such obvious gaps and indirections that their language is demonstrably not the transparent expression of experience. (The tight-lipped memoirs in *Life As We Have Known It* and the richness of rhetoric in Maya Angelou's autobiographies, make these very good for deconstructing ideas of language as unproblematic medium of expression.)

There are of course difficulties with a theoretically oriented course like this. If students don't like theory, it can be a struggle to teach, and there can be a great deal of silent resentment and anger in the classroom (see Culley and Portuges 1985: 209–17, 11–20); and even if they do like it, we have to keep from floating off into a paradise of abstractions. It has this year been a lively, stimulating group. Despite our theoretical and political difficulties relating to 'mainstream' English studies, we have paradoxically benefited from the English Board's lack of interest in feminism: because 'The feminist aesthetic' has been the only regular postgraduate feminist critical seminar, several English postgraduates researching in this area have gravitated to the group and have made valuable contributions to discussions. Clearly, this interest needs building upon – but that is another story.

The second course that I teach, 'Women and poetry', is an undergraduate course, and is more problematic – partly because unlike the other it is new, and I teach it by myself. The aims of the course when I set it up were first, to introduce students to a body of rich and exciting poetry which doesn't otherwise get taught, and second, to introduce them to a non-reductive feminist criticism including the work of Cora Kaplan, Mary Jacobus, and Margaret Homans. The material studied includes Victorian poets, American modernists, and modern British poets: Elizabeth Barrett Browning, Emily Dickinson, and Adrienne Rich are the key figures. I began the course by concentrating on the most recent poetry, thinking that students would find this the most approachable. This was, in fact, bad teaching strategy. The problem of how to read these women poets (the same problem that I've found in teaching 'The feminist aesthetic') has presented the students and myself with difficulties. For poets like Sylvia Plath, Denise Levertov, and Adrienne Rich are all deeply engaged with the traditions and methods of American modernism: contextualizing them is not just a matter of fitting them into background information, but of understanding what their poems mean and how they mean it. It is difficult to communicate this when students come to read Denise Levertov's poems knowing little about the tenets of American poetry: perhaps the names of William Carlos Williams and Wallace Stevens, but not much more than that, and a bit hazy even about 1960s anti-war radicalism and the differences between Levertov and Adrienne Rich as political poets.[5] It is not realistic to ask students to make good this deficiency by reading up their literary history: even if they had the time (which they don't: 'Women and poetry' is only one of four papers they will have to take in the annual summer examinations),[6] the university library still doesn't have the resources: book shortages are a constant problem on this course.

Meanwhile, seminars have tended to become either practical criticism sessions or impromptu lectures by me. (Options are taught by a weekly two-hour seminar, which can include some lectures, and in this case obviously should.) And the students, needing to make an intellectual framework for the course, often rely on an essentialist feminist argument that sees the poems as constituting a hidden subculture of women speaking and writing mainly to and about each other. This way of reading arises partly because, as with the Women's Studies MA, the course attracts feminist students for whom both interrogating their own experience and communicating with other women are important practices;[7] partly because of the common assumption that women write more directly from experience than men do (this assumption of course does not originate in feminism); and partly because the general absence of women's writing from other courses, except for nineteenth-century fiction, leads students to think of women's poetry as more separate from men's traditions and debates than it really is. But the main reason for students relying on essentialist notions of a unified female identity to tie together the poets they study is, I have to admit, that the structure of the course actually invites them to do so. Its aim of introducing 'a body of rich and exciting poetry' is valuable: literature courses *ought* to introduce students to the textual pleasures of poems they have not read before. But when translated into a necessarily selective syllabus, that 'body of work' rapidly becomes a static canon of women writers: a mirror image of the old canon of poetry from Chaucer to Yeats. I can testify that Toril Moi is right when she argues that 'a new canon would not be intrinsically less oppressive than the old. The role of the feminist critic is still to sit quietly and listen to her mistress's voice as it expresses authentic female experience' (Moi 1985: 78).

Am I saying that my sceptical colleagues were right to oppose this course, and that I should have done better to offer a unisex option on American modernism? No: the texts are well worth reading, even if the course had done no more than to introduce the students to the poems, even without a properly nuanced way to relate them to one another. But the problem of oversimplified essentialism isn't insoluble. As a teaching problem it isn't unique to feminism: it arises in different forms in courses on Marxism and literature, or literary theory, or even religion and literature – any course where students are given a theory, overtly or by implication, without having enough evidence to test or substantiate it. Furthermore, in its hegemonic form of universalizing the 'timeless insights of great literature', essentialism is implied in much straight teaching of English anyhow.

Unlike 'The feminist aesthetic', this undergradate course does not include much theoretical material: there is for instance no compulsory theoretical reading listed for seminars, though some is suggested. Clearly, it could help matters to direct students towards feminist theory: Cora Kaplan's *Sea Changes* and Toril Moi's *Sexual/Textual Politics* could both be valuable here. None of these books, however, is ideal as the mainstay of an undergraduate course: in their different ways, they all demand too much prior knowledge from the reader. Literary theory can have a hypnotizing effect on students instead of the stimulus it is meant to be. The best solution I can find is not adding a dollop of theory to the poetry mixture, but focusing seminars on texts whose language and form themselves raise relevant questions about identity and language, and then relating these to essays like Cora Kaplan's 'Pandora's box', and 'Language and gender', Nelly Furman's 'The politics of language' (Greene and Kahn 1985: 59–80) which the students can read for themselves. In the Easter Term we began with readings from *Aurora Leigh* and selected poems of Emily Dickinson, using these as reference points for the rest of the course and as different models of female poetry: the one claiming a poetic identity according to the Romantic definition; the other, by producing a multitude of ambiguous first-person voices, sometimes ironic and sometimes not, querying the notion of a single, stable identity. Both kinds of poem make it clear by their form and language that whatever they are, they are not straightforward expressions of the poet's experience – *Aurora Leigh* by the sheer bulk and range of its fictional narrative, Dickinson's poems by the variety of her speaking subjects. These have worked as reading models to approach Emily Brontë and Christina Rossetti: models also of the ways women have transformed the traditions in which they work. Students will have already done some work on Romantic poets such as Wordsworth and Shelley in their first-year course; and the course on nineteenth-century fiction, which most of them take or have taken, is also useful for contextualizing Victorian poetry.

The conclusion that I have reached both from teaching these courses and thinking about them for this chapter is that feminist courses need to be very clearly defined and tightly – though not inflexibly – structured, particularly if the teacher is, like me, an untidy person whose instincts are all towards free-ranging, unstructured discussion. It is, for instance, a mistake not to give lectures on an undergraduate course because one doesn't want to define one's teaching role as being the source of authority and knowledge – after all, especially for undergraduates, that *is* the teacher's role and importance. Not that this defines the teacher overall, but it is irreducibly part of our function, and to deny this is to cheat the students (see Culley and Portuges 1985: 203–8, 209–17). Similarly, it is a mistake to leave the direction of a seminar undefined in the name of flexibility, not because – to take a poetry seminar as an example – doing practical criticism leaves general issues hazy (it needn't); but because doing this provides no alternative to oversimplified generalizations. A feminist undergraduate course needs some lectures built in, to give students the information which will enable them to read texts in an appropriately nuanced way: it also needs a very coherent programme of seminars, with prepared questions about the literature that is to be tackled together with specified criticism and suggested theoretical reading.[8] And the need for coherence is nearly as great in a postgraduate course, even though postgraduate students don't need basic information in the same way. It is of course important not to be dogmatic:

students need to be free to disagree with their teacher. They can do this most productively if the teacher herself is clear about what she thinks and wants them to learn, and I have found that the best way of securing that clarity, since I personally am far from always living up to that ideal, is to build it into the structure of the course.

Notes

I am grateful to Kath Burlinson, Jane Forrester, Sue Jackson, Peter Humm, Sue Jackson, Sue Jonas, Lyn Innes, and Kate McLuskie for comments and advice on draft versions of this chapter.

1 'Eighteenth-Century Studies' is probably the most sexist of our 'basic' courses. Of those I have taught, 'Studies in American Literature' is almost as exclusively concerned with white male bourgeois writers but does include Emily Dickinson and Frederick Douglass; 'Nineteenth-Century Fiction' shares its emphasis about equally between men and women novelists.

2 Two well-known essays by American feminist critics approach this problem: Myra Jehlen's 'Archimedes and the paradox of feminist criticism', *Signs*, vol. 6, no. 4, 575–601, and Annette Kolodny's 'Dancing through the minefield: some observations on the theory, practice and politics of a feminist literary criticism', *Feminist Studies*, vol. 6, no. 1, 1–25. I agree, however, with Toril Moi that these feminist critics' arguments are very limited by their basically very traditional assumptions about what literary criticism should do and be (see Toril Moi (1985) *Sexual/Textual Politics*, pp. 70–5 and 80–8). Sandra Gilbert and Susan Gubar's *The Madwoman in the Attic* (1979) is probably the most famous and influential of all feminist statements of women's relation to tradition, but it is so long and expensive and exclusively concerned with nineteenth-century fiction that it could not be used in teaching unless I planned a course around it, which, given my disagreements with its partly essentialist approach, I would not wish to do. *Making a Difference: Feminist Literary Criticism*, ed. Gayle Green and Coppelia Kahn (1985) also usefully approaches the problem of women's relation to tradition.

3 The Board of Drama Studies has been teaching 'Women in the theatre', and the Board of Film Studies has been teaching 'Sexual difference in the cinema' (both optional courses) since October 1982. In addition, the courses that Single Honours Drama students take in their fourth (final) year, 'Directing' and 'Devising' include work on sexual politics in the theatre.

4   See, among others, Cora Kaplan's essay (1986) 'Language and gender', *Sea Changes*; Jan Montefiore (1987) *Feminism and Poetry*, ch. 5 'The lips that never lie'; Mary Jacobus (1986) 'Is there a woman in this text?', *Reading Woman*; Jonathan Culler (1980) 'Reading as a woman', *On Deconstruction*; Luce Irigaray (1985) *Speculum of the Other Woman* and *This Sex Which Is Not One*; Monique Plaza (1978) 'Phallomorphic power and the psychology of "woman"', *Ideology and Consciousness* 4.

5   'Woman and poetry' is offered to second- and third-year students. Second-year students will have done 'Explorations in reading' in their first year, which covers a selection of English and American classics from 1500 to the present, and three other interdisciplinary Humanities courses, most containing a literature component. None of our 'basic courses' at present covers modernism: 'Studies in American Literature' is a nineteenth-century course, stopping with Henry James. One other option, 'American writing in the 1920s', does cover American modernism so there is a fair chance that at least some of the third-year students doing 'Women and poetry' may know the American context.

6   'Women and poetry', like all other English options at the University of Kent is examined by essay: that is, there is a take-away paper on which students have three days to answer three questions with a word-limit of 5,000 exclusive of quotations.

7   The course includes non-feminist students as well, of course, and this year three men (out of twenty-two). I have found the essays cited above by Margo Culley and Barbara Hillyer Davis illuminating and helpful on the problems of teaching ideologically mixed classes.

8   Virginia Woolf's (1929, 1977) *A Room of One's Own* and her essays on women writers (*On Women and Writing*, ed. Michèle Barrett, 1979, London: Women's Press), Adrienne Rich's poetry, especially *The Dream of a Common Language* (1978) and her essays collected in *On Lies, Secrets and Silence* (1977) and *Blood, Bread and Poetry* (1987), and Eavan Boland's essay 'The woman poet: her dilemma', *Stand*, vol. 28, no. 1, Winter 1986–7, are all essential. As well as the books by Toril Moi, Cora Kaplan, and myself mentioned above in the text, the essays in *Making a Difference* (Green and Kahn 1985) also ask useful questions about the problem of relationship with literary criticism. Other important books are Margaret Homans's (1979) *Women Writers and Poetic Identity* and Alicia Ostriker's (1986) *The Thieves of Language: The Emergence of American Women Poets*; and for general stimulus, Gayatri Spivak's (1987) *In Other Worlds*.

9

'There's no such thing as "only literature"': English teaching in an anti-racist and multicultural context

Liz Gerschel and Susheila Nasta

Truth and consequences

When the mob swerved
at him
he screamed
'I'm not the man you're after,
I'm Cinna the poet,
I never meddled in politics!'

The mob knew better, 'Then tear him,'
it screamed back, 'tear him
for his bad verses!'

It was then he learned
too late
there's no such thing as 'only literature'.
Every line commits you.
Those you thought dead will rise,
accusing. And if you plead
you never meant them,
then feel responsibility
break on you in a sudden sweat
as the beast bears down.

(Edward Baugh 1978, in
Burnett 1986: 273)[1]

The title for this chapter from the Caribbean poet Edward
Baugh raises a familiar question concerning the relationship of

literature and politics. Not surprisingly, these issues are also central to discussions concerning multiculturalism, pedagogy, and practice in English departments throughout the country.

Teaching English not only involves teaching a subject with an intended product (so pointedly described in the Kingman Report), including the acquisition of control over the English language in its written and spoken forms, and some appreciation of the body of literature written in this language; it also acts as a vital means of conveying cultural mythologies and social values. Our approach to language, the literature we choose, and the issues we raise, whether in school classrooms, teacher-training courses, or English literature departments in universities, will reflect our own perspectives on issues such as Eurocentrism, anti-racism, high- and low-point cultures, sexism, and cultural diversity. As Lord Swann clearly recognizes in the brief guide to the main issues of the Swann report.

> The fundamental change needed is a recognition that the problem facing the education system is not just how to educate the children of ethnic minorities but how to educate *all* children. Britain has long been an ethnically diverse society, and is now, mainly because of her imperial past, much more obviously one. All pupils must be brought to an understanding of what is entailed if such a society is to become a fair and harmonious entity . . .
>
> Education has always been more than the reinforcement of the beliefs and values which each child brings to school, and there is now an acute need for a new dimension of tolerance and understanding, leading over the years to the eradication of prejudice and discrimination in society at large.
>
> (DES 1985a: 10)

Whilst this might be an idealistic vision, there is no doubt that the choices teachers make do have a profound influence on the development of their students' attitudes: what we teach is for life. It is remarkable, therefore, that a high proportion of literary courses in higher education and in initial teacher-training institutions in the United Kingdom fail to offer students the opportunity to engage with literature beyond the narrow confines of an ethnocentric approach. The result is a cycle of either exclusion or marginalization of literatures reflecting the culturally diverse and plural nature of modern society. In teaching as much as in writing, 'there's no such thing as "only literature". Every line commits you.'

This is not the place for a full discussion of the educational philosophy surrounding anti-racism and multiculturalism. However, some basic distinctions are worth making. The term 'racism', for example, signifies not only a personal manifestation of prejudice and power, but a system which underpins all the structures and institutions of society, by continuing to validate and enforce the values of a dominant culture. 'Anti-racism' is usually taken to mean a political position, reflected in policy and practice, which attacks such a construct of society. 'Multiculturalism' has had widely differing interpretations over the years, but it is by and large a liberal humanist recognition of a relativist rather than an absolutist approach to cultural diversity. Unfortunately, these two positions have often been seen as opposed, and, multiculturalism attacked as the tokenist inclusion of a 'non-white' text into a syllabus which stops short of a full cultural pluralism. At the same time, anti-racism can be misinterpreted and give rise to suspicions that literature is being used as propaganda or to the whole-scale rejection of literature outside a narrowly prescriptive context. As Peter Traves has said, a great deal of the hostility towards multicultural education is a waste of valuable energy:

> A direct and simple opposition between multi-cultural education and anti-racist education should not exist. Energy needs to be invested in forging a politicized pedagogy in which anti-racist ideology is linked to the best multi-cultural practice and where multi-cultural educational thinking is allied to committed anti-racist activity.
>
> (Traves 1987: 14)

The lack of central leadership from the British government on issues of education in and for a multi-ethnic society and the controversy surrounding this debate has led to the development of fragmentary and arbitrary policies and practice nationally. This *ad hoc* development can easily be illustrated by examining the present situation in higher education. For instance, many colleges of higher education and polytechnics purport to have effective multicultural policies or at the very least to observe their LEAs' policies. Although there are pockets of excellent practice, recent research on English departments in such institutions has shown that very few of them have systematically translated these policies into action in their curricula.[2] Equally arbitrarily, as independent institutions, most universities have no multicultural policy at all, although they may confront the issues in their courses. Whilst several of these institutions are actively engaged in the redefinition of English teaching, there seems to be little informed and consistent exploration of anti-racist and multicultural issues.

If we look at schools across the country we see, as the Swann Report (1985) has already shown, that the absence of clear policy objectives founded on firm educational principles has resulted in piecemeal implementation. This varies from areas in which there is a clearly stated LEA anti-racist and multicultural policy, effectively delivered in practice, to areas where there is the tokenist/assimilationist practice referred to above. In the most extreme cases the entire debate is quite simply seen as irrelevant, as the title of Chris Gaine's book on the subject, *No Problem Here* (1987), clearly indicates.

These attitudes are often reflected in the design of courses. For instance, if literature students on a BA course do not meet African or Caribbean literature until their final year and then only in an option, they are unlikely to find it easy to draw links between post-colonial literatures and a postmodernist world. Instead, they tend to see it as an esoteric and largely irrelevant study. If this experience were introduced and illustrated in mainstream courses from the first year onwards, the choice of a special study in non-European literature at a later stage of the course would provide fuller insights into the interrelationships between the development of literatures in the contemporary world. Similarly, pupils in schools who have engaged with a wide range of literatures as part of their English curriculum from their earliest experiences of reading and writing and story-telling, will be more likely to gain insights and pleasure from such literatures and to build on these as they continue their education.

Much of this relates to the status of the supposed 'traditional canon' of English literature. It is no easy matter breaking into any well-guarded inner sanctum, and it is a strange irony in the maintenance of the 'canon' argument that those who perpetuate it with high-minded aims to preserve the quality, history, and standards of 'British culture' fail to perceive the historic cross-cultural contexts of the canon itself. In the literature of this canon a mixture of cultural influences is nothing new. Chaucer, the 'Father of English poetry', drew on a number of international sources to shape the language and content of his tales; Shakespeare set his plays in Verona, Alexandria, and Troy and employed a broad linguistic and cultural range. No culture is static, and the transformation of existing languages and literatures has always been a feature of the development of new forms. As Salman Rushdie puts it: 'Cultural mixture, cultural impurity . . . is nothing new . . . impurity is the norm in the history of cultures . . . and notions of purity are the aberration . . . There is no such thing as a homogeneous culture' (Rushdie 1988: 35). If the traditional canon is in itself the product of cross-cultural influences, what does the current antipathy towards non-canonic literature really reflect but an opposition to cultural heterogeneity?

The Bullock Report, *A Language for Life* (1975), commented over ten years ago on the importance that the school's perception of the child's own culture and background has on his or her ability to learn:

> Immigrant [sic] children's attainment in tests and at school in general is related not only to language but to several other issues, particularly those of cultural identity and cultural knowledge. No child should be expected to cast off the language and culture of the home as he [sic] crosses the school threshold.
>
> (DES 1975: 286)

We all bring into teaching our own 'cultural baggage', usually packed into us at school and often, unfortunately, little altered by the experience of undergraduate literature courses and teacher training. Moreover, the vast majority of English teachers in Britain are white and very many will have been through the middle-class dominated channels of grammar schools (or top streams/bands in comprehensive schools) and universities. As teachers, we have a certain power in our classrooms. We can share this power by encouraging students to bring in their own areas of knowledge – story-telling in various languages or from other cultures, for example, or the works of writers from other countries or books that deal with issues that are relevant to their own lives and experience.

Indeed, unless students share in the process of making decisions about their own learning, the knowledge presented in the classroom will inevitably reflect and endorse the teacher's own values. If classroom teachers concentrate predominantly on texts written in standard English, pupils will obviously very quickly come to the belief that standard English is the only worthwhile form of English and that other forms have little value. If those pupils themselves do not happen to speak or write standard English as their first language or dialect, they will also begin to feel that there is something implicitly wrong with their own language. On the other hand, including texts written in or using dialects and Creoles demonstrates the value of these dynamic language forms and the literary uses to which they can be put, without undermining the crucial importance of teaching all pupils standard English as the language of power. Moreover, research has revealed that children who are offered the opportunity to maintain and understand the workings of their own languages and dialects are better empowered to gain control over other forms (Terrell 1977: 325–37).

It is important to deal with these questions directly, both at initial teacher-training (ITT) level and in in-service training (INSET). Our own experience in teaching on such courses in various parts of the country has made it apparent that many teachers deal best with the concepts and issues of multiculturalism and anti-racism by studying multicultural literature in ways, and at a level, appropriate to their own immediate circumstances. This approach has been variously interpreted in schools: sometimes two or three teachers (and sometimes larger groups such as whole departments, cross-curricular groups, or the entire staff of a primary school) have set about a process of self-education through literature. For example, English and humanities teachers in one secondary school in London focused on teaching themselves about Caribbean literature, because they wanted to recognize and respond to the changing population of the school. They introduced a programme of reading, research, and discussion, with the support of what advisory services their LEA could offer and also, on occasion, by involving local communities, parents, and writers. Some teachers have undertaken this learning experience before they have used multicultural literature in the classroom; others have taught themselves and their pupils simultaneously, although not always using the same texts.

The positive effect of this approach is two-fold. Firstly, teachers are able to examine their own positions and confront their own myths, assumptions, fears, and lack of knowledge, by establishing a direct relationship with a number of texts and broad themes – the ideological and mental effects of slavery, imperialism, and decolonialization, for example. Secondly the varied experience presented by a range of texts from different parts of the world will break down misguided assumptions created by inadequate labelling. An example is the frequently held view that 'Asian' literature is only literature stemming from India itself, thus ignoring the literatures in English stemming from the whole of the Asian subcontinent or the literatures of the Indian Diaspora, such as the literature of the East Indian Caribbean, Asian-British writing, or Indo-African writing. In addition, many powerful myths, such as the myth of the British Raj, will be more fully understood when taught and reconstituted within a historical context. A course on South-East Asian literature recently taught at Portsmouth Polytechnic to a group of B.Ed. degree students achieved precisely this. Beginning with an examination of commonly-held western myths of India, as reflected in Paul Scott, Kipling, and many others, the course attempted to adopt a bicultural approach. E. M. Forster's *A Passage to India* (1924) was taught alongside N. Chaudhuri's *A Passage to England* (1959); similarly Kipling's portrait of India was contrasted with that of R. K. Narayan. The East Indian experience in the works of Samuel Selvon and Ismith Khan (both Caribbean writers) was paralleled with that of African Asian writers, such as Peter Nazareth. The course then explored the Asian experience in Britain, by studying the short stories set in London's East End by Farrukh Dhondy and inviting the Asian woman writer, Ravinder Randhawa, to talk about her debunking of myths about Asians in present-day Britain in her novel, *The Wicked Old Woman* (1988). The course concluded with a dramatic presentation by students on a relevant subject of their own choice; one group chose to write a humorous play based around the mythical language of the east associated with the language of travel journalism and the hippy movement of the 1960s.

Approaching texts in this way enables students to begin to examine the roots of their own assumptions and to locate them historically; it also provides an essential and direct means of access to an alternative perspective from that of traditional English Literature: in the words of one intending teacher, 'Reading these novels and gaining a sensitivity to the different realities that the English language can convey made sense of two years of sociology.'

Introducing students to the notion of the power of language both as a builder of myths and as a transmitter of culture is an essential element of any literature course, but it is also a way of approaching the transient and hybrid nature of all cultures. In another course at Portsmouth Polytechnic, designed to intro-duce intending primary- and middle-school teachers to multi-cultural literature, the aim was to examine first and foremost the reproduction of either explicit or implicit racist attitudes. Students noted as many racist images as they could recall from their education or the media. They then discussed these, includ-ing labels such as 'ethnic minority', 'the racially disadvan-taged', and so on. We then examined some familiar literary myths: the story of Robinson Crusoe and Man Friday, for example, the relationship between Prospero and Caliban, and the use of stereotypes in *Uncle Tom's Cabin*. This involved some analysis of particular passages in group discussion, and was followed by close readings of several poems which highlighted these kinds of issues, such as William Blake's 'Little Black Boy' and Wole Soyinka's 'Telephone Conversation'.

The course then moved to close readings of a number of texts from Africa, the Caribbean, South-East Asia, and Britain (both Black and white). These included *Jane Eyre* (1847) and Jean Rhys's *Wide Sargasso Sea* (1965); *Equiano's Travels* (1789, 1967) and *Robinson Crusoe* (1719); *Annie John* (1985) by Jamaica Kincaid and *The Unbelonging* (1986) by Joan Riley; *The African Child* (1954) by Camara Laye and *Things Fall Apart* (1958) by Chinua Achebe. Whilst these texts are by no means fully representative, they served to open up a number of important questions. Perhaps the most shocking revelation, at the beginning of the course, was that only two out of fourteen students could actually locate the regions from which the writers came and put names to countries on a map of these areas. This made them aware early on of the Eurocentricity of their own school education.

The questions raised by the various group responses to the texts themselves, concerned issues such as how far *Equiano's Travels* (an eighteenth-century West African slave narrative) was influenced in its style and structure by the epistolary novel; related points of interest were the Black perspective on the Middle Passage and the descriptions of London during this period. The fact that a Black man wrote English fluently at this time astonished many of the students. The parallel reading of *Jane Eyre* and *Wide Sargasso Sea* introduced students to the interrelationship between slavery and the establishment of English country houses such as Thornfield Hall, and the need for the revisioning and retelling of history through the eyes of Antoinette Cosway (Bertha Mason) in *Wide Sargasso Sea*. In addition, the whole notion of 'the canon' was inevitably questioned. The African texts provided students with a view of the human effects of colonialism and the importation of Christianity on a small village community in *Things Fall Apart* and on the consciousness of a young boy in *The African Child*. Issues such as the disturbing influence of an imposed alien language on consciousness were raised in many of the books and the full impact of this kind of oppression explored through Hyacinth's mental instability in Joan Riley's *The Unbelonging*. Interestingly, students were keen to attempt to assess the 'quality' of the writing and debated at length the dangers of literature as propaganda when dealing with the rather overstated equation between gender, race, oppression, and madness in that novel, and were critical too of categorizing Black characters as victims.

These were only some of the issues which arose in the course (which also included a major input on the teaching of English as a foreign language). By the end of it, the students were not only more aware of recent non-British history but felt they had been introduced to a new and previously invisible world of literature. It motivated them to attempt to redress the balance in their own teaching and to avoid depriving their own pupils of a vital literary heritage.

If we want to teach English within an anti-racist and multicultural context, to the benefit of all our pupils and students, we must include the varied forms of English found in the English-speaking world and the literature of the Caribbean, Africa, Asia, the Americas, and southern Europe as well as the 'traditional canon', written, by and large, by white, male northern Europeans and North Americans. If we are to share power in the classroom, and share power in a society dominated by these values, we have to acknowledge the authority of Black and ethnic minority groups to speak for themselves through literature, and in their own language forms (Creoles and dialects and in translation) other than standard English. As Colin Prescod said at a conference on arts education in a multi-ethnic society: 'The basis on which the Black artist challenges the status quo is the authority of the Black experience' (Prescod 1985: 35). Salman Rushdie has described two main functions of Black literature under the heading 'giving voice': the first concerns the articulation of a 'body of rejected knowledge . . . knowledge which is known to be true within the black world, but which is rejected by its white shadow'; the second focuses more on the white community and becomes an exercise in 'shouting across . . . the gulf in reality, the chasm which exists between white and black perceptions of the world, their mutual world' (Rushdie 1988: 37). The first function involves a literature that bears witness, as in the work of writers such as Alice Walker or Maya Angelou and the second necessitates the development of new languages and forms in the redefinition of alternative realities. Rushdie does point out, however, the pitfalls of a self-consciously Black literature, which again invites marginalization to a 'white' literature assumed to hold the centre. One must also, of course, be aware of the numerous interpretations of the term 'Black'.

Despite the observations made earlier on the piecemeal realities in multicultural practice, it is important to note that schools, at both secondary and primary level, are much further advanced in their thinking than most institutions of higher education. In the past the demands of examinations and the limitations of set texts have often been used as an excuse for not changing the curriculum. It is easy to forget that examining groups are commercial enterprises selling a product and that teachers and pupils are consumers with a certain power of choice. Even in a restrictive climate in education, changes can be made. There is the evidence, for example, of what London University chose to call a 'Special Relief' [sic] paper on African and Caribbean literature, introduced into its A Level syllabus as a result of teacher pressure and demand. Amendments were also made by the London and East Anglian Examining Group to their proposals for GCSE as a result of the widespread dissatisfaction expressed by teachers prepared if necessary to switch boards.

The introduction of the unitary GCSE exam may be a blessing for all those committed to the teaching of multicultural texts, releasing teachers from the prescriptive hegemony of examination syllabuses. The Joint Board, an amalgamation of five new examining groups, states the following in paragraph 19 of its General National Criteria:

Avoidance of bias
Every possible effort must be made to ensure that syllabuses and examinations are free of political, ethnic, gender and other forms of bias.

Recognition of cultural diversity
In devising syllabuses and setting question papers Examining Groups should bear in mind the linguistic and cultural diversity of society. The value to all candidates of incorporating material which reflects this diversity should be recognized.

(DES 1985b: 19)

In the section on English literature, the National Criteria states:

Examining Groups may extend the scope of what is traditionally regarded as the canon of English literature in recognition that an awareness of the richness of cultural diversity is one of the rewards of the study of literature. The majority of the works must be literary texts originally written in English which may for example include American and Commonwealth writing, but works in translation may also be included . . . (Content: 2.1)

The works for detailed study need not be prescribed in a set texts syllabus of the traditional kind. For example, a wide personal choice may be offered in recommended reading of authors, themes, periods or genres. Works for wider reading may be suggested similarly. Examining Groups will need to ensure that the works for detailed study are of sufficient substance and quality to merit serious consideration. (Content: 2.2)

(DES 1985c: 5)

At GCSE and A Level, then, teachers are being invited to offer a greater range of literature both for detailed study and in evidence of wider reading. Some examining groups already include literature from various cultures (particularly from the Caribbean, with some texts from the Indian subcontinent and from Africa) on their lists. On syllabuses which are 100 per cent school selected, the possibilities for including literature from a variety of cultures are endless, and the choice may be deliberately made to reflect the literary and linguistic heritage of particular groups of pupils as long as the material selected is 'of comparable quality'. In the 'personal choice' areas of some syllabuses, such as the London and East Anglian Group's GCSE Open Study component, a student could choose to study the works of a particular author such as Rabindranath Tagore; compare the importance of place in works from different countries; focus on the emergence of Black women's writing in the 1970s and 1980s; compare two Caribbean novels of childhood, or two or three novels of exile. There is scope here for an examination of universal themes in a bicultural or multicultural context, or for a specifically culturally-oriented focus.

Teachers are therefore being given far more choice in the selection of texts for classroom use and with the greater emphasis on coursework assessment, greater freedom in the work they set. Yet, as Robert Bush has recently pointed out, 'the freedom to choose texts and ways of using them is also the freedom to use the same old texts in the same old ways, and there are many, many teachers who will continue to do so' (Bush 1988: 19). It is a freedom that cuts two ways and, as indicated earlier there are many schools where the notion of 'richness of cultural diversity' means little and the works of

writers such as Sam Selvon, Richard Wright, Olive Senior, or
Beverley Naidoo remain sadly unknown. Nevertheless, for
those committed to this field, the battle with the examining
boards is pretty much over (except for those such as the
Midland and Welsh Board who, as Robert Bush notes, largely
ignore the stipulation of the National Criteria). The onus for
promoting the reading of these literatures is now on the
teachers. 'If teachers want to introduce [African, Caribbean, or
Asian literature] there is really nothing to stop them', says Bush
rightly (Bush 1988: 19) but much more INSET work in this area
needs to be undertaken before the essential conservatism of
many teachers is overcome.

Concepts such as 'literary value', 'relevance', and 'freedom
from bias' might appear to be fairly straightforward, but, as
Michael Bennett has shown, problems can arise. Is Steinbeck's
Of Mice and Men (1937), he asks, 'invalid because it is racist or
valid because it exposes the racism endemic in the Depression?'
(Bennett 1988: 21). Whilst 'relevance' implies a need, does it
actually result in a re-evaluation of teaching aims? As readers
interacting with texts, the meaning stems as much from 'what
the text draws from us, as it is modified by how we, as readers,
limit it' (Bennett 1988: 21). It is part of the function of a teacher
to broaden and modulate these boundaries. However, this
broadening and sharing also involves 'letting something go' in
order that 'something else can come into being'.

This brings to mind familiar discussions in staffrooms and in
Higher Education Board meetings on, firstly, the 'impossibility'
of increasing the range of a syllabus and, secondly, the lack of
staffing resources to teach it. These discussions are usually
followed by pleas as to the unfamiliarity of the subject matter.
The frequently-voiced fear, 'I can't teach this because I don't
know anything about the background or the culture', is more an
excuse than a reason; the same would probably apply to texts
written in the fourteenth or seventeenth centuries. Having
taught GCE O and A Level syllabuses that included Dickens's
Great Expectations (1861), Thackeray's *Vanity Fair* (1848), and
the works of Thomas Love Peacock to pupils in a rural area of
Jamaica, one of the authors of this essay is constantly amazed at
the contrast between the enormous imaginative leaps expected
of those 16 year olds – and taken for granted by their examiners

– and the reluctance of those same examiners and some teachers to take a small jump into the literary unknown themselves.

It is not possible here to provide details on particular texts or to justify their literary merit. A good deal of research already exists in this area and extensive annotated bibliographies have been produced[3] by individual LEAs, professional groups, and organizations such as ATCAL (The Association for the Teaching of Caribbean, African and Associated Literatures) as well as in books designed for school use such as David Dabydeen (ed.) *A Handbook for Teaching Caribbean Literature* (1988) and Liz Gunner's *A Handbook for Teaching African Literature* (1984). It is more useful here to raise some of the questions English teachers in schools and in higher education will want to ask themselves in re-evaluating their courses, methodology, and syllabuses. A brief checklist of areas for consideration in a policy for teaching language and literature within an anti-racist and multicultural context might include the following:

* What are the language issues identified within the school/ institution?
* What discussion takes place between teachers and with students on the politics of language? Are the issues of colour, creed, class, and gender part of current discussion?[4]
* What place is given to standard English? Is it the only language form seen as acceptable for written and/or spoken English? Are all students taught that standard English, as the language of power and status, is necessary for their future success in Britain, but not to the exclusion of other language forms?
* What recognition is given to non-standard dialects of English and to Creoles? Are these recognized and heard as valid forms of communication? Are they accepted in literature and in students' written and oral work wherever appropriate? Are performing artists ever heard within the school or institution using these forms?
* What are the responsibilities of the department towards bilingual students learning English as a second language?[5] Do teachers ensure that bilingual students have access to texts and materials by reviewing their own teaching techniques and language? Is it understood that bilingual pupils

learn English most effectively through interaction with native speakers in the classroom?

* What strategies have been adopted by the English department to meet the cultural and linguistic needs of all their pupils? Has there been a policy for in-service training or deliberate self-education?

* How have teachers extended their own awareness of literature beyond the 'traditional canon'? Do teachers examine texts for racism and sexism and deal with these issues with students?[6] How do they share their information? Is there a regular review of resources and texts? Have they drawn on the students or community or advisory support? Are writers from ethnic minority communities invited into the school/institution to talk about their work? Are teachers familiar with specialist bookshops/journals?[7]

* Is there a conscious effort to move the literature taught away from the white middle-class male-dominated tradition and towards a 'decolonized' syllabus at all levels? Is there an anti-racist and multicultural approach to the literature taught at all levels in the school, including GCSE and A level? Are examining groups invited to accept non-traditional texts? Is literature by women and Black people part of the regular mainstream teaching of all teachers within the department and given equal status with the 'traditional canon'? Is 'tokenism' avoided?

* What links have been made with other subject areas within the school/institution to support this awareness and knowledge? Do teachers in relevant subject areas, e.g. history, music, art, drama, geography, social sciences, dance, and languages, know how the English department is approaching its work and what they are doing? Is there cross-curricular liaison and are there links in content?

* Who buys the books for the department? Who buys books for the school/institution library? What liaison is there between these areas? Do resources in the library support the courses? Is information shared? Is there a book-buying policy? Are community and specialist bookshops used? Are students and parents involved? Are there books in languages other than English/dual language texts? Are there book 'focus' occasions, such as Caribbean Writers'

Week or Books in Bengali Week, when writers and their
books are highlighted throughout the school/institution?

As English teachers we all recognize that stories carry mess-
ages: some are overt – historical tales, oral history, moral tales,
and fables; some are covert, and part of the hidden politics of
children's fiction. If part of the process of English teaching is to
help young people to develop, then we have to offer them the
opportunity to move from a limited world view encouraged by
an ethnocentric approach and towards a wider understanding
of alternative perspectives on the world. Racism is not innate;
no one is born racist. Racist views are absorbed early on,
influenced by the attitudes of parents, teachers, and others in
authority, images on television, in newspapers and comics, and
what children hear and see of the relationships between different
ethnic groups in society. Racism is not a permanent state of
being: it is learnt and it can be unlearnt. In the present political
climate in education, many schools are being denied the material and human resources to effect this. The teaching of arts and
humanities subjects and, in some, literature as an examination
subject, are being forced off the curriculum while extra support
is given to the areas of technology, commerce, and science. It is
therefore especially important to emphasize in schools, universities, and other institutions of further and higher education, to
students, parents, intending and practising teachers, and to
local education authorities in whose gift financial support lies,
that we are looking at a new concept of literature. Literature is a
fundamentally important tool of people's understanding of
themselves and others; it is also the voice of historical and
personal experience.[8]

As Her Majesty's Inspectorate put it in *English from 5–16: The
Responses to Curriculum Matters 1* (1986) literature alone offers the
opportunity to 'encounter language at its most highly wrought,
capturing, shaping and combining experience, thought and
feeling' (DES 1986: para. 36, 14–15). The literary experience
we offer in schools and institutions can only be enriched by the
writings of peoples who have themselves experienced the sort of
restrictions upon their language and freedoms that we are
currently facing, and who offer alternative perspectives to the
narrow view of education proposed by some sectors of govern-

ment. At its simplest, English teaching in a multi-lingual and multi-ethnic society must reflect its dynamic and changing culture and perspectives. In the words of Grace Nichols, Guyanese poet

> We have crossed an ocean
> We have lost our tongue,
> From the root of the old one
> A new one has sprung.
> (Nichols 1983: 80)

Notes

1 Originally published in *The Sunday Gleaner Magazine*, Kingston, Jamaica, 9 April 1978.
2 This observation derives from preliminary research conducted in 1988 by a project entitled AEMS (Arts Education for a Multi-cultural Society) funded by the Arts Council, the Gulbenkian Foundation, and the Commission for Racial Equality.
3 A particularly useful series of annotated bibliographies is J. Elkin and P. Triggs (eds) (1986, 1987, 1988) *The Books for Keeps Guides to Children's Books for Multi-cultural Society*, London: Books for Keeps Publications.
4 An interesting discussion of the English language as 'one of the prime carriers of racism' is given in O. Davis (1967) 'The English language is my enemy', *Dragons Teeth* 1:4, January 1980: 4–6, reprinted from *Negro Historical Bulletin* 30: 18, April 1967, USA.
5 It is important to stress that all teachers have a responsibility for bilingual pupils in their classrooms, despite the willingness of the Kingman Committee to abrogate this responsibility by referring to bilingual learners of English as a separate group with whom they are not 'primarily concerned' (DES 1988b: 5:17).
6 Particularly helpful starting points for such an examination of texts for racism are given in the World Council of Churches (1978) 'Criteria for the evaluation of racism in textbooks and children's literature and guidelines to be used in the production of non-racist and anti-racist books' reprinted in *Children's Book Bulletin*, 1 June 1979: 5–8 and by A. Prestwood (1980) 'Racism rating: test your textbooks', *Dragons Teeth* 2: 1, March 1980.
7 Useful journals include *Wasafiri* (ATCAL); *Dragons Teeth*; *Artrage* (MAAS); *Children's Book Bulletin*; *Multicultural Teaching*; *Multi-Ethnic Education Review* (ILEA).
8 For a fuller discussion of this question, see L. Gerschel (1984) 'Fictional people; political facts', *Multicultural Teaching* 2:2, Spring 1984: 44–50.

10

Dreaming the local: teaching popular cultural forms

Roger Bromley

My first concern here is to locate ways in which teaching popular cultural forms represents a challenge to existing modes of legitimizing and valuing knowledge. These existing modes have less to do with questions of value and distinction than with conserving the cultural power of particular academic practices. The teaching of popular forms has come under increasing attack from academics and others, mainly but not always from those on the right. Merely exchanging arguments about the forms themselves only serves to mystify the real motives behind these attacks, often launched from what has been called 'the platform of "high culture"' and originating in a set of deeply held assumptions about which forms of knowledge are appropriate for transmission in education, and which are not.

The structural context of these 'defences' of cultural power seems to me more important than what they have to say about *Dallas* or Barbara Cartland. For, above all, the struggle is about *forms* and the ways in which a dominant class, and its agents, strive to reproduce a particular cultural style as the only valid one. To offer some version of the popular as the answer to this kind of position is simply to invert it. Instead we need an approach which does not reduce questions of cultural reproduction to a canonic/popular slanging match.

In the name of 'excellence', a particular form of cultural

capital is defended for its inherent *value*; value being used here, as Bourdieu reminds us, both in the linguistic sense as 'distinction', and in the economic sense as 'scarcity' (Bourdieu 1984). These are key concepts underlying a deep anxiety among those professionally engaged in transmitting arbitrary codes in the guise of standards and scholarly objectivity. These professionals, trained in a limited but privileged range of skills often twenty or more years ago, have in some cases coasted on the strength of the 'scarcity' value of their skills and feel deeply threatened by the popular in whatever form it is presented, unless it has been previously validated by the 'academy' and its practices.

A tenured relationship with the dominant culture is often the only form of power made available to those cordoned off from real economic or political power. Underlying this particular relationship are a number of class assumptions which reserve 'distinction' and 'scarcity' for those who conform to a specific educational and cultural style. And beneath those assumptions lies a belief in capitalist social and economic relations which generate 'value' by enforced 'scarcity'. 'Rare', 'unique', 'great', and 'high' forms of culture derive their value from a particular economy, one which stratifies and excludes, and confers 'distinction' on those to whom it entrusts the task of reproducing and generating exchange value in the sphere of the cultural. In the academic world, value is a form of social capital dependent upon selection, assessment, limited access, and a number of different gradations. Part of my professional identity is derived from the power I have (or think I have) over these processes.

Popular cultural forms, by their very nature, whatever their content, challenge this model of legitimizing and valuing knowledge. Hidden within attacks on these forms, and their educational use, is a fear that extensive contact with the forms might lead to a 'deskilling' of academic practices, whereby forms of understanding and language will be liberated from their class expropriations and become accessible to a far greater number of people; so rendering obsolete the existing clerisy and its restrictive practices. The 'academic freedom' of selected cultural agents and sanctioned agencies is part of a remarkably cohesive and defensive structure.

Over many years now certain kinds of cultural production

and certain forms have become the sovereign basis of a particular intellectual orthodoxy and power, reproduced in specific social groups and in educational and other cultural agencies. It is those who have long enjoyed the power to select, classify, and order forms of knowledge in terms of specific gender and class assumptions who feel most threatened by collective modes of working, the open questioning of legitimizing processes, and forms of pleasure not yet codified or consecrated. Those who attack the popular in the name of supposed quality and academic excellence are living on the fast dwindling 'cultural capital' of an individualist system.

I have deliberately overstated these arguments because we need to make explicit the 'common sense' of elitism, its fossilized and anachronistic forms which have, in Gramsci's terms, deposited an infinity of traces in our cultural and educational practices without leaving an inventory. It is the purpose of this argument to suggest that the left must start asking questions about the seemingly natural and implicit forms which constitute so much of our academic practice; that it begin an inventory of the items which furnish the codes and styles of power, so as to demonstrate how criteria of 'excellence' are articulated with the ideologies of cultural conservatism. Dangerous, heretical, and unprocessed cultural mediations provoke the repressed doubts, anxieties, and insecurities of these 'guardians' – hence their aggression, violent rhetoric, and authoritarian tones: the armoury of their structures of command and continuity.

My view is that the actual content of popular cultural forms is secondary to the arguments about value. Ideally, these forms should be construed as a challenge to scarcity and cultural conservatism, and used to encourage a general disposition to increase the legibility of *all* cultural forms and the realization that *different* symbolic processes address and satisfy qualitatively different needs. However, it is well understood that a concern with the popular cultural representations of power, class, gender, sexuality, and race may unmask relations of power and of 'symbolic violence' uncomfortably close to those who enjoy 'delegate status' from a dominant class in the seemingly autonomous sphere of cultural and educational practice. I am not referring simply to the *Salisbury Review*, the *Spectator*, or those who would uphold the 'great tradition', but to those also in the public sector and who are sometimes even advocates of the experimental and 'radical'.

We may laugh at polytechnic lecturers turning their guilty pleasures watching 'soaps' into the subjects of discourse analysis, but we should be more anxious about those who suppress rather than those who ask questions thrown up by popular forms. We need to develop a whole new series of evaluative criteria for handling these forms; criteria based upon history, class, gender, race, and pleasure. Those who claim that popular culture is a narcotic handed to the people by a ruling political class which swallows it itself, need to step outside the frame of their own rhetoric and ask why they are content with being cultural 'insider dealers' for that same class. The 'popular' has, in these formulations, become simply an occasion for 'rubbishing' forms of possible 'dissent' (interestingly enough, it is invariably 'women's forms' which are violently attacked. The pun is intended since, to paraphrase Eddie Waters in *Comedians*, these jokers often hate women). It is a way of asserting the 'patriarchal binary thought' which determines some of the ways we think, and are thought in this society by relations of power. Rethinking the meaning of the popular must have as little to do with that approach as it should have with an 'uncritical romance with style'. The 'high' and the 'popular' constantly intersect at all levels, and it is this intersection which is seen as menacing. The popular is marked by instability and all kinds of contradictions, but it must not be used to stand in for the deeper instabilities, rigidities, and contradictions of those desperately sandbagging their own cultural power.

> If we spend so much time talking about unimportant matters, can we really be serious people?[1]

It is this intersection of the 'high' and the 'popular' which can be made to form the basis of a valuable teaching programme. In my experience of teaching 'popular' literature, the emphasis has been placed mainly on the generic features of texts and their relationship with ideologies. However, as is remarked elsewhere in this volume, newer concepts of ideology have established a measure of parity between texts from different cultural sites and levels, and this has helped to sharpen the ways in which the courses have been organized and taught. Apart from the relative isolation of popular texts from other literary/cultural forms, a concentration upon genre also led to a comparative neglect of the specific historical particularity of the textual productions. On the positive side, an approach through a cultural analysis which drew upon the resources of sociology, feminisms, anthropology, and social history extended the understanding of the 'popular' as part of a complex, contradictory, and shifting cultural process.

Changing colleges recently after teaching for many years in one institution, has enabled me to explore further notions of the 'popular' and to develop new courses. One such is a course called 'Popular fictional forms and cultural power' which is designed to examine the ways in which changing images of power and resistances to power are culturally mediated in the style, forms, and iconography of popular written and visual discourses, while at the same time exploring the social constructions of femininity and masculinity in specific fictional forms relating to power, desire, and pleasure. Some attempt is made at historicizing the approach – for example, the 'masculine romance' and the nation, the spy novel and the 'national subject' – but it is acknowledged that it is still informed by certain 'formalist' legacies. However, the shift of focus from genre to gender is an important one.

A second new course, 'Cultural forms and social relations: 1880 to 1930', is designed to demonstrate ways in which discourses and their interrelationships can form the basis of a meaningful field of study which includes both 'popular' and 'canonical' at points of intersection. The course attempts to explore the relationships between cultural forms, the representations of power, and social change in a period which was a formative one for British society, as well as being a time of profound transformation. The main focus will be on those texts/discourses produced, distributed, and above all, *popularized* within the framework of new processes of publishing, print technology, and marketing. Taking imperial modes of self-understanding as one basis of explanation for certain features of the period, the course will examine the representations of power, class, gender, and race in particular writings, many of which came to constitute part of the development of specific genres (e.g. *Dr Jekyll and Mr Hyde, Dracula,* and the adventure thriller).[2] The ideological categories of masculinity and femininity will be studied in the context of continuing struggles over the position of women. The aim is to historicize and 'periodize' cultural forms in their interrelationships and to develop a teaching approach which crosses disciplinary boundaries.

Using the 'boundary' metaphor in the different sense of local, national, international boundaries has led to the development of a number of ideas which have not yet found an appropriate teaching/learning framework. The 1987 Association for Cultural Studies annual conference, titled 'Beyond the nation – international perspectives in cultural studies' gave rise to thoughts about going beyond the 'nation' in terms of the presence (in Britain and elsewhere) of strong, but unempowered, 'regional' or 'local' cultures, inside but invariably 'outside' dominant versions of the 'national'.[3] The rest of this argument will be concerned primarily with thinking about the *local* as cultural space in which the popular and canonical could be seen to intersect, and will, finally, attempt to relate ideas of the local to the cultural uses of 'localized' Englishes in postcolonial societies, where 'nation-voices' have had to contend with the imperializing forms of the metropolitan nation.

Even in a small country like Britain national development on the cultural level has been very uneven. According to Hechter, national development is

> a process which may be said to occur when the separate cultural identities of regions begin to lose social significance, and become blurred. In this process, the several local and regional cultures are gradually replaced by the establishment of one *national* culture which cuts across the previous distinctions.
>
> (Hechter 1975: 5)

Although separate cultural identities may have lost *social* significance, a range of activities and expressive forms have been developed over many years to sustain and advance the *local* in terms of its symbolic significance. Language or dialects, belief systems, and lifestyles have all persisted, in differing ways, as the basis of cultural difference and cultural form. So-called peripheral cultural/signifying systems have often resisted attempts to transform them into the core, or metropolitan, culture. Often, of course, they are colonized and then commercialized as 'folk' artefacts.

It has been a feature of the 'peripheries' that, denied social and political meaningfulness, resistance and struggle have taken cultural forms – ritual, symbol, language, song, poetry, drama. In the 1930s a number of popularized fictions with a strong *local* inflection (works, for example, by Winifred Holtby, Walter Greenwood, A. J. Cronin, Howard Spring, J. B. Priestley) were produced in an attempt to use cultural forms to give *political* space to areas rendered economically and socially marginal. It may be that in cinematic and television forms these have become 'period romances' with their highly stylized aestheticizing of poverty, but at the time they were a powerful form for articulating the ways in which the 'local' had been left out of the 'national' development.

In the present, cultural expressions of the local may be a response to the historical experience over the last century and a half, of exile, emigration, and colonialism. John Berger, pointing to the fact that never before have so many people been uprooted, speaks of emigration as 'the quintessential experience of our time' (Berger 1984: 61). *Home* as the centre of the world in an ontological sense has become increasingly unstable and fragmented, 'to emigrate is always to dismantle the centre of the world, and so to move into a lost, disoriented one of fragments'. Even to those not in exile, the insecurity and fear of 'not belonging' is almost as acute. This is perhaps why the 'sentimental' genre (cf. the 1930s fictions referred to above, *Coronation Street*, *EastEnders*, etc.) is perceived as representing an attempt to reorganize culture (and cultural/symbolic power) from the point of view of the *local*. Where choice is increasingly prescriptive, the cultural may be, momentarily, the only site for reconstructing 'the centres of the world', of resisting political, economic, and psychological displacement. As Berger says at another point, 'the mortar which holds the improvised "home" together – even for a child – is memory' (Berger 1984: 57). Cultural forms with local inflections often have the effect of 'remembering' (in the sense of putting back together again, 'remantling') the 'untold story of a life being lived'. The effect is anamnesic, analogous to a form of cultural recall therapy. It is a way of *relocating*, defining a space, for those who, in the several senses of this phrase, no longer know their place.

Cultural localism – in whatever form – is not simply a means, therefore, of mediating national identity, but, potentially, a way of dismantling it. If we think of the *local* as a field in which possible meanings are generated and shared, then we need to attend to the extent to which 'belonging is the almost inexpressibly complex experience of culture'. In his introduction to *Belonging*, Anthony Cohen discusses the ways in which boundaries can be drawn at various levels of society:

> Thus I might choose to identify myself as British, Scots, Shetlander, Whalsayman, or as belonging to some particular kinship-neighbourhood nexus in Whalsay. The significant point is that with each 'ascending' level I increasingly simplify (and thereby misrepresent) the message about myself. At each descending level I present myself through increasingly informed and complex pictures. It should therefore be recognised that 'belonging to locality', far from being a parochial triviality, is very much more a cultural reality than is association with gross region or nation.
>
> (Cohen 1982: 11)

Arguably, representations of this cultural reality of 'belonging to locality', however mediated by the formulaic and the stereotype, challenge the ways we think, and are thought by, relations of power in capitalist society, and produce evidence of how different symbolic processes address and satisfy qualitatively different needs. The critical level in the popular is its construction of an emotional and cultural space in which a common belonging is affirmed and serially perpetuated. It is in this 'common belonging' that aspiration and possibility *culturally* become 'reality', symbolically overcoming alienation, difference, hierarchy, and distance. An imagined, local community has the power to *imagine* change in the world in which it is situated.

In a specialized and diverse modern society, the popular can represent the cultural equivalent of a face-to-face social system; it is a form of colloquial knowledge, a local cultural vernacular, not meaningful to those who hold power *but to those without*. It is a form of pleasure, consolation, and, intriguingly perhaps, even a

model of resistance. The 'composed gossip' (in Raymond
Williams's phrase)[4] of the popular cultural romance, edged
towards the sentimental and 'felt desire' though it might be, does
have continuities with irrepressible interests in the diverse lives
of other people, beyond the coercive shapes of hegemonic
representation. Only those who wilfully confuse the cultural
with the political, and misread ritual action as social action, can
fail to understand this. The popular *is* equivocal, inherently
unstable, and precarious; in its creative ambiguity it can
threaten code, classification, and structure (cf. Delderfield's
Diana) even if, narratively, it appears to resolve tensions by
restoring them (cf. *Rebecca*).

The particular narrative economies which perhaps a course
needs to focus upon are those in which the profane, organized,
differentiated, hierarchical, and role-structured society of
everyday power is relatively *weak*, and a wide range of social
possibilities in the crucible of the *local* are seen as *strong*. The
power of the weak is invested in symbolic forms of community,
undifferentiated democracies, and of sharing with 'people like
us'. The constructing of links of *affiliation* as cultural forms of
kinship is an important function of so-called 'soaps'.

In a society in which most privileged cultural forms have a
national and international articulation with specific resources
of power, some popular cultural romances, with their local
inflections, are recreation stories which propose a oneness, a
holistic and horizontally bounded society, a 'secular dreaming',
in the face of the fragmentations and injuries of gender, class,
and ethnicity beyond the horizons and boundaries of the local.
'Soaps' seldom refer to the 'national', not because they cannot
handle it, but because to do so would immediately 'trivialize'
the local and simplify and misrepresent the informed and
complex representation of the 'local' which is the form's generic
basis, its *raison d'être*. Read literally, or through a classic realist
prism, the popular is trivial and parochial, but a *creative* understanding sees it as a symbolic form of consciousness, and as a
'theoretical' proposition about the potentialities of *local* models
of social organization, networking, and 'storying'.

The popular, in order to be read effectively, depends upon a
number of conceptual categories or encodings. Ritual processes,
similarly, *mean* according to conventions, definitions, and

assumptions which originate in and are organized by *local knowledge*. Both are concerned with theories of power based upon representative service and sacrifice: a spiritual power in a secular society. The ideological frameworks of Delderfield's fictions and *EastEnders*, for example, are based upon codes of service and sacrifice, and a shared ethical symbolism. Another shared motif is the *memory* of a 'dialogic' time, a redemptive moment (cf. Ethel, Lou, Dot, and Dr Legg carrying out rituals and ceremonies of recall which 'look after' the local as a continuity in time and space. They have the 'power' to work in and change the world; they are the 'elders' of secular ritual). The individual is empowered but not for individualist ends. Both Delderfield's fictions and *EastEnders* originate in a secularized mode of Christian 'narrative'. The 'soap' partakes of the 'reality' of the parable – a specific cultural text with a symbolic resonance.

The petty bourgeoisie (often the 'owners' of real power in the local, and active in its organization, as in the Rotary Club) are conspicuously absent from popular drama of the *Coronation Street* or *EastEnders* variety. These are typological narratives of established patterns of living and traditional beliefs (or metaphorical constructs of 'ideal' forms of these) in which some of the central *ideological* affirmations of our culture – service, cooperation, sacrifice, community, love – *appear* to subvert the *realities* of power – coercion, monopoly, inequality, and individualism. The 'resistance' element (however attenuated) consists in the privileging of those values which, potentially, are anti-capitalist. Ah!, it will be said, that is precisely how the illusions of the powerless are sustained by the narcosis of power – but this is only true if the 'sentimental' is subject to an analysis based upon cultural absolutism.

In developing a course based on these arguments the analysis of typological narrative could be linked with the ways in which the differentiations of *common sense* can be seen in its tonalities which make it a fixed and labelled category, an explicitly bounded semantic domain, *as well as* a distinct and complex genre of cultural expression. Geertz regards common sense as a tangle of received practices, accepted beliefs, habitual judgements, and untaught emotions of 'colloquial culture'.[5] He treats common sense as a *relatively organized body of considered thought,* whereas it is an inherent characteristic of common-sense thought to deny this. Its unspoken basis is a claim that its components are *direct* expressions of experience and not *deliberated reflections upon it*. Common sense's status as 'just life in a nutshell' and its claim to represent 'how it is', in fact conceal how much it is an interpretation or representation of 'how it is', a culturally constructed gloss, or mediation, on the immediacies of experience. Common sense has become a central category of vernacular 'philosophy', and the conceptual root and paradigm of much in British cultural life, including 'soap'. It is part of the need to render the world distinct and habitable culturally, hence the development of what I would call 'axiomatic' narratives with their teleology and continuities drawn from the complex and contradictory resources of common sense.

All that has been said in the previous paragraph about common sense could be applied, by analogy, to works such as Delderfield's fictions and popular seriated dramas on the basis that, despite the 'realist' modes used, they need to be interpreted in subtler currencies than those commonly used. While the narrative forms of common sense ultimately register consistency, *en route* they celebrate contradiction and inconsistency. Common-sense wisdom is *ad hoc*, it comes in epigrams, proverbs, jokes, anecdotes, and moral homilies – 'a clatter of gnomic utterances' – and is never particularly consistent. Seriated drama reproduces this *ad hoc* quality *structurally* by its use of 'epigrammatic' set pieces which dramatically point a 'moral' in the form of narrative *exempla*. The structure is also close to anecdote, and the language homiletic and proverbial. Common sense deals in consistencies, patterns, frequencies, and regularities (to that extent it is formulaic) and when expectations fail to hold, common sense is not dissolved or paralysed, as it has developed 'cracker barrel' variables of thought ('fate', 'mystery', 'bad luck', 'throw of the dice', 'supernatural') which reinforce it as an absolute and dependable and *not* arbitrary system: that which 'everyone knows'.

Approaching the 'popular' as a form of common sense, or 'composed gossip', it can be seen as a medium of emotional speculation and experiment in a kind of 'social laboratory'. The language of the genre is 'particularity', familial and familiar (the exchange of first names codifies 'insiders' – titles are used for 'outsiders' and professionals – Dr Legg, Mr Wilmot-Brown, etc.). Based on small particulars and rapidly changing topics, it avoids the general. It could be argued that the genre is a catalyst of social processes in that it serves to pattern issues which might otherwise be vaguely or confusedly perceived at a local level. How a person 'watches' soap, gratifies their emotion, or serves their self-interest cannot be explained solely by reference to that person. The genre makes 'authentic' discourse out of the concrete, specific, and personal: its *mise-en-scène* is painstakingly authenticated. In academic (and male) discourse there is a privileging of the abstract, general, and theoretical, and the 'specific' has a low value, or is seen as 'inauthentic'.

By extension, it could be argued that the roots of 'soap' in 'inauthentic' discourse explains the primacy given to the female in the genre, because culturally (and ideologically) abstract thinking is customarily not associated with women. The genre is a dramatic space for the 'empowerment' of 'female' discourses, and resistances to the delocalization of social meaning. 'Soap' is a way of making *public* or shared what is conventionally ascribed to the private (cf. the use of the *public* house – 'the local' – and market-place as recurring sites to mark the entry of the female ritually into 'male' domains). It is a way of enlarging the world, not only for women, but also for the teenager (a high percentage of viewers) who are on the edge of 'experience'. In this respect, 'soap', like gossip, could be described as a form of 'healing' narrative; a way of articulating and speculating upon the unspoken. 'Soap', it could be argued, offers 'theoretical' models for 'emotional' enquiry; it involves a rudimentary hermeneutic act. Watching is far more interactive and open than is often claimed; *interpretation* is its essence. How often, for example, does a person construct their own problems via a fictional mediation? – for example, 'A friend of mine thinks she might be pregnant', and so on. It is not too fanciful to argue that part of the pleasure of 'soap' is its status as 'problem hypo-thesizing'. In the absence of 'real' community, 'soap' provides a context in which the powerless and the displaced can *imagine* 'community' (as an idea of collective interaction, *not* as a specific content) and find a narrative/representational form for their 'ordinariness', their 'trivia', 'chit chat', 'small talk', where the exceptional and the unique (the paradigms of an individualist culture) are 'eccentric'. 'Soaps' construct centres and patterns of belonging and intimacy, an 'ideal' neighbouring, ceremonies of moral speculation, based upon an excessive involvement in the 'here' and the 'now', but also with figures who bear in their narrative 'lives' continuity, private histories, oral traditions, traces of the *not-now* and the *not-here* (Lou, Ethel, the Karim Family).

As well as articulating values (or, rather, a space in which 'value' is on the agenda through a kind of ethical symbolism, or parable-ism), 'soaps' generate a sense of *local* power and control over boundary, space, time, relationship, future, and memory. This control over 'possibility' textualizes the power of women, and provides affirmations of self not in terms necessarily of the particularities (i.e. Kathy becoming a Samaritan, Angie leaving Den, the Queen Vic's ladies' darts team, and so on) but as narrative *symptoms* of activity and self-production. These are 'theoretical' models worked out in the *local* space of the culturally dependable *map*. They bear no more relation to 'reality' than the map does to the actual territory, or the architect's plan, or scale model, to a complex building, but the building/territory/reality needs the models for its theoretical articulations and calculations. You can take a roof off a model, move a motorway even, leave a husband, move in with someone, or take an overdose. The narrative 'models' are the 'other people' of ourselves, our subjectivities in stylized and hypothetical forms. They become an endless rehearsal, a mental and moral 'work out', a contextualization of ethical and moral decisions. Also, they form a base for insight and comprehension, a pleasurable site for human interchange as an exercise or role play, like ritual.

'Soaps' certainly echo in their construction received cultural stereotypes: they *are* edged with allegory, but cutting against it. They address those without social power and filling limited functions in the *public* world. If there are audiences of 20 million this does not necessarily suggest a passive population without taste, but a massive population without power: confined, narrow, and privatized within a rigid social actuality that is always there in its economic form. It is a population burdened by the specific and the immediate; for whom the *local* is the mediating instance of the national/international. People are not deprived

because they read tabloids or watch 'soaps', but the reverse.
The tabloid and the 'soap', beyond the specifics of content, offer
the possibilities at the level of structure and format (concrete,
personal, specific, and localized in inflection – 'homely') of an
alternative political culture. It will be said, however, that 'soap'
is part of the ideological hegemony, a way of keeping the masses
in their place by spinning fantasies of community (dated,
sentimental, parochial). Take these same masses out of their
living rooms into the National Theatre and the Bush (face-to-
face with fragmented, split, dispersed, and sub-Brechtian
dramas) and the masks of Thatcherism will soon be stripped off.

While not wishing to endorse any form of naïve culturalism, it
could be argued that one of the few sources of consistent *narrative
resistance* to Thatcherism is *EastEnders* and *Brookside*, based on an
ethical symbolism incompatible with unquestioned models of
family, enterprise, and property – a diverse representation of an
ethnically and sexually complex *local* society; exploratory,
tentative, and conditional in comparison with the 'certainties'
of *national* unity.

'Local, but prized elsewhere'

I began the previous section by referring to ways in which the
popular and the canonical could be seen to intersect as part of
a cultural analysis based upon concepts of the local. It is
not intended simply to place a number of texts alongside each
other (*EastEnders* with *Briggflatts*, for example, which would be
patently absurd) to be explored in *literary* terms, but by making
the local, regional, and peripheral the organizing principles of a
course, analysis would focus on the complex ways in which very
different discourses articulate or are articulated with the *local*.

In his *Epistle to a Godson*, Auden writes:

> A poet's hope: to be,
> like some valley cheese,
> local, but prized elsewhere.
> (Auden 1972: 39)

Using poetry as a base, questions of language, landscape, and
complex 'belongings' could be examined with particular reference to writers who have consciously identified their work with

region, locality, or cultural 'idea' – works such as Geoffrey Hill's *Mercian Hymns*, Norman Nicholson's 'Cumbrian' poetry, Bunting's *Briggflatts*, the work of Jon Silkin, the Orkney cultural 'mapping' in poetry and prose of George Mackay Brown, and recent Irish poetry.[6] Brian Friel's *Translations* (1979) which touched on so many aspects of language, local/national identities, transliteration, and cultural/political power, would be a seminal text. The emphasis in a course of this kind will be placed on the *local* as active and initiating, a continuing instance of cultural and linguistic diversity which acts as a reminder of the need to disengage the 'nation' from the 'state', and to reconstruct the 'national' out of its complex and multiple cultural resources in order to begin the process of *internationalizing* British culture. This process could be helped by extending or relating the course to a study of 'external' colonialism and ways in which writers have engaged the language, forms, and cultural power of an imperial nation.

In working with texts which ground themselves in the roots and sources of specific communities, analysis will not simply focus on topography, or matters of 'knowable' geography, but on what Norman Nicholson called 'the base and root of the living rock' of local habitations – on cultural space and time, history, tradition, order, and memory. The precise language used to register the local habitation very often draws upon international influences (as in Geoffrey Hill's poetry), or is shaped and refracted through images well beyond its immediate location. It is the *idea of the local* which is used as a form of cultural archaeology to meditate upon the 'home ground' and the informed and complex processes of history, labour, and class which have produced it. 'Newcastle is Peru', by Tony Harrison, is an example of this, as are Douglas Dunn's *Barbarians*, and more particularly, *St Kilda's Parliament*.

It can be argued that extending concepts of the popular to include those cultural forms using region, zone, or periphery as a *locus* of boundary-crossing activity, a space for seeing 'national unity' as 'notional unity', might become a matter of cultural and political survival:

> To survive at all, the desert dweller – Tuareg or Aboriginal –
> must develop a prodigious sense of orientation. He [sic] must

forever be naming, sifting, comparing a thousand different 'signs' – the tracks of a dung beetle or the ripple of a dune – to tell him where he is; where the others are; where rain has fallen; where the next meal is coming from; whether if plant X is in flower, plant Y will be in berry, and so forth.

(Chatwin 1987: 199)

At another point in *Songlines*, Chatwin notes: 'By spending his whole life walking and singing his Ancestor's Songline, a man eventually became the track, the Ancestor and the song' (Chatwin 1987: 179).

It is this 'prodigious sense of orientation', this 'naming, sifting and comparing', and this 'becoming' the track, the Ancestor, and the song which is at the root of much of the writing of two 'Caribbean' poets, Derek Walcott and Edward Brathwaite. I qualify the term 'Caribbean' because the work of both writers has an international perspective which, however, has a precise articulation in the local. 'Mongrel as I am', Walcott has written, 'something prickles in me when I see the word Ashanti as with the word Warwickshire, both separately intimating my grandfather's roots, both baptising this neither proud nor ashamed bastard, this hybrid, the West Indian' (Walcott 1970: 10). He writes of language:

The West Indian poet suspects the raw spontaneity of dialect as being richer in expression, but is not willing to sacrifice the syntactical power of English. Naturally enough, where the conflict is realized the poetry is strongest. That dramatic ambivalence is part of what it means to be a West Indian now.

(Walcott 1965: 252)

Walcott's *Midsummer* (1984) presents, in Stephan Feuchtwang's words, 'an intersection of references. One line of reference is to Rome, but others are not. Its intersection in the Caribbean creates another home for it' (Feuchtwang 1987: 126). Rome, the Renaissance, Henry James's Boston, Berkshire, and Warwickshire – sites and memories of different imperial moments – all figure in the poems, but they are dis*located* culturally and historically, broken off from their ethnocentric and Eurocentric space.

Midsummer works with an aesthetic–political dialectic which excavates a number of concepts about landscape, economics, history, race, time, naming, and memory – Walcott is not simply proposing a 'soft' pluralism, but examines the linguistic, formal, and cultural meanings of 'English' (as language, nationality, and 'hegemony'), 'European', the colonizer and the colonized, centres and peripheries, and the non-unitary subject. The work helps us to 'think' writing and the popular in new ways.[7]

Using this work as a starting point it should therefore be possible to set up another cross-cultural dimension of the course, one which sets out to challenge the Eurocentric and ethnocentric, as well as questioning the validity of 'nationality' as a meaningful premise for the study of literary cultures. The complex implications of talking about heritage, nationality, stereotypes, and imperial and imperialized modes of self-understanding have already been used as the basis for another course called 'Literatures in English' which looks at African, Caribbean, Afro-American, and Black British writings. (The existence of a firm College policy on multiculturalism and anti-racism, and a Committee to implement this and other policies, provides a necessary framework for this kind of development.)

In Edward Brathwaite's *History of the Voice* (1984), an account of the development of 'nation language' in anglophone Caribbean poetry, he talks about the ways in which the colonizer's language became the language of public discourse and conversation, of obedience and command, and in the process submerged the imported languages of the slaves. He shows too, however, how 'English' was being influenced by the underground, submerged, and 'popular' languages which themselves were constantly transforming into new forms – adapting to the new environment and cultural imperative of the Europeans, and exercising influence on the uses of English. The result of this process is what Brathwaite calls 'nation language' – 'sometimes it is English and African at the same time'.[8] The ways in which this 'repressed' has shaped 'Englishes' enables us to see that the 'prodigious sense of orientation' which marks inner-city Black culture is as crucial an instance of the *local* – the externally colonized 'migrated' to a position of internal colonialism – as any of the more traditional (particularly rural) understandings of spatial organization and perception.

In *X/Self* (Brathwaite 1987) Brathwaite represents the intersection of four landscapes – European, African, Amerindian, Maroon – in a series of poems which cross and recross the boundaries (local, national, and international) of cultures in order to demonstrate how much is based on a culture that is personal – 'i-man/Caribbean' – and how much multifarious and internationalized, a matter of learning and education.

In this work, 'colonization' ceases to be an explanatory metaphor and becomes a territorial, cultural, and experiential 'fact' – complex, varied, shifting, historically specific – as well as an episodic, discontinuous, and multiply inflected 'narrative'. *X/Self* opens out from the Caribbean onto a world view, a view informed, by European and classical cultures as well as by the New World and by Africa. The 'X' is both the brand of the slave – X/ex-nomination, ex-self – and the 'self' at the crossroads – of empires, nation, village, languages, and histories:

> embrace
> him
> he will shatter outwards to your light and calm and history
> your thunder has come home
>
> ('Xango')

It is this 'shattering outwards' from the 'local', this flowing to and from 'other' cultures which the teaching of the 'popular' has to engage:

> bop hard bop soul bop funk
> new thing marley soul rock skank
> *bunk Johnson is riding again.*
>
> ('Xango')

Notes

I should like to express my thanks to my former colleagues at Portsmouth Polytechnic, and to new colleagues at the College of St Paul and St Mary, Cheltenham, who have in different ways made possible many of the ideas and schemes outlined here.

1   Patricia Meyer Spacks (1983) 'In praise of gossip', in Morris Freilich (ed.) *The Pleasure of Anthropology*, New York: Fawcett, 153–70. Much of this section is deeply indebted to this extremely stimulating discussion, including the use of particular concepts and

phrases. To avoid cluttering what is essentially a descriptive account, I have not footnoted all these 'borrowings', but am using this general note to acknowledge the value of her argument.

2   Special emphasis will be placed on 'deconstructing' the texts of late nineteenth-century imperialism in order to examine the use of race, class, sexual, ethical, and nationalist discourse. My phrase 'imperial modes of self-understanding' refers to the west's representations of itself in the terms of 'authenticity', 'authority', and 'knowledge'. Two texts have proved particularly useful in understanding these processes: Malek Alloula (1987) *The Colonial Harem*, Manchester: Manchester University Press, and Benita Parry (1987) 'Problems in current theories of colonial discourse', *Oxford Literary Review* 9, nos 1–2, 27–58.

3   I am indebted to conversations with Brian Doyle for some of these ideas.

4   Raymond Williams (1985) *Towards 2000*, Harmondsworth: Penguin, 146. The last chapter of this book, 'Resources for a journey of hope' summarizes precisely what Williams, who died in January 1988, left as a legacy to those of us influenced by his ideas and inspired by his political witness, especially in a period when 'dialogue' and 'difference' are little valued in our educational system. Williams's novels, particularly *Border Country*, *The Fight for Manod*, and *The Volunteers* would form an important part of any study of 'nation' as a cultural–ecological community.

5   Clifford Geertz (1983) *Local Knowledge*, New York: Basic Books. The discussion on common sense draws extensively upon Geertz, and the same practice has been adopted as in note 1.

6   Two useful introductions to the poetry which will form the basis of this kind of course are Anthony Thwaite (1985) *Poetry Today*, London: Longman, and John Williams (1987) *Twentieth-Century British Poetry*, London: Edward Arnold. The thoughts expressed here owe something to both books.

7   Interestingly, Walcott's latest collection of poetry (1988), *Arkansas Testament*, London: Faber, is divided into two sections – 'Here' and 'Elsewhere' – but the distinctions between the two are constantly blurred, checked, and subverted.

8   It is this simultaneous, intersecting and inextricable quality of the local/national/international, cross cultural which is at the centre of what is being proposed here. Obviously, questions of cultural imperialism and the power of transnational corporations will also form a crucial dimension of this kind of study.

PART III
Case Studies

11

'I see the murderer is a skilful door opener': investigating autobiography and detective stories with 11 to 18 year olds

Steve Bennison and Jim Porteous

> Holmes answered the phone. He was smoking a pipe, wearing tweed trousers and he had just had a shower so his hair was wet. Holmes came straight to the scene of the crime and started looking for clues.

At the risk of over-simplification, we could see English teaching for 11–18 year olds being pulled in two directions. On the one hand, the liberal 'progressive' tradition, at its most extreme operating only in terms of the free play of individuals' imaginative expression untrammelled by convention and structure, either textual or social. On the other hand, the current forces demanding a rigid adherence to the acquisition and accumulation of facts and 'skills'; represented by the proposed imposition of a National Curriculum with testing at 7, 11, 14, and 16 of pupils' knowledge 'about' language, *Animal Farm*, *David Copperfield*, or whatever else strikes the Secretary of State's fancy as a desirable benchmark.

The majority of present English teaching for 11–18 year olds attempts to steer an eclectic course between these two extremes whilst remaining, in general, within the liberal tradition. This article describes three examples from one partial attempt to construct an 11–18 English curriculum that tries to extend and question this moderate liberal 'progressive' approach in order to develop a third, very different pedagogy, centred on notions both of discovery and of control. It aims to provide students with methods of discovering the ways ideological structures and forms of power operate in textual and social discourses, ways which can then be contested and used. The three examples describe work carried out in the first year (by 11 year olds), at GCSE by fourth-year students (14–15 year olds) and at A level, in an 11–18 city comprehensive and the neighbouring technical college.

By describing the teaching and learning practices below in empirical terms we can also illustrate and analyse the three main processes upon which the work is based. Through the course of the three examples there are related movements in the pupils' learning: 1 from classroom practice, to a gradual under-standing of theoretical concepts, to theorized practice; 2 from the student's sense of 'myself' as a writer, to a practice informed by an understanding of narrative structure, to a theoretical grasp of criticism and discourse; 3 a developing understanding of subjectivity: moving from me, to the self, to the subject.

Amongst the tensions encountered during this work, for both teacher and student, are those between the liberal 'progressive' appreciation of individual experience and a knowledge of ideological operations in the realm of subjectivity; between creative writing and genre; between practice and theory. We shall be discussing the reading and writing of autobiography and detective stories, two genres concerned primarily with questions of control and disclosure, with limited freedoms within given discursive structures, and with the construction of the self and of social power relations in the 'real world' as well as in the textual or 'fictional' world. The work thus involves learning how this power operates, how these controls are and can be exercised.

> 'Aha!' cried Debbie Holmes. 'I've got a pretty good idea, all I need is for him to confess. I don't think it will be too difficult. In fact it will be easy.'

Despite this confident extract from one girl's story, planning and writing a short detective story is a fairly sophisticated task for 11 year olds, regardless of their apparently familiar ac-quaintance with the figure of Holmes and other detective fictions and characters via television. A quick summary of how this work was introduced and organized demonstrates how the class overcame and solved problems on a practical basis and how, through this process, new questions and issues concerning the operations of different types of control were raised and addressed. The class first wrote a brief description of their room at home and next evaluated how accurately this reflected their sense of themselves. They found that the descriptions gave a confused impression, for 11 year olds, even if not sharing a room, do not generally choose their own furnishings, wallpaper, carpet, and so on. In this investigative frame of mind they next wrote a short story in which a female or male adult detective (wittily named Ho(l)mes) enters a room and, by examining its contents, tries to identify the inhabitant's character and habits: at the close the owner appears and Holmes's work is shown to have succeeded or failed. Although this work is initially based around a topic comfortably familiar in English classrooms, here the preliminary work on 'my room' raises from the outset ideas about, for example, signs and disclosure, rather than concentrating on the writers' personalities, wishes, etc.

Having now set up the ideas of a detective, clues, and false signs a possible structure for a short detective story was worked out. No published detective fictions were read at this stage, but the class did discuss Tony Hancock's *The Missing Page*, screened the previous weekend. A simple plot was decided upon, divided into three chapters. The detective was first asked to help prove that a character accused of a crime, who was 'obviously' guilty, was actually innocent; then followed the investigation; finally the results of the inquiry were announced. The class set about devising their own stories within this basic structure; the name Holmes was retained as it offered convenient associations as both a model and a stereotype to parody. Time was first spent drawing up lists of characters and locations and sorting out a feasible plot with likely suspects, clues, red herrings, a map of the scene of the crime, etc., and the class confirmed details they would include (for example, weather, characters' appearances, tone of voice) – the conventions of realism generally and of the genre in particular. The class then wrote their stories individually.

'There's no time for jokes! There's a dead body in my room and it's Sir George – my husband!'

'Are you sure?'
'Of course I'm sure! I slept with the man for three years and you ask me if I'm sure!'

At first sight this work does not appear to be radical, with its plot based upon a civilized return to an established order and peopled by an engaging collection of strangely youthful aristocrats, shifty menials, and plodding policemen and involving the consumption of large amounts of food. As writers, however, the class were performing some significant and quite radical work in relation to the control they could exercise, as well as discovering the limitations imposed by the structures they were operating within. Usually sited in a pre-1980s era, with mansions and servants, these stories are clearly alien to the writers' personal experience; the need to construct a logical plot in the third person also served as a distancing device. The writing had also to be decentred, away from the immediate and the self, and its effectiveness considered mainly in terms of the effects on the readers, the rest of the class, who would expect it to conform to the basic conventions of the genre. For example, the vocabulary had to suit the various characters and the historical and class settings, clues had to be inserted, false trails laid: to this extent the writers had to erase themselves from the fiction they were producing in order to possess a greater control over it. Furthermore, because of the generic conventions, there was another quite radical and complex distancing procedure at work: to produce one fiction – their story – the writers had first to construct the story of 'what really happened', which is itself then almost erased and only disclosed at the end by the detective: this control was achieved through the conscious use of generic narrative strategies.

'Mr Holmes, are you going to write a story about all that's happened?'
'Maybe, I don't know, Miss Robins.'
'How did you work it out?'
'Elementary, my dear Miss Robins, elementary.'

On a technical level the class produced, after much labour, surprisingly good narratives; rather like, on another level, the interrogative work of the successful detectives. And just as the detective gains knowledge, so too, perhaps, the class gained some 'useful knowledge' through their work about some aspects of control and the use of power. Obviously, this is a central theme within the narratives they constructed, wherein the adult detective deploys investigative abilities. Working within controlled and structured contexts – as pupils of a teacher, writers of a genre, and so on – permitted the class to recognize these controls and to then exercise aspects of the same type of control over their texts and what they revealed to their readers. Often this sense of control is reflected in a heady exhilaration apparent in their writing, something demonstrated during the time they spent reading and discussing each others' stories when they were produced in 'published' form, typed, and covered. The following extract demonstrates an ability to work within the conventions of the genre and to exercise a shrewd manipulation of the emergent knowledge disclosed to the reader, on a parallel with Holmes's own creative detective work:

Holmes knocked on the door. An old lady opened it.
    'Hullo. I'm Holmes, you called yesterday about the murder.'
    'Oh yes, come in. You're just in time for tea.'
    'Thank you, but I'm not very hungry. I am a bit thirsty.'
    'I'll make you a coffee.'
    'Thank you.'
    'Come and sit down. Here's your coffee.'
    'Ah, where is this dead body?'
    'In the dining room.'
Holmes looked at the body.
    'It seems like he was shot.'
    'Yes, he was shot.'
    'When did you hear the bang?'
    'Oh, last night. I was doing the washing up when suddenly I heard a shot. I dropped the towel and rushed into the dining room but I was too late – the killer had gone.'
    'Was it a man or a woman?'
    'I couldn't tell really. All I saw was a brown coat disappear through the glass doors.'
    'Were they open at the time?'
    'No, I closed it in the evening.'
    'But they're open now, aren't they?'

'I'm sure I closed them.'
Holmes looked at the door.
'I see the murderer is a skilful door opener.'
'He must have been,' she said.
'I wonder if it was a man,' he said.
'Pardon?'
'Nothing,' he said.

In the past the kind of freedom enjoyed by many teachers in constructing such courses has often been suddenly stifled by the need to prepare students for external exams. The advent of GCSE, particularly for departments which have adopted syllabuses assessed entirely by coursework, does allow teachers and students to circumvent these previous restrictions to a certain extent. 100 per cent coursework assessment returns some form of control back to the teacher: within certain minimal restraints teachers have a vacant space to work in, which they can fill as they wish according to individual taste, department policy, or consortium or examining group guidelines. At worst this might result in a *laissez-faire* vacuum, at best teachers can begin to construct coherent courses which allow for an integrated continuation of earlier English work into the examination years without undue external diversion. It is possible to incorporate, for example, a constructive approach to writing involving drafting, revising and editing, collaborative group work, and the study of an unrestricted range of 'texts' of all kinds. The space is available, therefore, to continue a form of interrogative, investigative work – as on language, genre, narrative – and which can now at GCSE address itself to wider questions of control in relation, for example, to representations of gender, race, schooling, and individuality.

The GCSE coursework described below is, ironically, on autobiography, which appears to be a quintessentially 'personal' genre and which occupies a celebrated position in 'progressive' liberal English teaching. This work, however, though based on necessary 'progressive' initiatives, seeks to develop further the implications of the first years' detective-story writing, investigating the way that autobiography is constructed as narrative and not as unmediated self-reflection, and how the discourse of the genre is part of contemporary ideological constructions of the self. Uncovering and investigating both the generic and social processes of this construction marks the beginnings of a politically useful knowledge, a conceptualized 'making strange' of what appears to be natural and universal – the self. Obviously, students aren't sent sobbing from the classroom bewailing their theoretical status as mere ideological constructs, any more than the first years as writers are invited to consider themselves as feeble amateur contributors to a generic treadmill. Just as the first years are encouraged to take pride in their individual achievements so GCSE students are encouraged to see their individual experience as valid and important. Questioning one's experience doesn't negate it: but any new understandings that remain only abstract concepts unrelated to social reality can themselves be of little value.

The fourth-year class began this section of the course by reading a short published autobiographical piece by a student at the end of her schooling (Leitrim 1979). Although this was the story of an unconventional life it was noticeable that the narrative conformed to familiar generic conventions in terms of form, mode of address, chronology, and causal development through fixed stages. Experimenting with their own autobiographical writing the class recognized the need to work within generic conventions regarding how the past is imagined, selected, and ordered, and how the present self is implicated in the representation of a past self. The past is constructed as a narrative, as a story with order, values, and a hierarchy of discourses: the past 'I', clearly, is the central character of the narrative, controlled and structured by the dominant discourse of the present writer. At an obvious level this was seen to involve decisions about which experiences of the text's central character were to be altered, emphasized, or suppressed altogether. This issue of levels of knowledge and disclosure has clear links with the detective-story writing by the first years. Whereas what was at stake for the first years was the creation of a successful detective story, now it was the students' own sense of self that was on the line. This process of 'making strange' was carried further by relating a brief autobiographical experience in the third person; the resulting stories emphasized the essential similarity between autobiographical and fictional constructs. If autobiography is constructed this way, to what extent is one's own sense of self similarly manufactured?

The class went on to apply some of these ideas to a selection of community publishing and to a detailed study of a full-length autobiography, *Between High Walls* by Grace Foulkes, an account of a working-class childhood in Edwardian London.[1] The purpose here was one of analysis as opposed to celebration and empathy or seeing the text as a historical document. Appreciating that it did not offer an unmediated record of individuality, the class identified the controlling structures of the text and the life it described, of which the author herself may not have been aware. After further discussion, focusing on questions of gender and class and on the author as a selfless domestic provider, the class wrote an essay on the ways in which the author presented her childhood and, in particular, considered her construction as a working-class mother as disclosed by the text. This reading exemplified how controls, both generic and social, operate in the construction of story and self.

With another fourth-year class this area of study was developed by reading an extract from an autobiographical piece by a school student and noting how the narrative construction depended on the technique of condensing three or four major incidents into a 'normal' school day (O'Connor 1979). This in turn led to an extended piece of writing, based on prepared interviews with older relatives or neighbours, in which reminiscences of separate vivid moments from schooling were set within a convincing, realist context of everyday domestic, classroom, and playground activity. To stress the extent of the generic construction (and thus of the self in the text) these pieces were written not as biography but as first person autobiography. The class were manufacturing a self in their writing for a person they knew which was patently different from the person's own account, thus disclosing a process similar to that of all autobiography.

At A level the current dominant approach to English Literature is essentially concerned with 'the personal', replacing an impersonal course in received taste and judgement. Study is expected to take place in an autobiographical or declarative mode in which the central subjects are the controlling authors, whose texts are created to make manifest their opinions, ideas, and feelings, and the students, who should grow and develop through a proper personal response to the authors. This liberal humanism is especially prevalent in the new, more 'progressive' syllabuses such as the AEB 660, which whilst allowing space for a range of approaches and teaching methods, are still grounded in an unqualified celebration of individuality, reflected in the syllabuses, exam questions, and markers' reports.[2] The demand that students declare themselves as subjects is especially apparent in the fact that the felt quality of 'authentic' engagement, empathy, and so on in their response – as opposed to critical interrogation – is considered crucial. Some examiners have a magical intuitive ability to recognize an unknown student's 'personal voice', and reward it in preference to writing which applies theoretical concepts, which is dismissed as either 'regurgitated' or 'sociology'. Indeed, rather than 'making strange', the dominant direction of English at A level is towards 'making natural', whether of texts, readings, or the students themselves.

In the commercial study-aids designed for A level students, the students and the texts in question (through their main characters), both seem to share a common goal: a striving towards maturity, tolerance, understanding, and an achieved formal, social, and moral unity, based around apparently natural oppositions such as social/individual, public/private, and male/female. The 'personal', when most authentic, is integrated into the social norm: this applies, inevitably it appears, to the characters in the text and, implicitly, also to students, whose 'personal response' will be suitably rewarded if it matches the culturally approved ways of reading.[3]

One of the consequences of this remorseless individualizing of both author and student is to depoliticize both. A particularly grim example of this was on show in the following 1987 AEB 660 exam question: 'Illustrate from *Songs of Innocence and Experience* Blake's awareness of social and political injustice. Have you found this an attractive quality in his poetry?' As Pierre Macherey and Etienne Balibar have written, 'literature is historically constituted in the bourgeois epoch as an ensemble of language – or rather of specific linguistic practices – inserted in a general schooling process so as to provide appropriate fictional

effects, thereby reproducing bourgeois ideology as the dominant ideology' (Macherey and Balibar 1978: 84). However,
although this is true in general it does rather bleakly neglect
the possibility of small-scale oppositional interventions.
It is still possible to use the space afforded by coursework at A
level (as at GCSE) for more radical work, which can in fact be
used to question the assumptions upon which the syllabus itself
depends.[4] The following two examples of coursework at A level
for the AEB 660 syllabus, on autobiography and detective
fiction, indicate an approach that uses the same theoretical
basis as the previous work with first and fourth years; applying a
now explicit analytical critical practice to texts and their reproduction, particularly in relation to their function as ideological
discourses.

As at GCSE, the work on autobiography began by breaking
down the distinction between fact and fiction and studying
autobiographical narrative as a highly selective construct; in
this case we used Orwell's *Down and Out in Paris and London* and
Homage to Catalonia. After reading, independently, a number of
other texts and looking at various snippets together the group
then produced a chart indicating a whole range of questions and
problems concerning ways of writing and reading autobiographies. At this stage the group read and discussed brief
extracts from a wide range of texts (including *In Search of a Past*, *I
Know Why the Caged Bird Sings*, Freud's *Introductory Lectures*, and
Nietzsche's *Ecce Homo*).[5] What emerged as the main issue was
the status of the text as a construct which was itself constructing
an ideologically recognizable version of the subject and of
subjectivity, presented through the privileged discourse as the
subject of the narrative. To what extent, for example, did the
controlling 'I' recognize itself as a material construct, in both
textual and historical and social terms? In this respect the A
level students were now doing a more explicitly theorized
version of the fourth-year work. The group next worked on
categorizing modes of autobiography (and approaches to the
reading of autobiography) in a simple form – liberal humanist,
psychoanalytical, and, closely related to each other, materialist
and feminist – each mode constructing a different version of
subjectivity in textual and social terms.

The last piece of work undertaken by the group as a whole sought to apply a basic theoretical concept of ideology to the opening few pages of *The Autobiography of Mark Rutherford*, an apparently extreme version of the humanist autobiographical mode (Rutherford 1881). With some planned prompting the group noted the narrative manoeuvres through which the individual 'I' as both child and present writer was constructed; how Rutherford is presented as both typical and special, how he places himself in history as a present relic cut adrift from a Utopian past made up of an imaginary community of early communists ('There was absolutely no competition') scuppered by the expansion of capitalism. The group also picked out the ways in which Rutherford introduces a range of 'sub-texts' ('The Word' and sermons in chapel, writing in school, family letters). The effect of these was to privilege his own writing, by contrast, as a 'real', 'personal' text clinging to a precarious existence and thus of especial value (as he is himself). It also proved impossible to determine from internal evidence whether the text was autobiography or fiction! This work on autobiography demonstrated how our sense of subjectivity is materially produced and reproduced in textual and social contexts, that 'I' and 'myself' are ideological and political terms. This is most apparent when a text represents subjectivity as essentially natural: the silence on this issue declares a bourgeois individuality in its most political form.

This approach to discourse and ideology was developed later in the course in analyses of *Tess of the d'Urbervilles*, *The Tempest*, *Persuasion*, and others, especially in relation to issues of gender. One student concentrated on autobiography for her individual extended essay required by AEB 660 and wrote on changing representations of femininity in *Jipping Street*, *Truth*, *Dare or Promise*, and *Landscape for a Good Woman*, looking at issues of motherhood, 'naturalized' female roles, and expectations in and out of the home, as well as at the changing and increasingly oppositional understandings of how subjectivity is constructed.[6]

A similar approach informed a study of Raymond Chandler's *Farewell My Lovely*, also for AEB 660 coursework. This was part of a term's work on 1920s and 1930s USA, which considered essays and short stories by Hemingway and Scott Fitzgerald, *The Great Gatsby*, *The Grapes of Wrath*, *Waiting for Lefty*, reportage and political writing, films, photography, and popular songs. The general idea was to look at a range of ideological responses (conscious or otherwise) to the social and economic upheavals of the period and at how these were mediated through the available generic discourses, which were themselves sometimes transformed in the process.

Before starting the work on *Farewell My Lovely* the group first read Doyle's 'Charles Augustus Milverton' from *The Return of Sherlock Holmes* and discussed Catherine Belsey's comments in *Critical Practice* (1980) on the gaps in the text, in the hope of establishing a method of analysis which could be applied to other writings. The study of *Farewell My Lovely* began with an attempt to situate the text in the history of popular crime fiction and to consider the way that this reflected the historical difference between the worlds of Holmes and Marlowe. The shift from dastardly individual villains to a sense of widespread social 'corruption', for example, is readily apparent in the gangster films of the period which the group had watched. Other basic contrasts were noted, as between an assumption of fixed and agreed values and a new sense of all-pervading brutality and cynicism, and between the cerebral fireside analysis of clues and the professional detective's direct personal involvement in the world of crime. Using a rather crude Lukacsian explanation these changes were traced to contemporary developments in modern capitalism and bourgeois values.[7]

The Chandler novels are useful in the way that their slightly untypical self-consciousness and the hyperbolic nature of the texts draws attention to themselves as constructs. As a 'window on the world' *Farewell My Lovely* has already been made strange: this caused initial problems in that it seemed little more than a jokey puzzle, but its knowingness helped undermine any possibility of an innocent reading of the text as uncorrupted 're-alism'. The group spent two weeks reading and discussing the novel; making detailed stylistic analyses of selected passages; considering the function of the iconography and the humour; composing witty parodies; constructing lists and diagrams to show binary opposites and structural conflicts. We looked at, for example, the conflicts between individualism and a structured society; the tight humour of individual episodes and the diffuse structure of the overall plot; the strict moralizing and detached cynicism; the '*femme fatale*' and the 'good woman'; the hero's ambivalent shifts between involvement and distancing, machismo and self-mockery. The text, we concluded, seemed to offer no convincing ideological response to the social and economic developments of its period, just a troubled individualism, one that knew itself to be powerless in the fact of impenetrable structures, but which retained a bemused, moralizing sense of detachment. (A seamlessly stage-managed course would, no doubt, have drawn out telling ideological parallels on the site of the textual 'I' between Marlowe and Mark Rutherford . . .)

Alongside this the group watched two film versions of Marlowe and a recent television adaptation, noting the very different reproductions for different audiences and times. The group went on next to study *The Great Gatsby* and, for their coursework, wrote an essay drawing out significant connections between the two texts. As with the work on autobiography a wide selection of related texts was available for individual reading and one student subsequently chose to write her extended essay on three Dashiell Hammett novels, applying ideas encountered during this part of the course.

At all three stages the students' work encompassed a far wider range of materials and activities than detailed in this account, with no separation between literary and non-literary texts, written or otherwise, or between reading and the students' own writing. The theoretical principles which encouraged this variety required at the same time, however, a quite specific form of teaching and learning. At A level, for example, this approach does not deny students opportunities for open debate (as any classroom observation would confirm), but it does contest the liberal assumption that 'it's all a matter of personal opinion' by revealing some of the implications of competing readings, theories, etc. In this structured process of discovery and control, and discovery of control, the most important unifying factor, one which exists in a paradoxical alliance in the classroom with a respect and concern for individual students and their learning, is a continuous questioning of textual and social discourses, including that of individuality itself.

'I think I'll go and ask Lisa a few questions,' Holmes said.

He found Lisa sitting in her bedroom reading a romance story.

'Lisa, here you are,' said Holmes. 'I just want to ask you a few questions about the murder. What happened?'

Notes

Thanks to our colleagues and students past and present, and members of Bristol LTP and the Avon branch of NATE with whom we discussed and argued about many of these ideas. An earlier account of the first-year work was included in a collection of papers written for the SCDC National Writing Project.

1   See, for example, Stephen Humphries (1983) 'Radical childhood in Bristol 1889–1939', in Ian Bild (ed.) *Bristol's Other History*, Bristol Broadsides; and *Bristol As We Remember It, A Bristol Childhood, St Paul's People Talking*, all Bristol Broadsides; Grace Foulkes (1976) *Between High Walls: A London Childhood* in *My Part Of The River*, London: Futura.

2   For details of the AEB 660 syllabus see Stephen Bennison and Jim Porteous (1987) 'An ordeal of personal compulsion? English 14–18', in *Changing the Subject: LTP 6.*

3   See also Alison Light (1983) 'Feminism and the literary critic', *LTP* 2: 70; and Terry Eagleton (1985) 'The subject of Literature', *The English Magazine 15*.

4   The Avon Branch of the National Association for the Teaching of English is currently working on a proposal for a new A level in Literary and Cultural Studies which would make a complete break with the traditional ideology of A level English Literature.

5   Ronald Fraser (1984) *In Search of a Past*, London: Verso; Maya Angelou (1984) *I Know Why the Caged Bird Sings*, London: Virago. The group also looked at snippets and extracts from a range of other autobiographical texts including *A Sort of Life*, by Graham Greene; *Autobiography*, by Harriet Martineau; *Confessions*, by Jean-Jacques Rousseau; and *Memoirs of My Life and Childhood*, by Edward Gibbon.

6   Kathleen Woodward (1983) *Jipping Street*, London: Virago; Liz Heron (ed.) (1985) *Truth, Dare or Promise: Girls Growing Up in the Fifties*, London: Virago; Carolyn Steedman (1986) *Landscape for a Good Woman; A Story of Two Lives*, London: Virago.

7   Loosely based on the more sophisticated arguments in Ernest Mandel (1984) *Delightful Murder: A Social History of the Crime Story*, London: Pluto Press; and Ken Worpole (1983) *Dockers and Detectives*, London: Verso.

12

Changing literature at A level

Margaret Peacock and Elaine Scarratt

It is no surprise that new, working definitions of literature are being introduced in comprehensive schools. The child-centred approach to learning, developed in the lower school, plus open access to sixth-form education, have challenged long-accepted and deep-rooted assumptions about the content and pedagogy of A level English. We start from the assumption that literature and criticism, at least as represented up to now on A level syllabuses, have had a predominantly white, male, and middle-class bias. As long as students studying English were also white and male and middle class there was little chance that this would be changed. Terry Eagleton in his introduction of *Literary Theory* points to the same feature in I. A. Richards's tests of student responses to unidentified poems at Cambridge in the early 1920s:

> one is struck by the habits of perception and interpretation which they [the students] spontaneously share – what they expect literature to be, what assumptions they bring to a poem and what fulfilments they anticipate they will derive from it. None of this is really surprising; for all the participants in this experiment were, presumably, young, white, upper or middle-class privately educated people of the 1920s ... Their critical responses were deeply entwined with their broader prejudices and beliefs.
>
> (Eagleton 1983: 15)

Comprehensive education, with its opening up of A level to a much wider spectrum of society, has freed literary study from this narrow perspective. Our A level students, coming as they do from a wide variety of middle- and working-class cultures, either of which could be white or Black British, Asian, Afro-Caribbean, Chinese, Vietnamese, or Turkish, amongst others, bring different assumptions, prejudices, and beliefs to literature, which are both challenging and rewarding.

Not that the acceptance of this cultural richness has been automatic. We might conceivably have viewed our own task as that of helping those ignorant of the 'Great Tradition' to accept the values inherent in traditional A level. That we have not is owing partly to our understanding of our pupils' needs and partly to our sympathy with developments in recent literary theory. We felt that the traditional A level syllabus with its hierarchical view of literature derived from nineteenth-century Romanticism and Leavisite elitism was too restrictive. A brief sketch of the terms in which English was introduced into the secondary curriculum will help explain our rejection of the traditional approach more fully.

There seems to be an assumption that because there is a 'Great Tradition' of English literature there is also a 'great tradition' of English teaching. But in fact the subject was introduced into mainstream education less than one hundred years ago and A level appeared only in 1951. Rather than evolving from some artistic or literary practice or as a result of wholly altruistic motives, the subject was established for largely political, social, and religious reasons at a time of marked social turbulence and moral uncertainty. In the process of establishing a national education system (for boys), influential educationists such as Matthew Arnold and Robert Lowe sought to curb the insurrectionary potential of a 'raw and half-developed' working class (Arnold 1869, 1963: 105), and so maintain social order.

With the failure of religion as an agent of such control, Romantic criticism and the study of literature, particularly of poetry, swiftly moved in to take its place. Poetry was seen in this tradition as a divine, moral force and this view, coupled with a claim such as Wordsworth's that the poet had the power to bind 'together by passion and knowledge the vast empire of human

society as it is spread over the whole earth, and over all time'
(Wordsworth 1802, 1977: 881) echoes through education documents at the end of the nineteenth century and into the first
thirty years of the twentieth. The self-improving qualities of
English were continually stressed in this period and were soon
joined by an explicit belief in the ability of literature to promote
empathy between lower and higher classes. As the Spens Report
put it: 'it should be possible for the spread of a common habit of
English teaching to *soften the distinctions* which separate men and
classes in later life' (para. 222, our italics).

The Newbolt Report (1921) and then the Hadow Report
(1926) and the Spens Report (1938) confirmed the view that
class differences need not be a cause of strife if the working class
could be brought to identify with their superiors via an acceptance of the 'diviner' nature of great literature. The desire also to
inspire a sense of duty and patriotism can clearly be seen in the
texts effectively prescribed by the Board of Education. These
were consistently heroic and masculine, and included epic
poems, pantheistic Romantic verse, biographical essays on
great men, sagas, voyages, heroic adventure novels (but no
social realism), Shakespeare, and patriotic songs.[1] Pupils were
given 'suitably graduated series of exercises' (Board of Education 1904: 1) and were 'taught to understand, not to criticise or
judge' (Board of Education 1910: para. 36). The object was
appreciation in a literal, slavish sense: pupils memorized and
copied carefully-selected passages of great literature, composed
essays on subjects already tackled by great writers, and then
compared their efforts with the originals.

When therefore F. R. Leavis and *Scrutiny* intervened in the
study of literature, they entirely changed the form and manner
of literature teaching in schools. Leavis's 'practical criticism'
was 'unafraid to take the text apart' (Eagleton 1983: 43), or 'to
criticise or judge'. However, although Leavis's critical method
represented a new departure, the training in sensibility and
discrimination he encouraged, linked with a critique of mass
society, was fundamentally consistent with earlier thinking.
Indeed, a Leavisite approach informs much teaching today. At
the same time, of course, alternative methods and positions
have emerged. One such is the so-called 'English as language'
paradigm which came to fruition in the 1960s in the work of

Barnes, Rosen, Martin, and Britton, in LATE (the London Association for the Teaching of English) founded in 1947, and NATE (the National Association for the Teaching of English) in the late 1960s and 1970s.[2] This tradition with its emphasis on the heuristic role of language rather than literature and its sharp distinction 'between using the mother tongue and studying it' (Britton 1973: 14) has informed our own approach and our aim to encourage our pupils' confidence in the process of discovery and in their own opinions. The related concept of 'language as personal growth' outlined in Britton's *Language and Learning* (1970) similarly helped us respond to the cultural pluralism of our student intake. In Stephen Ball's description, this model 'stressed the need for English teaching to begin with the pupils' performance and to be related directly to their experience. Social and personal relevance were being stressed as the main bases on which personal growth would be achieved' (Ball 1985: 68). The idea of 'personal growth' has been responsible for some notorious slackness and error, and we have tried to avoid this by stressing what Bennison and Spicer recently describe as both 'affective *and* intellectual "personal responses"' (Bennison and Spicer 1988: 34, our italics).

The coming together of different cultural assumptions and values in the curriculum and classroom has therefore required a redefinition of literature. But in schools this redefinition is only 'new' at A level. School English departments have been aware for many years of the cultural diversity of their pupils, and have broadened the curriculum in the lower school to take advantage of it. This means of course that our students begin their A level English course with very different expectations of what literature is all about than those given only a traditional diet of Shakespeare, Dickens, Austen, and perhaps Conrad. Included in the Kidbrooke English fourth- and fifth-year curriculum is a course called 'Language and power' which aims to develop an awareness of language as a conveyer of social and political ideologies. Students discuss accent and dialect, the language of advertising, how sexism and racism operate in language, and how children's literature can be a powerful medium for conveying assumptions about the class structure of society. This awareness together with the background study of a wide range of teenage fiction by black and white authors, and some experience of analysing the media, forms a strong foundation for the kind of A level study we now offer. The way is then open for an active investigation of various and changing literary texts rather than a passive appreciation of static 'great' works. In this we would agree once more with Terry Eagleton:

> All literary works . . . are 'rewritten', if only unconsciously, by the societies which read them; indeed, there is no reading of a work which is not also a 're-writing'. No work, and no current evaluation of it, can simply be extended to new groups of people without being changed, perhaps almost unrecognizably, in the process; and this is one reason why what counts as literature is a notably unstable affair.
>
> (Eagleton 1983: 12)

It is this instability which informs our choice of texts, the way we teach them, and what we want our students to investigate about literature. This is not to say that we promote subjective interpretation; the group rewriting of a text will always be a product of the active reading process of the varied members of the group, collectively negotiated (with or without teacher intervention), leading to *one* rather than *the* interpretation of a text. We want pupils to explore, to exchange responses, to interpret, and to become confident in their critical ability, and in the process to see literature not as god-given and designated 'good' by someone else, but as a socially-determined construct open to interpretation and reinterpretation, by themselves as well as others. As Nick Peim writes: 'English is not about learning or knowing an object in the conventional sense. It is more about mastering a discourse; having available appropriate responses' (Peim 1986: 13).

How, then, does all this translate into an A level English course? It would not be true to say that the traditional A level syllabuses available to us until recently prevented this kind of approach, but they certainly did not encourage anything other than the acceptance of 'Literature' with a capital 'L' – as established by tradition and long-standing critical opinion. The double expectation of a conventional, and therefore acceptable – but yet original response produced the perverse search for obscure poems on the 'Practical Criticism' paper, and an unhealthy insecurity on the part of our students. The most frequent question we remember students asking when we followed the London A level syllabus was, 'What will the examiner do if he [sic] doesn't agree with what I've put – with my interpretation?' We certainly didn't set out to give the impression that there was an 'answer', but the wording of the questions, the fact that the examination was a 'testing' rather than an exploration, the invisible arbitrator whose name we didn't even know – all combined to make the student feel that her or his response was being set against a prescribed interpretation and judged accordingly.

We needed, then, a syllabus which provided greater freedom of choice and approach and we found this, several years ago, in the AEB Alternative Syllabus, which is assessed through two end-of-course examinations – Paper 1, Practical Criticism; Paper 2, Open Book Set Texts; and Paper 3, a coursework folder: each awarded equal marks. There are other similar courses now available.

The open-book nature of the examination is integral to our approach. Our experience with O level literature had already taught us this. The memory work which is unavoidable in an examination where texts are not allowed in the examination room, can only be inhibiting to the kind of thinking we wish our students to develop. One of our students, who decided to take a second A level English syllabus after getting an A grade in the lower sixth on the AEB course, discovered how different the learning process is. Here are some of her comments:

> artificial situation – detailed criticism without the text? Who does that? It becomes an exercise in reduction and organis-ation – dividing work into components – glorified filing – less personal input for students – say you can only learn, say fifty quotes over four books – roughly twelve from each book – it is unlikely that opinions will differ wildly over the twelve sentences that represent the book best. The essays turned out will probably be fairly standard.

As she also comments, it becomes a game of 'guessing the question' and learning a certain amount by rote, whereas in an open-book examination a 'far greater appreciation of the author's work is gained by the in-depth detailed study which is necessary to build up the knowledge and ability to answer "on your own"'. At the same time, it has to be said that the AEB examination does not completely eradicate the anxieties generated by sitting any examination. Having the texts to refer to does, however, encourage the students to think and write in the ways in which they have become accustomed.

It is in the third paper, however, that the main difference from the traditional A level lies. This is a coursework folder which has to contain eight pieces of work on six different texts, one of which must be a Shakespeare play and one a work of non-fiction. The set texts are chosen by teacher, or student, or both. In addition to the eight pieces students must include a 3,000 word essay on a topic of their own choosing, requiring the study of two or more texts.

It is significant that coursework assessment at A level was a long time coming, and we are aware that it is still looked on with suspicion by some universities. It was, however, one of the main reasons why we changed to our present syllabus, and we defend it absolutely. We would, in fact, like to see the board offering 100 per cent coursework syllabus. This is not, of course, because we want to 'help' our students write their essays (a criticism we have encountered) but because it allows for what we consider to be the only real process of thinking and communicating thought. Students can develop the process of drafting and redrafting they have begun in the first to fifth years, a concept of writing which is at the heart of the English course in these years. They can try out methods of expression, test out their ideas in writing and build the confidence to be original without the daunting and limiting prospect of either their first thought, or their learned response, being judged and graded. In the history of examinations there can have been few original ideas, yet in coursework essays we find them all the time.

It is not only the coursework component that is important, however, but the fact that we can, together with the students, choose the texts for study. The degree of choice allowed varies from school to school (or college) – some, we know, allowing students to write all eight essays on texts they have themselves chosen. At the moment we select six texts at the beginning of the course, but also encourage students to submit their own choices, or those negotiated with us. Currently, some of the books chosen for individual study and possible inclusion are *Marilyn*, *Kinflicks*, *The Women's Room*, *One Flew Over the Cuckoo's Nest*, *An American Dream*, *Rebecca*, and *Ministry of Fear*.

As we said, a strength of our A level groups is that they consist of students from a wide ethnic and cultural background, though the traditional list of set texts did not allow us to develop and use this strength to any great degree. This diversity of cultural background, therefore, was something which informed our choice of coursework texts right from the beginning. If we were to allow for, even encourage, a new definition of literature, we had to validate that claim by including the kinds of texts not previously considered appropriate for study at this level. We included, then, works by black writers, women writers, contemporary writers – Alice Walker, Maya Angelou, Fay Weldon, Toni Morrison, Paule Marshall, James Baldwin, Maxine Hong Kingston, Trevor Griffiths, Sarah Daniels, John Fowles, Monica Dickens, Joe Orton – works untried as far as the canon is concerned, but which have consistently elicited excellent work and vociferous arguments in their favour from our students.

It is perhaps the most demanding and most exciting section of the coursework – the long essay – where we see the most positive response to studying this kind of contemporary literature. Three thousand words is often daunting at first to some of our students, but we are constantly impressed at how quickly they find what they want to write about, engage with their texts, and write very interestingly about complex issues. The confidence they eventually feel, and the freedom to construct their own readings can be conveyed by a few of the titles they have chosen:

> 'The clash of conventional hopes and unconventional desires in *Who Lies Inside* by Timothy Ireland, *Giovanni's Room* by James Baldwin, *Nights at the Circus* by Angela Carter, and *Rites of Passage* by William Golding.'

> ' "The triumph of goodness over evil is a pre-requisite for the success of the popular novels of James Herbert and Ray Bradbury." An analysis of reader expectation in popular science fiction and horror literature.'

'Life for West Indians in the Caribbean and London from 1939 to the 1950s as seen in *A Brighter Sun*, *Turn Again Tiger*, and *The Lonely Londoners* by Samuel Selven.'

'An examination of how three women struggle to achieve a sense of self in a male-dominated world in *The Bell Jar*, *Girls in Their Married Bliss*, and *Martha Quest*.'

Not all students choose to write about contemporary literature, but a couple of topics about earlier texts will serve to illustrate how they approach established texts in a new way:

'A comparison between modern and traditional Gothic literature. A study of "The Bloody Chamber" and "Company of Wolves" by Angela Carter, *Otranto* by Horace Walpole, and *Frankenstein* by Mary Shelley.'

'*Not* love at first sight – the difficulties of developing compatibility and fulfilment in relations between men and women as described in the novels *Jane Eyre*, *Pride and Prejudice*, and *Emma*.'

We include this list of topics, not simply because they indicate an interest in contemporary works not usually considered 'Literature' at this level, but because they are a product of another essential and growing aspect of the course: namely, independent reading. We make our own reading an integral part of the course from the beginning, in a way in which we always intended to but never did very successfully, through pressure of time to get through the set texts and teach the proper organization of material. Now we start off with a book list – which gets longer every year as we add our own and our students' discoveries. During the first week, every student has to choose one book, and is given a fortnight to read it. At the end of the fortnight, each student reports back to the rest of the group. Quality of insight and skill at reporting naturally varies, as does enthusiasm about their choice but the amount of cross-fertilization never ceases to amaze us. By the end of the sessions, most students have a long list of books they 'must read', and nobody feels that time has been wasted, though we haven't been slogging through texts. This kind of session happens periodically through the course, giving rise to discussion on a very wide variety of books: from Mills and Boon, to works such as *Tristram Shandy*, *Tess of the d'Urbervilles*, *The French Lieutenant's Woman*, and Bob Geldof's *Is That It?*.

What methods, then, do we use to make our students readers who are no longer consumers but 'producers' of a text? First, in order for a student to get inside a text and make it her or his own, the barriers between the reader and the text have to be broken down; texts must not be seen as inviolable. The relationship between teacher and taught, similarly, must change; the environment must be supportive and open enough to allow for students to risk interpretations, which often, of course, means exposing their thoughts, and therefore making themselves vulnerable. The framework the teacher builds for this relationship is therefore extremely important. She or he initiates an activity or a task, stimulates the discussion but has to learn to take more of a backseat from that point on, and give the students freedom to work through ideas.

The process of breaking down the barriers between reader and text begins right from the beginning of the course. The introductory session begins not with a set text, but with a wide variety of extracts, such as the openings from novels, to encourage students to look at narrative techniques, different relationships between writer and text, writer and reader, reader and text. Students start, then, to look at how they and others read, to question essential relationships, and to see that a text can be broken up, interpreted, and analysed. We introduce them to the wide range of writing which loosely comes under the heading 'novel': some Dickens, some George Eliot, some modern novels, some feminist novels, authors who consciously set out to draw the reader's attention to their reading – Italo Calvino, for example. It all serves to convey, from the start, that this course will not be 'taught' in the sense that the teacher will tell them what is important and therefore what to write about. Instead, it conveys that we want them to explore what this thing called 'literature' is: to appreciate its range and parameters, to ask why readers' values differ, and so on. We also move very quickly to discussing a range of poetry – something few pupils will have very much experience of. Our first aim here is to show that studying poetry can be enjoyable, and that it can develop their *own* creativity. In this context, we can start to 'play around' with poems. 'To His Coy Mistress' for example, is translated into a modern setting, using the poet's arguments and (if possible) the style, or the tone; or the woman's reply is put into verse. It's fun, it's comical, and very effective in helping the cohesion of a new group. More importantly, students are studying poetry without the usual inhibitions.

We aim to help the students to see poems as constructs, and to understand the choices a poet makes during the creative process, and one method that we find helpful in this is what we call, variously, dismembering or deconstructing a text. It is particularly useful when poems are not immediately accessible, as in the following examples which illustrate approaches to the anthology *Bread and Roses*, a text written by and for women. This is the set anthology for the open-book 'Practical Criticism' paper and proved difficult for both students and teachers. The way these suggested approaches were produced is also significant. What follows is taken from a long list of suggestions on how to tackle this anthology, put together not just by Kidbrooke teachers, but by teachers of the course from many schools, gathered together at one of the regular moderating meetings. This collaborative method, within and outside the department, is central: teachers feel less isolated, they are able to talk through new approaches with other teachers and the Chief Examiner, new methods and ways of working are shared and validated, and confidence grows immeasurably. This, then, is a short extract from that list of suggestions:

1 Cut up and reconstruct poems. Particularly suitable for this are: Michelle Roberts's 'Out of Order, Out of Chaos' and Nicki Jackowska's 'The Meeting'. (Reconstruction is an interesting exercise. Often students will argue hard for their own poem being 'better' than the poet's. They have, of course, made their own meanings from it, while getting inside the language used.)

2 Poem 'consequences'   a All read the same poem.
   b Each person writes a comment or a question on a sheet of paper.
   c Each sheet is passed on to the next person, who answers the question

> and/or writes another com-
> ment . . . until the sheet is re-
> turned to the original person.
> d Group discussion.

3 The students read around the class. Each person reads
up to a punctuation mark, then makes a note on the
significance of what they have read.

A similar approach is seen in this extract from teachers' notes,
produced within the department for the same anthology:

'Aurora Leigh' by Elizabeth Barrett Browning

This is interesting because it contains two voices: that of the
woman poet privately celebrating her creativity and that of
her male cousin dismissing her work as middle class female
nonsense. It needs careful re-reading but relates well to the
poems already looked at. *In pairs* students select lines which
either ring bells in their own experience, or which could be
linked clearly to the previous poems. Or, *in pairs*, they read
Section B. One reads and the other butts in and answers,
either as Aurora or herself.

'Autumn' by Christina Rossetti

The poem is cut up into what seems to be its natural though
irregular stanzas. Each stanza is stuck on a piece of A4 paper
and everyone is given a different coloured felt-tip pen. The
sheets are passed around and the task is to respond in some
way to the stanza in front of you by circling words, phrases,
writing comments or questions. This task worked well, provoked a lot of discussion and prompted their own essay title:
'With reference to two poems show how the section "We Who
Bleed" seems preoccupied with the notions of strength and
isolation.'

The wording of the title, at first glance, may not seem remarkable, or different from many A level questions, but it in fact
differs from the 'norm' in two distinct ways: firstly, it was made
up collaboratively by the students; secondly, it was formulated
after discussion, so it is a condensation of thoughts and ideas,
already discovered by the students, who in this instance are not
being asked to prove somebody else's critical point. This

method is central to our mode of teaching, since it avoids testing students as much as possible, and instead sets up situations that demand their active participation and independent thinking.

It must be evident that there is very little of 'teacher talks, students take notes' going on in these exercises. (In fact, bills for sugar paper are getting as high as those for A4 lined.) *The Wasteland*, for example, becomes a collage of images cut from magazines, stuck on for display and discussion; significant quotations from *Hamlet* are built up by a group on sugar paper and used to focus the attention of the rest of the class on what the play seems to them to be saying about women, for example, or relationships, or the family, or whatever strikes them as important. By concentrating in this way on words, phrases, images, and links between them, students make their own meanings, and find the confidence to explore them publicly. We also find that by working with a text in this way, students get to know it well, so that their writing is full and convincing.

The methods we use are, of course, familiar to our students, for many of them will have learned from our practices in the lower school. Role playing is one example of this. As well as acting out scenes in *The Crucible*, for example, students may take on the parts of the characters and in turn cross-examine each other on motivations, feelings, and relationships. Or, this method can be used to look at 'gaps in the text' of a novel: Tom's proposal to Lydia in *The Rainbow*, for instance, can be successfully explored dramatically so that the tension of the episode can be more directly experienced, and the significance of what is *not* said thrown into relief.

One of our jobs as English teachers is, of course, to make accessible to students some of the experiences which they will not have had first-hand. Occasionally, we can find ways of helping this process along outside the classroom. Faced with Ursula's first experience of teaching in *The Rainbow*, we decided that some students might like to prepare and teach a lesson to a first-year class. Those who took the opportunity (in pairs, we might add, because they didn't like the idea of being totally exposed, on their own) found it not only interesting and even enjoyable, but were able to compare it very fruitfully with Lawrence's perceptions about authority, individuality, and about imposing one's 'will' on a 'mass'.

It would be true to say that we have learned a lot from collaboration with drama teachers in schools and with actor–teachers in our local Theatre in Education group. Their methods are effective in getting to grips with texts in the classroom. Even more interesting, however, has been the use of role playing to open up and examine the political nature of literary texts. The most memorable example of this was when the Greenwich Young People's Theatre collaborated on a day's role playing for our Summer School for lower-sixth A level students. The theme of the week was 'Literature and Society' and we wanted a way to introduce students to the complexities and wide implications of this, before immersing them in intensive studies on particular issues. The programme was so effective that it is worth describing in some detail.

The programme was called 'Culture Shock', and all the students (about 100 of them, from schools all around south-east London) were divided into different sections of an imaginary society. The country in which the scene was set bore a close resemblance to Ulster, in its relation to a controlling state and in its political structure. The town was called Moreside, and the occasion, the Moreside Arts Festival. Several groups, such as the People's Liberation Party, the Westland National Party, The Heritage (the official Arts' magazine, whose resemblance to *Scrutiny* was noted by staff, if not students), had to decide their priorities for the programme, and put them forward to the Moreside Arts Association. They were given a long list of possibilities, ranging from overtly political AGIT-PROP theatre, to 'high culture'. During the day various unforeseen situations orchestrated by Theatre in Education members arose – such as the arrest of the nationalist poet – which were designed to prevent easy solutions, and make everyone reassess their decisions. The extent to which the students threw themselves into this programme was shown not only by the fact that they kept going in heat that exceeded 90°F but by their production of numerous statements, magazine articles, whole magazines, and even their own political poetry. They grappled, all day, with huge political and artistic issues. What does 'artistic achievement of the very highest quality' mean? Is all culture necessarily political? Why is Bach 'art' and the Sex Pistols not? Or are they? If a political poem gets its message across forcefully, does that make it 'good', and thus good enough to be included in any Arts festival? Is everything traditionally considered 'Literature' middle class? These are not easy questions, but the students certainly began to appreciate their implications, to see that value is political, and that literature is produced by people who live in society, and are therefore part of the organization of that society.

Obviously this kind of programme, excellent though it is, can only be a rare event given the kinds of constraints we work under in schools. And it would not be effective if its message were totally alien to the students. Its strength lies in the awareness students develop through such intensive role playing, and the way this helps crystallize ideas already present in their A level course. On a more mundane level, students discuss political perspectives all the time: is a Marxist interpretation of *Othello* justified? What is a feminist interpretation of *Jane Eyre*? Is a non-political interpretation of *The Grapes of Wrath* possible? Is D. H. Lawrence sexist, and if so, is his work of less value? Do we only think Alice Walker is 'good' because she is trendy?

We think that if our students leave school, having at least raised questions on these issues, then they will have got far more out of their A level literature course than they would have done if they had studied eight books, in depth, and known only what all the critics have said about them. There are also times when the students question or even object to the texts: *Bread and Roses* has provoked strong adverse responses, for example. Some students have felt that it's 'all about black, feminist, lesbian, single-parent mothers', some male students have felt alienated by it because they perceive its main message to be 'women are great, men are bad', others have felt that 'birth and periods' are not poetic subjects. The strength of the resentment in our students has challenged our teaching methods and, as we have mentioned earlier, since it is such a difficult, provocative, and stimulating text, this means we have to constantly discuss how we can make it accessible. It also challenges the students to develop a more critical stance so that they don't react purely personally to what they perceive. Nobody said that exploring what constitutes 'literature' and developing one's understanding of it is easy.

At the end of all the sugar paper, all the discussion in small groups, all the role playing, all the deconstruction of the text, however, what is actually assessed is only what the students commit to paper. For the writing of essays, of course, is still necessary. There has been considerable change, though, in the kind of written response required, and therefore in the kinds of questions or tasks set. This is as true in the examinations as in the coursework. The emphasis has moved a long way from the universal, all-embracing quotation plus 'Discuss' which so often elicited a mechanical or a learned response. Preparation for the examinations is no longer a matter of trying to anticipate the questions, and of making sure the students have enough material to answer them; we are confident that the questions set will demand understanding and will allow for individual and informed answers. In this context, it is significant that each set book in the examination has two kinds of questions set on it: one which is directly related to a section of the text (which students are required to reread before answering) and one which requires a more general approach. Students can choose to do all questions of the former type if they so wish.

Some examples will illustrate how the questions provide the opportunity for students to engage with the texts, to show what they really think, and prove themselves capable of following through a close and interesting argument.

As You Like It
Either: What do you think is Shakespeare's attitude to love in the play? Discuss this by focusing on what you think at least three characters have learned by the end of *As You Like It*. Draw most of your evidence for your answer from Act V.
Or: Examine carefully the role of Jacques in Act II, scene vii, by paying close attention to the speeches he makes in this scene. Go on to show what significance you think this episode has in the play as a whole.

The Grapes of Wrath
Either: What do you think Steinbeck gains or loses from interspersing his narrative of the Joad family with his less specific 'inter-chapters'?
Or: What do you find interesting about this passage

from the middle of the novel? Analyse the ways in which Steinbeck presents this episode, commenting on themes and ideas which you find important in the context of the whole novel, and indicating the features of Steinbeck's style which help convey the passage's impact: 'It ain't no use,' Noah said. . . . 'Take your breath in when you need it, an' let it go when you need to.'

[All such passages are quoted in full in the examination paper.]

The Duchess of Malfi

Either: Examine closely the final scene of the play, Act V, scene v, from the Cardinal's speech beginning, 'I am puzzled in a question about hell'. Analyse the ways in which Webster creates intensity and dramatic interest in the scene.

Or: By looking closely at the portrayal of Bosola and the Duchess, explore some ways in which Webster presents the conflict between good and evil in *The Duchess of Malfi*.

So far we have concentrated on the kinds of answers encouraged in the examinations. In the coursework, as well as writing about particular sections of text, or the questions which the students themselves formulate after discussion, we have also been able to develop imaginative responses, along the lines of those used in the first to fifth years. Like other schools which encourage this kind of writing about texts, and know it to be a way of eliciting quality of perception, awareness of literary style, and depth of analysis, we wavered at first about whether we should allow our students to submit it for assessment. The Board states in its handbook that one of its tasks is to 'maintain comparability with other Advanced Level syllabuses', and of course we wished for this too. Our worry was that our students would be penalized for not submitting only critical essays. We have been very pleasantly surprised: we took the risk, and with great success. Not only were our students not penalized, but many got the highest possible grades for creative work. It is a pity that there is not space here to include some of the more entertaining pieces. The following will give some idea, however.

In one example, a student supplied a missing scene from *Mill on the Floss*, capturing George Eliot's style, tone, relationship to audience, and her relationship to text just as well as she could have done in an analytical essay. In another, a student submitted a discussion between several people after the opening night of *Death of a Salesman*. A third was a description, in the style of the novel, of what happened in the woodshed in *Cold Comfort Farm* (a great favourite and one of the reasons why we keep choosing this novel as a coursework text); while a fourth consisted of a dialogue between Egyptian servants about Antony and Cleopatra.

Although we have tended in the past to advise our students to put only one or two such pieces in their final coursework folder, we have been very pleased this year to hear that the Chief Examiner would accept a whole folder of creative work – on the very sound basis that the best criticism is creative.

This leads us to the last, but extremely important aspect of the course: the close communication not only between a group of schools using the syllabus, but between ourselves and the Chief Examiner. Schools are grouped into consortia, and regular meetings (two or three times a year) are convened by the Chief Examiner. One of these meetings is always to discuss the previous summer's papers, and here we are able to criticize questions, talk through how students answered, and make requests for the next year's papers. The second meeting is more general, and allows for discussion of teaching methods, the suitability of set texts, proposals for new ones, and the induction for new teachers to the course. Each school takes along a range of students' work, which is then exchanged and assessed. The issues raised are not easy. What distinction should be made between the lower-sixth essay and the more mature upper-sixth essay? Do we differentiate between those texts chosen by students on their own and essays written totally without teacher intervention, and those done under closer teacher supervision? When it comes to final assessment, at the third and fourth meetings, the folder, of course, has to stand on its own merits as a representative selection of the student's work, and the grade given accordingly. We are encouraged to look for those qualities of perception and understanding which we consider worthy of A level, and to mark positively. (We have to admit that the really difficult ones – those written by students for whom English is a second language, for example – are put in the 'can't decide' file for special attention by the Chief Examiner.)

We have found it impossible in this essay to divorce our teaching methods and styles from the particular course we have chosen to follow. Two things must be obvious by now: that high commitment from the teachers involved is essential, but that the rewards are great. The collaborative approach, both within the department and between schools, is not only satisfying, but involves constant reappraisal and analysis of what we are aiming at and achieving.

There is no getting away from the fact that education is political, or that examinations exist to grade the workforce. The notion of the 'real' A level student is still with us, but the increasing numbers of students who are not white and middle class who are choosing to do A level literature is having a salutory effect on teachers who wish to redefine and reappraise both literature and education. The Avon NATE A Level Working Party is now also questioning whether literature should be studied as a subject divorced from, and by implication, thought to be superior to other contemporary media. They write:

> To insist that students see literature as the central and superior form of cultural production is simply to delude them and to stifle the interaction between their study of literature, their own cultural formation, and their understanding of contemporary society.
>
> (Bennison and Spicer 1988: 30)

The Working Party is proposing a syllabus which is overtly political and which challenges the characteristic specialization of A levels. They plan for students to examine a vast range of cultural forms in the light of core concepts so as to gain an understanding of 'the whole area of cultural production and reception as a single unified field' (Bennison and Spicer 1988: 31).

We began on this same theme with a quotation from the introduction to Terry Eagleton's *Literary Theory* and would like to end with one from his conclusion, titled 'Political criticism'. Writing about the influence of the women's movement and the study of working-class writing, he says:

> These areas are not alternatives to the study of Shakespeare and Proust. If the study of such writers could become as charged with energy, urgency and enthusiasm as the activities I have just reviewed, the literary institution ought to rejoice rather than complain. But it is doubtful that this will happen when such texts are hermetically sealed from history, subjected to a sterile critical formalism, piously swaddled with eternal verities and used to confirm prejudices which any moderately enlightened student can perceive to be objectionable. The liberation of Shakespeare and Proust from such controls, may well entail the death of literature, but it may also be their redemption.
>
> (Eagleton 1983: 216–17)

We would like to think that this process of liberation and redemption has already begun in alternative A level studies.

Notes

An earlier version of this article appeared in *Literature and History* 13: 1, Spring 1987, 104–14.

1 Recommended texts included, for example, *Lays of Ancient Rome*, *The Fairie Queene*, Plutarch's *Lives*, Southey's *Life of Nelson*, Prescott's *Selections from Mexico*, Froissart's *Patriotic Poems*, the *Tales of King Arthur*, *Ivanhoe*, Macaulay's *Essays*, and *Biographical Sketches of Great Characters*. Lists of this kind were introduced in 1904 and appeared in subsequent Board of Education reports until well into the 1930s. See J. H. Davison (1988) '*Why boys underachieve in English*' (unpublished Ph.D. thesis, Goldsmiths' College, University of London) for further discussion of the questions of class and gender raised in these paragraphs.

2 See, in this tradition, D. Barnes, J. Britton, and H. Rosen (eds) (1969) *Language, the Learners and the School*, Harmondsworth: Penguin; J. Britton (1970) *Language and Learning*, Harmondsworth: Penguin; N. Martin, *et al.* (1976) *Writing and Learning Across the Curriculum 11–16*, London: Wardlock Education.

13

Teaching creative writing
Zoë Fairbairns

I love watching *Masterclass*. This is a TV programme in which a distinguished musician teaches a gifted student. I am not knowledgeable about music, but I know what is going on as the teacher worries away at small, subtle points, niggles and nags, coaxes, comforts, praises, criticizes, and challenges the student to give her or his best; to try that note once more; to question, to repeat, to do it *again*, not because it was done badly before but because it could be done better; and because if it is worth doing, it is worth doing in such a way as to strive for excellence.

All this makes for beautiful music and enthralling television. An equivalent programme about writing would not be so enthralling. Unlike the making of music, writing is not a spectacular activity. Musicians use carefully-crafted instruments which are often huge and gleaming and demand muscular exertion, controlled breathing, and sweat. The sexiest word-processor cannot compete with that, and anyway many writers still use pens. In writing, the exciting developments take place in the privacy of the mind, beyond the reach of cameras or audience. The physical act of writing is ordinary, everyday. Documentaries about famous writers are more likely to show them going for walks, eating and drinking, or talking to the camera than they are to show them writing. When a writer is writing, there is nothing to look at.

This may be why so many people who take for granted the desirability, indeed, necessity, of teaching music, art, dance, sculpture, are suspicious of the idea of teaching creative writing. 'You can't *teach* people to become writers,' they declare. 'Writers are born, not taught.' And then, suspiciously: 'How do you do it, anyway?'

Approaches to teaching creative writing

I have been teaching creative writing since 1972, usually on a part-time, freelance basis, at venues including primary and secondary schools; colleges and universities; men's and women's prisons; women's centres, bookshops, community centres, and adult education centres, some of them residential.

Sometimes I work alone, sometimes in partnership with another writer/tutor. Students have ranged in age from 4 to 80; in ability from those who have difficulty forming a simple sentence to those who already have books in print; in motivation from those who want to make (or develop) careers as writers, to those who believe writing will be helpful as a form of personal psychotherapy. There are those who have an idea for a book which they hope will change the world for the better and want to know how to write it; there are those who turn up for the creative writing class because Church Architecture is full. Some students are already bewildered by the intensity of their passion for writing, and want some help in harnessing and directing it; some are simply curious. Others have time on their hands (because of retirement, unemployment, or the departure of people they used to spend time looking after) and want to rediscover something that interested them decades ago.

Sometimes school students will turn up to hear what the Visiting Writer has to say because their teacher told them to and anyway it makes a change from English; and many prison inmates will welcome the opportunity to leave the cell, be it to cook in the prison kitchens or write poetry in the education block; but by and large anyone who comes to a creative writing class may be assumed to be a volunteer.

Anyone who comes to a creative writing class may also be assumed to be a writer.

I use the word 'writer' (in this article, and when teaching) to mean not simply 'anyone who writes' but 'anyone who writes with care'. A writer rewrites; a writer is not content to have the words spill from brain to paper in any old order, but sees the first draft as merely the beginning of the job. A writer is not content to be approximate about meaning, but strives to be exact. A writer writes it again. And again. And (quite possibly) again, learning a bit more about writing every time. A writer measures the success of a morning's work not simply by the pile of perfect pages produced, but by the fulness or otherwise of the waste-paper basket.

Whatever the age or background of students, I always stress this because I want to steer a path between two widespread, false, and damaging assumptions. One may be summed up as 'A writer is that glittering charismatic person I saw on the *South Bank Show* and could never be me.' The other is 'We are all writers.' We (the human race) are not all writers. We (the participants in a writing workshop) are.

Writers want to be better writers, and this means rewriting. Successful rewriting demands time and space, and I always discuss, fairly early in any course, the ways in which time and space can be claimed. Some writers can claim it by spending less time on leisure activities, social life, or hobbies. Others have to make riskier choices, perhaps moving from full-time to part-time employment, or spending less time studying, or reducing the amount of domestic service they are prepared to provide for their families. The choice is theirs, but no student will be able to make the right choice who does not believe that writing is important. But it's a vicious circle, because students won't believe writing is important enough to claim time for if they don't think they are making progress.

The first job of the teacher of creative writing is to break the circle.

One way into the circle is to get students writing now.

I have known students, particularly adult students, to be appalled by the discovery that the creative writing tutor expects them to write something, and to do it now. They were expecting something entirely different, a lecture on literary theory perhaps. But I know of no literary theory that makes writing easier. The only way to do it is to do it. I am not talking about 'jumping in at the deep end'; people have been known to drown in deep ends, and I don't approve of drowning students. They can start at the shallow end and if they don't want to jump in they can go down the steps.

Going down the steps

In this section, I will describe some of the writing exercises I use in workshops. Their purpose is to get people writing. Anyone who says thereafter 'I can't write' or 'I can't get it down on paper' can have it pointed out to them that they just have.

I also give some examples of how the exercises have worked in practice, in different groups. They are only examples and not generalization. It has not been my experience that (for example) male prisoners respond to a particular exercise in one way and young women at school in another. The individuality of the writer frequently overrides the setting, and this is as it should be.

To say this is not to say that writers exist and work outside society, or should, or could. It is to say that it is very difficult to write anything whilst self-consciously looking over one's shoulder at social context, or the group's expectations, or those of the tutor, or even one's own politics. What has been called 'inspiration' is not some sort of effortless magic; it is what happens to a writer who, after ninety-nine days of hard slog, finds on the hundredth day that it's a little bit easier and rather exciting.

The satisfaction of discovering that one has written exactly what one meant – that one has found one's writing voice – can only be earned by paying attention to that voice, and withdrawing a little way from other people's. For the writer who wants her or his work to contribute to social change, this withdrawal will only be temporary, but many writers find it essential.

When setting exercises, then, I stress that students should not ask themselves 'What does the tutor want?' but move off in their own directions as soon as they feel ready to. What the tutor wants – what this tutor wants – is as many different responses as there are individuals in the class.

Some of these exercises are my own invention. Others have been borrowed from other tutors and sometimes adapted. I use them in my own work. Writing exercises tend to circulate like folk-songs, losing and gaining bits, sometimes retaining their essential character, sometimes becoming unrecognizable.

Word power

Writing well means choosing the words that have the power to express what the writer means, and arranging them in such a way as to enhance their power.

This requires awareness of the power of words.

I ask students to write down five words that taste good. (If you, the reader of this piece, feel like trying some of the exercises as you go, please do.) I use the term 'words that taste good' rather than 'the names of your favourite foods' not only because some words taste good which are not the names of foods but also to stress the power of words to evoke a physical response. Anyone who doubts this should read a well-written cookery book when feeling hungry, and note what happens to the stomach and the salivary glands.

When everyone in the group has written their five words (mine might be *coffee*, *sea*, *butterscotch*, *kisses*, *orange*) they read them aloud as a list, one person after the other. No critical comment is required because the beauty of this exercise is that it is impossible to get it wrong. The most surprising choice of words – *purple*, for example, or *fog*, or *victory* – are often the most pleasing. People who may be anxious about reading a piece of their writing aloud can probably cope with reading aloud a list of words, so that particular sheet of ice is broken.

'Five words that taste good' can be followed by 'five words that taste horrible', 'five words to make you anxious' (*overdraft? overweight? father? hangman? AIDS?*), 'five words to make you wistful', and so on. Very young children, and others whose writing skills are limited, can say or dicate the words. A group of 4 year olds responded with great enthusiasm to 'five words that taste horrible' (or 'five words that make you feel sick' as they preferred to put it), extending their choices beyond the names of disliked foods and on into bodily functions, fluids, and disorders (human and animal) such that some of us really did start to feel sick . . . but that's the power of words for you. Words are precision tools and as writers we have to respect and use them as such.

Implied stories

Some people attend writing workshops because they want to know how to get ideas for stories. Many assume that novels, and even short stories, have to be meticulously plotted in advance. This is the approach of many writers whom I admire, but I prefer to start with something fairly uncertain and explore it through drafting and redrafting until a story emerges.

From the 'word power' exercise it is relatively easy to move to sentences that will have a particular effect. Students are asked to write a sentence which, if said to them, would worry them. Examples could include 'There's probably nothing to worry about', 'I'd like to see you in my office', and 'I'll tell you about it when you've finished eating'. The reason these sentences are powerful is because of what they do not say; the implied story behind them. The exercise is to take the sentence as the first sentence of a story and write the story.

A woman in her twenties in an adult education workshop took 'There's probably nothing to worry about' as the first sentence of a story about a mother being told that her baby is ill. She was pleased with her story, as was the group; she felt that if I had asked her specifically to write about a mother being told that her baby was ill, she would not have been able to do it, but the line 'There's probably nothing to worry about', with its vagueness, sharpness, familiarity, and possible deceit gave her a way into material which might otherwise have been unmanageable.

She volunteered the information that the story was autobiographical, but I would never ask a writer this question, or make any assumptions about it. The connection between a piece of writing and 'what really happened' is subtle and complex, and many people will be inhibited from writing imaginatively if they think their audience is always going to assume that the story is about them.

Running

People don't run for no reason. If someone is running, the chances are that he or she is (a) pursuing, (b) being pursued, (c) training, (d) late, or (e) competing. In any case there is certain to be high emotion and an implied story.

Students are invited to leave their desks and go running. They can run along the street, across the playground, down the corridor. If disability or ill-health prevent them from running, they can be asked to move as quickly as they reasonably can. They need only do it for about a minute, but the point is to do it very self-consciously, observing their sensations and thoughts. This develops the skills of closely observing that which is everyday and ordinary. In fact nothing we choose to write about is ordinary; if it is ordinary, why write about it? We look for what makes it different and therefore interesting.

Once students have been for their run – while they are still out of breath – they are asked to sit down and, without discussing it, without thinking too much or editing or forming complete sentences, write what they remember about the run and what they are feeling now. If the energy of physical movement transmits itself to the writing, and it usually does, stories and poems will emerge.

On a writing weekend for teachers, a man wrote about a home handyman discovering that he lacks the vital tool to finish a job and rushing down the road to the DIY hypermarket, hoping to get what he needs before the place closes. The group enjoyed the account, but felt (as did the author) that it didn't really go anywhere. After some discussion the author discovered that what he really wanted the man in the story to do was run to the DIY shop . . . and keep on running, run away from home because he was fed up with his family. That really is a strong beginning, containing as it does domestic comedy (incompetent Do-It-Yourselfer), personal crisis (a man feeling trapped by marriage and parenthood) and a great and recurrent political and moral dilemma: the needs of the individual versus the needs of the group (is personal unhappiness a good enough reason for walking out on a family, and if not what is the unhappy person to do?).

None of this was planned in advance, and this story again illustrated the point that it is the *practical experience of writing* that generates ideas and enables the individual writer to find the voice, style, and form with which he or she is most comfortable. Whatever the writer's political commitments or social purpose in writing, I believe that the best way to begin a piece of fiction is with a single, familiar, manageable human dilemma. If the writer's beliefs are held strongly enough they will usually take care of themselves. This man's story wouldn't have been nearly as interesting if he had set out to write about 'Masculinity in Crisis', even though that, as it turned out, was his subject – but it started with the writer going running.

Food

Students are asked to write a description of somebody eating.

The sight may be poignant (the handing out of rations at a refugee camp); disgusting (a drunkard eating spaghetti by hand); sexy (a pre-seduction dinner, spiced with uncertainty); frightening (something involving poison); symbolic (food as power, school dinners as an aid to discipline, commercial wheeler-dealing over a business lunch) . . . Food is used by human beings for much more than nutrition, and almost anything that can happen, can happen over a meal.

I've said that I don't generalize about students' work, and I don't; but it is noticeable that men are more likely to write about the pleasures of eating, while women are more likely to write about anxiety. A 16-year-old student in an all-girl group wrote a terrifying account of a day in the life of a girl who cannot control her eating. The author used the suspense tactics of a thriller writer to keep her readers on the edges of their seats over whether or not her heroine was going to break open a packet of biscuits. Another girl in the same group confined herself to a close description of eating chewing gum, but even that created anxiety: would she be caught and forced to throw the gum away?

When discussing the work, we had some discussion of food, feminism, and fat. I suggested that they write an account of someone enjoying food. Of six girls in the group, only two did this exercise. One wrote about a man enjoying a steak; another wrote about a woman enjoying cooking.

Half my age

Whether or not we write autobiography, whether or not we disguise it, our memories and experience are an important resource. But inviting students to write about themselves can raise problems.

I once invited a group of prison inmates to write about their first day at school. They informed me that I reminded them of the prison psychiatrist and I gathered that this was not a compliment. They had seen my suggested writing exercise as an intrusion on their privacy, and a possible source of pain.

Prisoners are not the only people who can be hurt by memories and it is difficult to write well when it hurts. The aim of the exercise, therefore, is to provide space for writing on that subject which is so endlessly fascinating – ourselves – while not allowing that space to become too threatening.

I ask students to identify and concentrate on the year when they were half the age they are now. I then ask a series of factual questions about that year and ask them to write down the answers. The questions might include 'Who was Prime Minister?', 'What was your address?', 'Who else lived there?', 'What did it cost to rent a flat or buy a house or go to see a film?', 'What films were on?', 'What would you have worn to a party?', 'Which wars were being fought?'.

This is not a quiz and it doesn't matter if students get the answers wrong (no one will check). The point is to concentrate on facts and details which will evoke a time in the student's life, a time which, with a bit of luck, will be distant enough for them to have perspective on the things that happened, but not so far away as to have been forgotten.

The point is to cover a page with a list of details any one of which may trigger a story. When students have done this, I ask them to start a story set in the year when they were half the age they are now. The story can be fact, fantasy, or a bit of each. It can be about themselves, someone they knew, or someone imaginary. All or any of the details they have gathered from memory may focus their attention on a day or a moment, tune them into the atmosphere of the time and give them a range of alternatives.

Some stories written in response to this exercise do indeed consist of autobiography in its rawest state: an account of an unhappy love affair, for instance, or an assault, or a bereavement. But it is the student's choice to write on those themes. If the themes are painful or threatening, there are safer alternatives already on the page. Any one can be picked up, turned over, examined, fiddled with, and turned into a story. The year when you were half your present age may well be the year when a tragedy occurred in your life, but if you don't want to write about that there may be as rich a tale to tell about the day you touched someone who had touched one of the Beatles.

A woman in a feminists' writing workshop once said: 'I don't have any difficulty writing about things, describing them, getting the details; but I don't know how to make them important.' Many people identified with this view, but it seems to me that trying to make our writing important is a bit like trying to be funny: the harder you try, the less likely you are to succeed. There are no important themes in fiction and no unimportant ones either. The writer should tell the story she or he wants to tell, and, more often than not, importance will take care of itself.

These exercises, and dozens like them, provide useful ways into writing, but that does not mean that they are exclusively for new writers. I use them in my own work; for example, if a story-line appears to be getting bogged down, if I can't decide what a character is going to do next, I give them a meal. People reveal so much about themselves by the way they choose, obtain, and eat food that I am almost invariably back on course by the time they have finished eating.

Short, self-contained exercises get the writer writing. The next stage is rewriting.

Criticism and rewriting

When the poet Robert Graves left school, his headmaster's parting words were 'Remember your best friend is your waste paper basket.'

Unkind as these words may sound, they contain a great deal of truth. The writer who hates the sight of a full wastepaper basket – looking upon it as a symbol of failure and wasted time – will never feel comfortable about rewriting. It is much better to see it as a friend to whose care the writer consigns those early drafts which are no longer needed because they have discharged their responsibility to prepare the writer to write the final draft.

It is for the writer to decide what goes into the wastepaper basket (or its electronic equivalent). I respond to students' work as critically as seems to be appropriate, but if the student does not agree with my comments, she or he has the last word. This does not mean 'don't listen to criticism' – people who will not listen to criticism should not go to creative writing classes, and they certainly should not venture into the world of publishing – it means that it is for the author to decide which criticism is valid and useful and which is not.

Children, and the child in all of us, often expect teachers to 'tell us how to to it'; to pronounce that we have got it right or wrong. There are subjects to which this approach is appropriate, but creative writing is not one of them. Notwithstanding those writing schools which promise to refund your fees if you don't earn them back from writing whilst following their courses (and they must know something I don't know, offering a guarantee like that) I do not believe that people can be taught to write in such a way as to be 'publishable'. A publishable manuscript is a manuscript that a publisher wants to publish, and since tastes and needs vary from publisher to publisher, publishability cannot be reduced to a formula that can be taught.

Rewriting does not mean turning a piece of work into something completely different in order that it will sell; it means exploring a range of possibilities. Ideally a creative writing group provides a safe space for this exploration.

Whatever the age or background of the students there are ground rules for keeping the space as safe as possible.

Nobody is forced, or even persuaded, to read their work aloud if they do not wish to do so. In the absence of free photocopying, reading aloud may be the only practical way of sharing work among a group, but students may ask others to read their work, or not share at all.

Positive comments come first, and should be specific. 'Brilliant!' is nice to hear but not very constructive. 'I liked the way you used short, hard fast words to suggest running feet' is better.

Negative comments should be accompanied by positive suggestions: not 'that was long and boring' but 'There was a lot of repetition in that chapter; how would it be if you cut here and here?'

The writer is not called upon to defend her or his work. It is better just to listen and think. No one can force the writer to make inappropriate changes. The safety of this knowledge frees the writer to explore such rewriting possibilities as:

Cutting. Is every single word doing a job? Words that mean nothing should be cut. Short words should always be favoured over long ones. Opening paragraphs are often no more than verbal throat-clearing and can be cut. Many writers repeat themselves at the end of a story or poem, just to be sure that everyone has got the point. It takes nerve to cut here, but it is often beneficial.

Viewpoint. Is first person better than third person? How many narrators should there be, and how much should the narrator know? Should the narrator comment or participate? There is only one way to find out and that is by trial and error; it is often useful to rewrite from a different point of view to see which works better.

Clarity. If the writer is writing for an audience, it is the writer's responsibility to communicate clearly with that audience. If workshop members don't understand a writer's work, that could be because they weren't paying attention, but it could equally be because the writer was being unnecessarily obscure. The writer must know and understand what she or he is trying to say, otherwise how can a reader hope to do so? Early drafts will often serve to clarify the writer to the writer's self, but the final draft is for the reader.

Pace. The events of a single day can fill a book or be summarized in a phrase. As with viewpoint, the only way of finding the right pace is by trying different approaches and seeing which works.

Building up atmosphere. This does not mean going on for pages and pages about the sunset. Sunsets have been done, so the writer who has not got something truly original to say on the subject might do well to keep off it. Atmosphere comes not from weight of detail but the right detail. An attentive workshop audience can often spot the right detail sooner than the writer can, and bring it to the writer's attention.

Dialogue. Many new writers are nervous of dialogue. Capturing the structure and quality of a person's speech is difficult and indirect speech seems safer, for example: 'He ordered me to fetch him a cup of tea.' There is nothing wrong with that, but direct speech *is* more direct: ' "Tea," he commanded. "Now." ' It is also more economical – four words replacing ten.

The list is endless. The point is to enable the writer to develop a feel for his or her own style, for what can be done now and what is better left alone for the time being. Writers become aware that, however they write it, they could have written it differently. This awareness is unlikely to do much for the peace of mind of someone who, in the words of a student, has taken up writing 'in order to relax' but it is the only way of developing creative writing skills.

Why teach creative writing?

The process is difficult to explain or understand; the demands are enormous; the rewards are uncertain; the profession is overcrowded.

So why teach creative writing?

In the context of secondary schools, one reason for teaching creative writing is that it is on the syllabus. The *GCSE The National Criteria for English* (HMSO 1985c) require that students be given opportunities to 'develop a variety of styles of writing . . . [including] narrative writing and an imaginative response to a range of stimuli and experience'. The authors of the document note somewhat nervously that ' "Open" kinds of writing are necessarily more diverse in the opportunities offered to candidates, and the approaches adopted . . . [and this] may create difficulties in comparing the candidates' performance' but the requirement is nevertheless clear. 'Course work . . . offers more realistic conditions for drafting and redrafting with access to source material and it allows for the sampling of a greater variety of writing.'

Some teachers' response to this requirement is to encourage creative writing as a means to the end of better critical writing; others see it as an end in itself. Under Writers in Schools schemes, professional writers are sometimes brought into schools to work with students, and also with teachers. Many teachers, charged with the responsibility of helping students to write creatively, are in fact very anxious about creative writing themselves. In the London Borough of Bromley, I have, with other writers, been running writing workshops for teachers as part of their Grant Related In-Service Training. Students see writers teaching and teachers writing. Everyone studies and, in the context of workshop sessions, everyone teaches. As writer-in-residence at a primary school, I recently took part in a Writers' Evening for parents. Children aged between 8 and 10, their teachers, and I as a local writer, presented our work. Elsewhere I have run writing workshops for parents, not simply so that they can help their children, but to enable them to discover something of their own creativity.

A teacher in a writing workshop once recalled how she, as a child, had written a story. Her teacher's response was to draw a red line from the top left hand corner of the page to the bottom right and make no further comment. Having had this experience in childhood, she was understandably anxious about reading a story aloud and having it discussed by colleagues. It emerged that everyone in the room (myself included) had experienced cruel criticism of our work as children, and this had made us anxious about even constructive criticism as adults. These revelations were extremely useful for the workshop, because we concentrated on responding to work with honesty but also with respect for the feelings of the author. We discussed the importance of doing this with children's work, recognizing the ease with which children can be hurt by the thoughtlessness of adults in authority over them.

I was able to draw analogies with the writer/editor relationship. Some editors do cast themselves as boss/teacher/parent and this arouses anxiety and resentment in writers. Ideally, the editor is the writer's colleague, criticizing and making suggestions on a basis of equality. In commenting on students' work (be these students teachers themselves, or 6 year olds) I point out that I am doing no more than is done with my work by editors. Teachers, students, writers, can all be editors to each other. Whenever possible, I take my own work-in-progress into the schools where I work, and ask my students to act as editors for it.

It is frequently pointed out that library shelves are full of books by great men and great women who never went to creative writing classes. But it is equally true that most writers have been helped on their way by mentors of one kind or another, and, in the case of contemporary writers, these have often been found in writing groups. Determined new writers probably do not need directing, but they can benefit from serious and respectful attention, validation, and encouragement. When the new writer is a school or college student, she or he may also gain in the purely practical way of being allowed time – serious study-time – to pursue what might otherwise have to be treated as an outside interest. Tomorrow's adult writers are in today's classrooms.

Also in today's classrooms are tomorrow's literary decision makers. These are the people who, much more than writers, will wield power over what gets recognized as tomorrow's literature: the publishers, the booksellers, the critics, the academics, the givers of awards, the arts administrators, librarians, teachers of English, customers in bookshops. I am not suggesting that all these people should be writers – heaven forbid. But one of the worst professional experiences a writer can have is to fall into the hands of an editor who knows nothing about writing but is determined to tell the writer how to do it anyway. People who are going to exercise power over writers can only benefit from the experience of writing something.

Another reason why writers such as myself teach creative writing is this: I do it for the money. I mention this not in order to introduce an unwelcome element of vulgarity (it has been said that the main difference between amateur and professional writers is that when amateur writers meet for a drink they talk about style and form; professionals talk about pounds and pence) but because one of the first things I try to establish in a writing class is that writing is neither a sacrament nor a form of neurosis; it is a job of work. For me, teaching writing is part of the job of being a writer. In terms of pounds paid per hour worked, it is the better paid part.

There is no one way of being a writer. There is no generalization about writing that cannot be disproved. There are no absolute standards, guidelines for quality (aesthetic, political, or commercial), definitions of success, career structures, qualifications, disqualifications. Creative writing might, therefore, be seen as the supremely unteachable subject. And yet it gets taught, and self-taught, and learned and done. All the student writer can be offered (and that includes the student writer in all writers) is a range of alternatives, and an environment in which it feels safe and rewarding to try them.

Notes

Writers in schools. Schools, colleges, community centres, and other organizations wanting to employ writers to run workshops or courses can either write to the writer they want (c/o his or her publisher) or contact the Literature Officer of their Regional Arts Association. RAA's can often supply lists of available writers, and subsidies for visits. Addresses of RAA's appear in the *Writers' and Artists' Yearbook*, published annually by A & C Black, London.

Writing courses for adults. Evening and daytime classes are often run by adult education institutes, university extra-mural departments, and such bodies as the Workers' Educational Association. Public libraries will usually have details. Residential courses are run by the Arvon Foundation; brochures can be obtained from the Arvon Foundation at Totleigh Barton, Sheepwash, Beaworthy, Devon; or the Arvon Foundation at Lumb Bank, Hebden Bridge, West Yorkshire.

Books on writing. There are two schools of thought on this point. They are mutually contradictory and I subscribe to them both. The first takes the view that reading books about writing is an excuse for not getting on with one's own. The second finds any writer's account of her or his processes fascinating, stimulating, informative, and therefore useful.

I never produce lists of recommended books for writing courses, but if I were to they would include, from the Arvon Foundation's *Way to Write* series, titles by Fairfax and Moat (1981), Kitchen (1981), Paice (1981), Baldwin (1982), and Aiken (1982). If students ask me, as they often do, about my experiences with publishers, rather than go on all night I refer them to my own autobiographical essay on the subject (Fairbairns 1987). Brande (1983) and Weldon (1985) have produced companionable explorations of the craft of writing. So did Trease (1961) but his book, which I treasured and made full use of in my teens, is long out of print.

14

Another park bench: autobiography, knowledge, and popular education

Denise Hayes, Peter Humm, Lesley Massey, Douglas Norsworthy, Penny Price, Nikki Slater, and Paul Stigant

Seven authors of one chapter need a word or so of explanation. Saying something about the way the seven of us worked on this collective essay is the best way to introduce the experience and purpose of the course on autobiography which it describes.

Peter Humm and Paul Stigant are the two teachers who initiated the autobiography course in 1984; Denise Hayes, Lesley Massey, Douglas Norsworthy, Penny Price, and Nikki Slater are five of the first group of students who joined the course in that year. All five subsequently went on to join the BA Humanities degree at Thames in 1985. There were a further seven students who attended regularly, six of whom went on to undertake degree or further study in the Polytechnic or elsewhere. Other students came and went, for one reason or another, throughout the year. This essay is the product, not only of the experience of the course, but of later discussions about it and in particular two meetings, (one of which we tape-recorded) to consider what we wanted the essay to be about. Paul Stigant then put the ideas of the group together in written form, which was then circulated for further comment and discussion. This is a revised version of the original essay on that discussion.

We have tried then to reflect in this essay the uncommon experience of co-operative working developed in the three terms of the course. This has sometimes made it difficult to maintain the conventional distinction between an authorial we and the reference to the actual experience of seven authors. Moving between the collective and individual experience, between we and I, is perhaps the best evidence of what we all gained from this course.

'Knowledge is Power' proclaimed the mast-head of the *Poor Man's Guardian*, the unstamped and illegal newspaper of the 1830s. It is worth beginning this essay with that fact from Britain's political and educational past for at least two reasons. First, the course on working-class autobiography which this essay is in part about began by looking at the writings of people recalling their lives in the early decades of the nineteenth century. But secondly, as the course developed it became much more than an academic study of autobiography; it became a sharing of experience and knowledge that in its differing ways, for all of us, proved liberating and empowering. In fact, the course was very much a shared experience that reiterated in the 1980s the slogan that 'Knowledge is Power'. That power came in many forms and was different for all of us, whether we joined the course as students or as teachers. For some of us it was the power of self-confidence, the power to make major decisions about where our lives were going. The evident importance of the course to the students gave the teachers the power to argue that 'sub-degree' teaching was equally as important, and considerably more rewarding and exciting than the majority of under and postgraduate courses to which the Polytechnic was committed. But the course empowered in one other important way: it came to involve not simply the giving, receiving, or sharing of knowledge, but also the production of knowledge.

The course itself was one of a number run by Thames Polytechnic under the general title of 'Polystudy'; the intention of those courses being that they offered a range of subject matter all appropriate for people wishing to return to study. These courses were (and are) not 'Access' courses in the strict sense of that word, though the possibility of further degree study has always been there for those willing and able to take it up. The course on working-class autobiography, first offered some four years ago, was begun by the two teachers involved as an extension into the classroom of their shared interest in Literature-and-History. Both teachers, as two of the editors of the journal *Literature and History*, have long been concerned that the issues of interdisciplinary study and of the boundaries of these two subjects were not being sufficiently explored in the classroom. This point was important: *Literature and History* was an academic journal, the problem was how to translate this kind of 'elitist' work into the kind of useful knowledge that Polystudy students would find relevant and exciting. A course on working-class autobiographies from the early nineteenth century to the present seemed to offer real opportunities for this to happen. It had, as it was initially conceived, several major advantages. First, there were significant problems or questions that could underpin the whole course: why do people write (need to write) their autobiography, and more particularly what does this mean when they are ordinary, not famous, men and women? How has the writing of autobiography changed over the last 150 years? What kind of literary forms and styles have been employed in the process? Secondly, it was hoped that the topic would have an immediacy, and the reading be less threatening, for people returning to study and very likely to be lacking confidence in their academic abilities. Another advantage was that there existed two excellent books both edited by John Burnett that brought together extracts from working-class autobiographies of the nineteenth and early twentieth centuries (Burnett 1974 and 1982). Class discussion of the reading the group did each week could constantly shift between and bring together issues of literacy and historical significance: autobiographies by their very nature are both literature and history. Finally, reading and discussion could often be focused upon a particular theme: family, childhood, work, poverty, gender, politics, race.

All this, however, represented only a collection of broad expectations and objectives; neither Peter nor I, though we both had been teaching in higher education for over a decade, knew quite what to expect. We both went into the enterprise lacking confidence. This lack of confidence is worth reflecting on. It was something shared with the rest of the class but left unspoken. Indeed, it was only as students came to admit their lack of confidence, and came to argue, as everyone contributing to this essay would argue, that confidence was one of the major things the course gave them, that the two teachers could begin to confront their own uncertainties. But this is not to argue that the two teachers gained one kind of confidence while the students gained another, rather it is to point to the way the notion of 'confidence', so often stressed as one of the main objectives of return-to-study courses, is itself a complex and many faceted state.

When we all came together to prepare for and write this essay we began to realize that though we all could, and wanted, to use the term 'confidence', we none of us quite meant the same thing by it. Nor was it something static and fixed. It came and went. Increasing confidence gained during weeks of class discussion and debate, evaporated for many when the time for writing the termly essay came round. It was something that had to be built, and rebuilt, though each time on perhaps slightly different foundations. It was, therefore, cumulative but its growth was hardly based on a straight progressive line. Nor, scarcely surprisingly, was it all acquired during just one year of Poly-study. For Nikki, it was a second year course on the Humanities degree – Gender and Society – that gave her the confidence to challenge the structures of male power. Equally, Doug insists that confidence was not something that came to him suddenly, he has no recollections of a momentous change, just a gradual process, but it is, none the less, something he can measure. His decision to take on a degree course stood in marked contrast to his earlier decision to join Polystudy; it was a 'positive' decision based upon a growing confidence in his own abilities.

Confidence would, in fact, appear to be a word all of us involved in the course have used in describing and addressing wider changes that took place in our perceptions of ourselves. Looking back it seems obvious now that a course on working-class autobiography would be a particularly appropriate academic study within which this could happen. Discussing the value that ordinary women and men placed upon their lives, discussing the relevance of their experiences both in terms of their own societies and our own, inevitably produced a focusing in on the problem of what was both unique and general in our own lived experience. It also raised the question of to what extent personal experience is relevant to academic study. One major objective of an academic education, it can be argued, is to develop the skills of abstraction, conceptualization, and generalization; to enable people to think and analyse outside the confines and limits of personal experience. Indeed, this is clearly the objective that informs most (if not all) course design and *teaching* in humanities and social science degrees. It can, and of course does, produce major problems for students (and teachers who care to confront it) in and outside the classroom. How relevant or desirable is the use of personal experience in a classroom discussion on Plato's *Republic* or industrialization and the family? Should such discussion not centre on the hard 'facts' of the subject or the (equally distancing) consideration of theoretical positions and premises?

These problems, we want to argue, are central to any discussion of the meaning of education and people's experience of it. It is certainly an issue brought into sharp relief on return-to-study style courses. Students on such courses have usually been failed (in both senses of the word) by education at an earlier point in their lives. Usually, of course, they blame themselves and not the educational system for this failure. And yet 'education' remains important, is perceived as being important to them; they are prepared to give themselves another go at it. What is actually happening is that the teachers, and the system of education they represent, are being given a second chance. Recognizing the situation as a second chance, as a 'fresh start', places (for the teachers, as well as the students) even more emphasis on the importance of getting the educational service offered right. For ultimately it is less a matter of what academically a particular course is about than what it signals about the meaning and importance of education more generally. As Doug said in our discussions for this essay, the autobiography course was for him most memorable, not for its academic content, although that was now important, but for its creation of a learning process that recognized and valued every contribution from teacher and student alike. That 'learning process' needs consideration.

There are no easy answers to the problem of how, in the learning process, personal experience can be married to the abstraction of knowledge. However, we would want to insist on a necessary relationship between the two. This is not to argue for an anecdotal presentation of evidence, or for the creation of general 'truths' solely on the basis of individual experience. Rather, it is to claim that knowledge acquired through education should be a kind that enlarges the importance of experience by reassessing and contextualizing it. All that we have said so far points to the way the learning process on the autobiography course involved a reassessment of ourselves, and hence our experiences, and a contextualization of those experiences in relation to the individual writers we were discussing and the history that surrounded them. It also involved a further contextualization in our relationships with everyone else in the class. Different voices, different individual reactions to a piece of writing under discussion, different interpretations of our relationship to that piece of the past, sharpened but also relocated our own sense and knowledge of the world.

In terms of how this happened on a week by week basis the readings chosen for the class discussions were particularly important. John Burnett's two autobiographical anthologies were especially appropriate because both dealt with writings by ordinary, 'unknown' people. One of the benefits of Burnett's extracts was the time span they covered (nineteenth and twentieth centuries); another was the range of literary forms employed by different writers. The extracts were also short and it was a revelation to all of us how the group could spend two hours in often intense discussion over only a few pages. From an early stage in the course the group read through and beyond the 'text': to discuss what a particular writer was not saying, and why; to compare one writer's technique with another; to consider what to us in the late twentieth century was strange or familiar in the lives and wider society a writer was describing. It also became important to the group to consider why one writer appealed to some in the class but not to others. The complex problems of the relationship between author and audience was thus established early on. So, for example, in one class we looked at Syd Foley's contribution to Burnett's *Destiny Obscure*, 'Asphalt'. We first compared Syd Foley's use of the short story to the more conventional autobiographical narrative in his wife Alice Foley's best-selling *A Child in the Forest*. Discussing the fictional devices Syd Foley uses to tell his story (the entrance of the 'evil' stepfather that divides his childhood, in two, the little victory that Syd shares with his mother over her husband that climaxes the story/autobiography) led us to consider the relationship between 'fact' and 'fiction', literature and history. Class discussion could, therefore, on the basis of one short piece of writing (although in later classes we tended to discuss whole books) explore difficult issues around the construction of knowledge and experience; autobiography as 'literature' and 'history'; and as an individual mediation of the problems of the relationship between the past and the present.

What was important in all of this was the way individual contributions in discussion built into a sense of collective knowledges. On numerous occasions members of the group would say that after their 'private' reading of a piece of writing they had a particular interpretation of it, only to find in class that others had responded differently, and that this then required a reassessment and a rethinking on their part. Indeed, listening to the contributions of others was important in other ways: when the ideas of the first and then the second person to speak were taken seriously it encouraged others to test out their thoughts. Trust and confidence is infectious, and when students gained these, it encouraged everyone in the group to value one another's contributions. In fact, as one member of the group said, 'sitting together discussing an autobiography written over a hundred years ago, I had the impression that we were feeling our way towards a truth, a truth that we, to some extent, were creating'.

Yet what exactly was the role of the teachers in this learning process? Obviously it is important. As already implied, any class will take its cue from teachers as the figures of authority, as the apparent source of the knowledge that really matters. However much Peter and I would want to argue that we learnt just as much as everyone else – which we did – and that, therefore, we were sharing this learning process, our position in class was different from that of the students. Teaching, and, in particular, the quality of teaching, was something we all discussed for this essay. It was, and is, something extremely difficult to talk about. What is it that makes for the sense that a course has been well taught? What is it, more importantly, that goes on in a particular class that makes it well taught? These are important questions, especially in higher education, where they are seldom seriously discussed. Too often teachers will throw the problem back onto the students: a class does, or does not work, because of the quality of their contribution. But, as we have already argued, the quality of that contribution depends, perhaps in large measure, upon the 'trust and confidence' which it is the teacher's responsibility to generate. And that requires not only listening to and taking seriously every individual contribution, but also keeping an open mind on what 'truths' and knowledges any particular class may come up with. There is a nice difference between getting a good discussion and asserting a firm control over the direction that discussion takes. As one member of the autobiography group said: 'I believe that both Peter and Paul subtly orchestrated our discussions in order to bring out the best from them; but I also believe them when they maintain they exercised little control over the direction those discussions took.'

Everything we have said so far points to the fact that 'knowledge' in itself has little meaning, perhaps little value, unless the context in which that knowledge is constructed and acquired is itself given value. Hence the importance we have attached to the collective and creative atmosphere of the autobiography course; to the growing sense of trust and confidence in each other that was built up; to the feeling that here were 'knowledges' to be discovered, not learnt from a body of facts that already existed. Our discussions in preparation for writing this essay returned time and time again to these three points. Essentially we were talking about the production of knowledge as a collective endeavour and achievement, and not a matter of individual genius. Significantly the autobiography course did not, as so much else in education does, end in an examination. It did not end up pitting student against student, or teachers against students, in terms of grades. The final weeks of the course were spent in producing and editing our own collection of autobiographical writing. It provided a creative – and for some of us a painful – space in which to explore our own chosen autobiographical style, and to recognize that writing about oneself is no easy matter (especially after reading and dissecting the examples of so many others). What we produced was an interesting and diverse collection of autobiographical extracts that themselves repaid consideration as pieces of literature and history. Moreover, our coming together to read and discuss each other's pieces was itself a further celebration of our collective endeavour and achievement, our trust and confidence in each other.

And yet to recall this is to emphasize immediately how different the context in which we produced knowledge on this course was (is) from that which governs education in the main. This issue cannot be ducked. Not only does it raise, once again, the question of the value and purpose of graded assessment in education, but it problematizes even further definitions of 'knowledge'. Could the knowledge we discovered and acquired on this course have possibly been the same had everyone known there was to be an examination, to be passed or failed, at the end of it? But, on the other hand, is there any point – in good Thatcherite practice – in 'thinking the unthinkable' and arguing that the production of knowledge in eduation can only be improved and knowledge itself changed by the removal of graded assessment? We do not aim to answer those questions here except to mention one point that came up in our discussions for this essay. Was the Humanities degree a different experience from that of Polystudy, we asked? Doug expressed the difference in this way: 'What I found more difficult on the degree course was the loss of that "creative" feeling that had inspired and sustained me during the Polystudy course. This was replaced by a far more "business-like approach" that got things done . . . but some of the sparkle went out of learning.' What produces, we wonder, that 'business-like approach' to education?

Perhaps, however, that question can be put another way: is there anything wrong in a 'business-like approach' to education, one that gets things done? That all depends on what you believe the acquisition of knowledge is for. And that of necessity makes knowledge and education a political issue. This essay began by recalling the *Poor Man's Guardian*'s claim that 'Knowledge is Power'. The newspaper was part of a political campaign being waged not just for the freedom of the press, but for the freedom of knowledge, and for the right of working people to gain a knowledge – in fact an education – that would help in their liberation. Liberation, it was believed, depended upon the *right* kind of knowledge – 'really useful knowledge' – a knowledge that would enable working people objectively to analyse their society, and hence the reasons for their oppression. Such knowledge, it was argued, would not be supplied by their governors and rulers. If knowledge remains power 150 years later, how far is it still part of a process of liberation? Indeed what process of liberation, and where do the experiences we are describing in this essay fit that process?

The process we have described is a kind of personal liberation; individuals being freed to recognize their potentials. This is doubtless something that most people would applaud, but as Lesley argued, as a woman this is not necessarily the same thing as being freed to *achieve* that potential. An uneasy and uncertain relationship exists between the potentially liberating world of education and that of waged work or the home. It would be comforting to be able to think of the four years of first Polystudy and then the Humanities degree as some kind of free space of personal exploration and discovery. Of course it is not quite like that. The ivory tower of higher education these days constantly interacts, and has to negotiate with, the equally demanding and probably constraining world of the family. This is particularly the case for the kind of students who come onto degree courses via Access and return-to-study routes: mainly, though not solely, women with children. Their experience of student life cuts across the conventional wisdom or image of 'the student'. Knowledge and education as a means to personal liberation is then a somewhat abstract notion unless defined more specifically in relation to the wider variety of students now in higher education.

None the less the question 'liberation for what?' remains. Is it utilitarian in the most obvious sense of getting a (better) job? Or, is it that plus something else? It is easy for teachers with fairly secure occupations to argue for education as something valuable in itself; something that offers students many ways to self-improvement. But this is to leave the slogan 'Knowledge is Power' open to a whole variety of meanings, and to tie it fairly tightly to *individual* development. And yet what we have described in this essay is a course of study that succeeded because students did not feel isolated individuals struggling to acquire 'knowledge', but members of a group working with and helping each other to succeed intellectually. Hence, while the group now contributing to this essay all made it onto the Humanities degree, that has not yet diminished a feeling of regret for those other students who, for whatever reason, never joined the degree. There is inevitably a contradiction here: in education we measure success individually, yet our teaching practice and philosophy is collective – we expect ideas to be shared and developed by people thinking and discussing together. To argue, therefore, for the success of the autobiography course we have to face this contradiction: not, perhaps, for the course itself, since it never sought to measure one student against another, but in terms of the value of this course when the experience of most other courses in higher education preaches a different kind of reality. We have argued that the autobiography course justified the claim 'Knowledge is Power' in some of the right kinds of ways. It empowered us individually but it also produced a situation in which people sought to help and support each other not just academically but with personal problems and crises as well. Other forms of study in higher education also produce these benefits. Lesley and Nikki are clear that they enjoyed and benefited from four years of study and not just the three years of the degree. But the production of knowledge works differently on a degree course. It is more 'business-like' in the way it is packaged and presented; it is more tightly structured and courses have far less individual freedom to develop unchecked by the demands of the whole degree. We could just leave it at a recognition, even a celebration, of the difference. But this would be dishonest about the politics bound up in the claim that 'Knowledge is Power'.

The forms of knowledge, the testing of knowledge, and the presentation of knowledge are very much a political issue, as we know only too well in this period of the most inaptly named Great Education Reform Bill. (And it is worth noting here that the *Poor Man's Guardian* opposed the other so-called Great Reform Bill – that of 1832 – on the grounds that it gave power to the landlords, the merchants, and the manufacturers but not the working classes.) If knowledge is power then who controls and determines the nature of knowledge is all important. In part, however, the struggle also remains, as in the nineteenth

century, access to knowledge. Both these points are important
to the experiences of education we are discussing in this essay.
Many students on return-to-study courses are at a very particular point in the educational spectrum of our society. Institutional state education has for the most part failed them up to
the age of 16; another form of institutional state education
potentially awaits them. Return-to-study courses exist, of
course, within the constraints of state provision. But those
constraints need not be the same as exist for degree courses; nor
is the student's relationship to the course the same. Because of
these factors a much greater space exists to free the production
of knowledge from the boundaries that usually enclose it. Space
exists in fact for students to begin to control and determine the
kind of knowledge they want discussed. Penny recalled during
our discussions of the course, for example, the way individual
students in the group began quite naturally to suggest texts for
the class to consider. She also recalled how her advocacy of Han
Suyin's *Love is a Many Splendoured Thing* met with a very mixed
reception: a sign not merely of the class's confidence in discussion by this stage of the course, but of its ability to challenge or
welcome a particular contribution to our developing knowledge. A small example, perhaps, but an indicative one and
representative of student-centred initiatives throughout the
year and succeeding years of the course.

How justified then are we in referring to Polystudy at Thames
Polytechnic and the autobiography course in particular as an
experiment in, and example of, 'popular education'? We take
popular education to mean the struggle of ordinary women and
men to gain an education in a society which, while it might not
in the late twentieth century actually deny them one, certainly
provides it in forms that many find alienating or unacceptable.
We take it, therefore, to be an education that represents an
alternative (both in the way it is provided and what is provided)
to that which is generally on offer. Popular education has a long
history, and working-class demands for 'really useful knowledge' in the 1830s is an early expression of it. Much has changed
since the 1830s, not least the enormous expansion of the state
education system, and while alternative forms outside this

system have continued to exist, the major site of the struggle for a popular education has been within the arena of state provision. As we have argued, Polystudy style courses have a very particular, perhaps unique, place in further and higher education: within the system, they are not bound by it to the same extent as most other educational provision. Here issues of access, content, control, and context come much more within the power of those teaching and attending the courses. Hence the courses themselves offer a greater opportunity to those wishing to search out alternative educational objectives and philosophies. It is, therefore, in the nature of these objectives and philosophies that the politics of Polystudy resides.

The first thing to say about the autobiography course as an experiment in popular education is that its subject matter was, in part, intended to be about just that: popular education. It is impossible to read working-class autobiographies of the last 150 years without recognizing the struggle for and value which working people have placed upon knowledge. More importantly, however, these experiences and desires spoke directly to the students who likewise valued knowledge and had to struggle to obtain it. There existed here, then, a direct link between aspects of the course's subject matter and the students' own lived experiences. It was important also that other themes developed in the course picked up not just students' own experiences but related these to wider historical and on-going struggles. Hence we looked at autobiography as a form of class, as well as individual consciousness; we discussed questions of gender and the gendered nature of writing; in later years of the course we focused more sharply on issues of race and black experience. It has to be said that it did not always work out the way the teachers intended: Nikki, for example, does not remember the course being about gender at all. Behind all this, none the less, there lay the political assumption we believe has always motivated popular education: that knowledge has little value unless it can be used to help people individually and collectively to understand, analyse, and change the world in which they live.

To say this, of course, is to describe a course beloved of all ILEA and 'trendy-left' education-bashers everywhere. Those who feel this way will have yet further proof in this chapter of what is wrong with education today. Their arguments are probably ones that those struggling for popular education in the past would recognize: that it is partial and biased; that it does not provide a hard, rigorous, or disciplined approach to knowledge; and that it does nothing educationally to equip people to live or work in the wider world – in the language of the early nineteenth century – that it does not prepare them for their 'station in life'. What those struggling for a popular education know, on the other hand, is that theirs is *not* the dominant voice; it might be a voice that offers an alternative, but it remains very much a marginalized voice. Moreover, they are also acutely sensitive to issues of partiality and bias: why, after all, provide alternative perspectives if the dominant ones are the sole fountains of truth? Or, finally, why make the knowledge acquired through popular education 'soft' or 'easy' when that knowledge will find itself constantly under challenge and attack? The threat offered by the forms of popular education we are describing comes, of course, not from the fact that it is the dominant voice in the production and the re-production of knowledge, but from the fact that it resists control and incorporation, and that it asks the unpalatable questions.

There exists now, then, as much as before, a need to promote popular education. The problem remains, particularly in the days of the GERBIL, what strategies are available for its promotion. How, especially within the area of state educational provision, can the vital issues of access, content, control, and context be taken into the hands of ordinary people? In higher education, we would like to suggest, by making access, and particularly the qualifications necessary for access, a contentious issue; by calling into question what the guardians of knowledge – the teachers – claim to be the essential knowledge for any degree or course; by allowing other experiences, those of the students for example, to prise open the prevailing definitions of what people really need to know to be 'educated'; by recognizing, as the present government has recognized, that the institutions of education are themselves political sites of struggle. Now clearly we are not claiming, nor would we want to claim, that our autobiography course represents anything major in this struggle. It is no more than one course, one kind of educational experience. But in so far as a small group of individuals could come together to effect change, to alter the parameters of their own lives, and issue an example of what was possible to others, then, the autobiography course was far more than sixteen people sharing a Friday morning at Thames Polytechnic. As teachers and students what was open to us was this little corner of the education system. There are many such corners, particularly in higher education, where the issues of access, content, and control in particular, can be met and confronted head-on.

This essay has sought to describe an experience and to locate that experience in a historic and on-going struggle for knowledge. Not knowledge in the abstract, though that has always been part of the struggle as well, but more pointedly a particular kind of knowledge: 'really useful knowledge'. It is part of the struggle that each generation defines and redefines what it means by really useful knowledge and how it produces it. The preparation for and writing of this essay was part of the experience we are describing. The individual and collective gains we have made have been immense, and because of that we make no apology for the rather celebratory tone of this whole essay. But that tone comes also from the fact that we know this is by no means the only experience of this kind. Others have discovered, and are discovering, 'really useful knowledge'. The alternative voice may at times appear muted, but it is still there.

And our title? When we collected together at the end of the course our own autobiographical writings, someone suggested that we called the collection 'The Park Bench' because until *then* her most extravagant ambition had been to have her name on a plaque on a bench in the park. This, then, is our second park bench.

15

Taking it seriously: teaching popular culture

Margaret Beetham, Alf Louvre, and Brian Maidment

Introduction

The following chapter arises out of our experience of collaborative teaching in the area of cultural studies. The processes of writing, like the processes of teaching which we describe, have involved discussion and debate as we tried to work out common ground. In what follows we have sought to describe this common ground but have not tried to eliminate difference of voice. We would want to assert the importance of this; although we work as a teaching team we have very different styles and emphases. Our students, too, come from different positions and make sense of the course in different ways, a point we return to in the last section.

The cultural studies described in this chapter are pursued in two main areas of the English section's work. Firstly, they feature as a major component (between a half and a third) in the work of English students on the Humanities degree. Here a compulsory course called Culture, Society, and Text is taken alongside other English courses which are mainly genre-based. Secondly, they feature as an interdisciplinary core (roughly a third of their work) for students on a single honours degree in either English Studies or Historical Studies. Students and staff from both disciplines meet together for joint lectures and seminars in these 'common courses'. Much of this chapter, especially the discussion of texts in the central section, refers to work on the second year common course, Culture, Ideology, and Social Change, which deals with the late eighteenth and nineteenth centuries.

Making the syllabus

The legitimacy of studying popular culture

Classic definitions of ideology, as superstructural and hence reflexive, as class-based misconception, or, more generally, as 'false consciousness' often led to the dismissal of modern popular culture by the orthodox left. According to Gorky speaking at the 1934 Russian writers' congress – orthodoxy with a vengeance this – American popular literature was overwhelmingly about gangsters and prostitutes, it reflected corrupt values, and encouraged individualist illusions. Worse still, popular culture was (and is) – dramatically – a commodity, the illusions made profits. Marxists with those reflexes were in remarkable coincidence with Leavisite Liberalism: there was a shared dismissal of contemporary popular culture in the west as corrupt and the 'masses' were seen as passive and vulnerable. And yet, remarkably, both groups placed faith in a literary canon (albeit differently composed) somehow immune to and above these pressures.[1]

Such determinism – popular culture the bi-product of ideology (itself the epiphenomenon of class, which in its turn takes shape from the economic base) – was in our time most famously attacked by E. P. Thompson. His stress on agency in the development of class consciousness led to a new evaluation of all kinds of cultural artefacts – diaries, newspapers, autobiographies, ballads, cartoons – which, he claimed, were part of a heroic popular culture in the early nineteenth century (see Thompson 1963).

Recent challenges to the dualism of base/superstructure, economy/ideology made by Gramsci, Althusser, and Foucault have also lent new weight and point to studies in popular culture. When ideology is seen as having its own material existence, as 'signifying practices' relatively autonomous from other social practices, or in terms of the discourses of power/

knowledge (which do not articulate but constitute the subject) then, in some respects at least, a very much more positive problematic emerges.[2] Artefacts of all sorts are now to be read in terms of their specific ideological effects. As the work of *Screen* sought to demonstrate, all sorts of genres and sub-genres – verbal and visual (and within the visual: dramatic, cinematic, and televisual) – had their own particular effectivities: the interpellation of the subjects in any one discourse, in some ways confirming and consolidating what others offer, yet has its distinctive sources of pleasure and identification.[3]

Such emphases have sustained and been sustained by an increased interest in literary-critical theories – which have themselves generated engagement with artefacts once regarded as trivial or negligible.[4] More significantly, newer concepts of ideology tend to create an equivalence between texts from different cultural sites and 'levels'. Canonical literature is now increasingly read in terms of ideologies and artefacts from popular literature, and popular culture in general is seen as having no less significant specific effects, as likewise creating 'positions', promoting values, and, perhaps, as gestures of cultural intervention or subversion of the same status as the acknowledged texts. Because popular, because of their quantitative reach, in fact, these artefacts can be seen as more 'significant'.

Material for studying popular culture

It is a small step from here to the cheerful confirmation (with Barthes) that literature is only 'what gets taught', to the rejection of literature as somehow self-selecting according to immanent value. The consequences of this position, however, need recognizing. For it implies the rejection too of any polemical counter-canon (of the alleged 'real' or 'repressed' culture). Such constructions, after all, depend upon a (now contested) essentialism, the notion that popular cultural artefacts simply 'express' alternative values or experience.

So one arrives – positively, if chillingly – at the definition of the field of study as 'discourses and their interrelationships'. Such a definition has three major consequences for cultural studies.

1 Potentially there is a boundless field of study, empirically vast; from the texts of orthodox literary criticism to those of

more usual concern to the social historian or anthropologist. A modest illustration: a recent seven-week study bloc on the mid-nineteenth century included a temperance pamphlet, chapters from Darwin, Smiles, Mrs Beeton, and some extracts from medical textbooks (on sexuality), as well as the work of Tennyson, Gaskell, Ruskin, and the popular writer Jean Ingelow. Disciplinary boundaries are in the circumstances fragile – for one may well go beyond self-consciously 'literary' discourse. The inevitable question, of course, is 'which are the significant discourses, and why?'

2 When material is not canonical (and not then, apparently, self-selecting) it is chosen as symptomatic – that is, as significantly related to other phenomena (most commonly class, gender, race, or, more blandly, 'social developments'). Often, significantly, the relation our courses emphasize is between popular or 'sub-literary' artefacts and what might elsewhere (and in the period under study) be treated as canonical texts. So, the work of nineteenth-century artisan poets is read in relation to the Augustan or Romantic models they often embraced, Beeton's *Household Management* held alongside Ruskin's *Of Queen's Gardens*. The 'other phenomena' to which the artefacts from popular culture are related are for us often in the first instance textual and discursive phenomena. We can't assume an unproblematic historical discourse and relate our texts to that, without turning them once again into mere reflections. Because the struggle for meanings and values takes place actively in discourse, the texts studied function not just as secondary evidence for 'shifts' or 'developments' described elsewhere – but as instances, as parts of the process of class or gender assertion. Part of the impulse for the textual analysis we make is, precisely, to define the ideologies of the day: these are not taken on trust from a prior account.

3 Such a project requires a reflective self-conscious mobilization of theory – literary-critical and historiographical. Both textual interpretation and historical explanation are at issue. Investigating 'mid-Victorian stability', for example, we are concerned to read popular and 'influential' texts for the values and identities they profer but, concerned also – necessarily – to weigh the relative significance of such cultural intervention. This inevitably means reviewing contending histories. The

concepts that inform the histories – notions of hegemonic struggle, the 'disciplinary society', 'the triumph of the entrepreneurial ideal', the politics of prosperity – and their underlying historical stances – are not used as fixed reference points but provisionally, as liable to critical consideration and testing.[5]

We must recognize, then, the interdependent relationship of textual studies with theory (neither guarantees or underwrites the other). And yet also that the selection of material (which texts? which discourses?!) depends upon some prior, and in the broadest sense political, perception of what is significant in social development, however provisionally and self-consciously held.

A historical range

With these motives, these interests, this level of theoretical concern what is the reason for examining popular culture in the *nineteenth* century? Couldn't these be advanced with more immediacy in a wholly contemporary study? The degree in which these studies are sited adopts the predominantly nineteenth- and twentieth-century focus traditionally associated with courses studying 'the making of the modern world'. There are then pragmatic reasons for the range of our studies: readings of nineteenth-century popular culture (in second year) lead into equivalent studies of twentieth-century material (in third year). This has the virtue of constructing contexts and parallelisms so that, for instance, studies of the contemporary popular press are informed by earlier attention to its 'radical', 'improving', and 'commercial' variants in the nineteenth century. Such consecutive study, the prior exposure to older popular artefacts, helps, too, to temper excessively affective reactions to contemporary works.

Over and above specific parallels between nineteenth- and twentieth-century material, a stronger claim is that we are examining significant continuities in terms of cultural processes in general. To put it more bluntly – that many aspects of contemporary popular culture have their origins in the nineteenth century. Studying the developing relations between elite and popular modes, the burgeoning power of the market, the recurrent movements of ideological accommodation or resistance (and the traditions they establish), the shifting patterns of ownership and access, and the relative stability or otherwise of generic conventions as these features have developed over the centuries, should create the perspective necessary for contemporary evaluations. As for the significance of the 'culture industry' in maintaining social cohesion, winning consent, or accommodating resistance – as these varied phrases indicate, that can never be a matter of objective description but of historiographical and political debate.

The strongest claim in defence of such a range of study is less to do with continuities and similarities than with difference. Content matters. For such a breadth of study works to affirm the changeability, the historical relativity of key presuppositions about gender, class, race, childhood, self, sexuality, art, work, and so on. These are in due course, cumulatively, revealed as constructs rather than eternal or natural. If no particular academic or theorized 'history' is – or can be – assumed as gospel, the historical imagination, the recognitions of change, conflict, otherness is, we hope, endorsed and encouraged.

Focus

We hope we have suggested how our syllabuses try to disavow any unproblematic history as hermeneutic key – how they try not to see texts as reflections. But the historical 'solutions' that might be held at bay in particular blocs of the syllabus inevitably insinuate themselves in the overall framing of the course (even the blandest phrases – 'the making of the modern world' – carry their ideological charge!). We have tried to be aware of the implications of different sorts of focus, each of which brings its own pedagogical promise and difficulty.

Chronological survey (The investigation of discourses in relation to socio-economic changes and their impact on gender, community, and class formation over, say, several decades.). With this focus the institutional sources and the ideological constituences of chosen discourses can be established in detail but the volume of historical data can swamp the attention given to generic conventions at work in the discourses. Attempts to correlate discourse and class (or gender) are weakened, the more data there is to suggest the complexity of, say, class composition or gender definition. The tendency of the chronological focus is to set data against perceived pattern – to collapse into historical empiricism.

Epochal analyses (The ideological effects of the text considered in an extended time scale, over centuries.). In the course of a 'chronological' or 'conjunctural' study, those dimensions of the text *not* exhausted by reference to the immediately preceding or succeeding decades might be focused on. A strategic intervention might be made to emphasize certain long-lived generic conventions surviving despite centuries of thematic or stylistic innovation: conventions that work to proffer the most fundamental versions of personal identity. For instance, in the late nineteenth century, certain novels could be examined as 'boundary texts' – exemplifying the pressures at work in, and, despite the most self-conscious interventions of their authors, the continuing hold of the 'realist' fictive mode (Arthur Morrison's *The Child of the Jago* for example). The danger with this focus – even temporarily adopted – is, of course, formalist deduction: the effectivity of discourses extrapolated from their abstract analysis rather than demonstrated in concrete historical action.

The conjunctural focus (Attending to selected 'moments' rather than complex chronological narratives, giving due weight to enduring, 'organic' aspects of the crisis, including ideologies established over centuries rather than decades – yet also examining the particular balance of forces of the moment under study.) The conjunctural focus seems to avoid both excessive empiricism and excessive formalism. Cultural patterns can be discerned that are distinctive and specific to the conjuncture rather than ubiquitous. Potentially the most elegant solution, this focus is pedagogically the most difficult – for texts and discourses are subjected to so many different contexts that they can be fatally overloaded. 'Horizontally' they may be examined in relation to economic, political, and ideological forces; 'vertically' in relation to the hegemonic crisis typically chosen for conjunctural study *and* in relation to long-term epochal traditions. The greater the number of contexts and interpretations, the greater the temptation of simplistic and mechanistic readings that have, at least, the virtue of clarity!

The boundlessness of cultural studies returns, in a different guise. There are endless numbers of texts to choose from, and, having chosen, endless numbers of contexts in which to read them. We exaggerate, of course: but only the more firmly to reject the exasperated (and fashionable) relativism of deconstruction. For this 'boundlessness' is not a valid excuse for returning (as so many do) to rereading the established classics. Recognizing that nothing selects or frames itself we should rather accept the responsibility. It is up to us.

Choosing the texts

The 'boundlessness' of cultural studies makes the selection of texts for seminars more than usually fraught, especially for interdisciplinary common course work where neither the literary merit nor the historical significance of a document will guarantee its inclusion. Indeed in some respects the distinctive and distinguished texts that would ordinarily receive attention within the parent discipline (literary criticism or history) might be disqualified precisely because at the moment of reading they privilege one group of students over the other. Inevitably, there are a variety of considerations underlying decisions in the construction of the syllabus: about what gets read and when. We can list these as pragmatic (influenced by pedagogic concerns), polemical (shaped by beliefs that there are important presuppositions about cultural value that need interrogation), and conceptual (deriving from our collective sense of how the field of cultural studies should be drawn). Needless to say, these considerations inevitably overlap.

For pedagogic reasons we try to choose texts which can be perceived as 'problematic', either self-evidently so (because of formal unevenness or unconventional origin or because marginal in the record), or made so by their situation in the course (*Of Queen's Gardens* read alongside *Happy Homes and How to Make Them*). By their inclusion or their juxtaposition such texts are meant constantly to remind students that the rules of analysis and assessment they mobilize elsewhere (in specialist courses) do not necessarily apply here. These courses offer alternatives to conventional literary and historical diets (novels and ballads, essays and journalism, famous manifesto and long-lost tract) not out of a puritanical or aesthetic drive toward 'difficulty' for its own sake but, precisely, to draw attention to the process of interpretation and its numerous possibilities.

On the other hand whilst 'problematic', the texts should not be dauntingly arcane. Ideally, they should be accessible for students from backgrounds in either discipline. This, of course, raises the question of 'context' – how much do you need to know to deal with a problem text? – though it is important to challenge the assumption that 'context' equals 'background' (and will hence be the exclusive preserve of 'historians'). Students of English, for instance, might contribute to the sense of 'context' by referring where appropriate to the history of literary forms and modes related to the text under scrutiny; or by establishing its linguistic register, or by bringing to bear a knowledge of the discourse in which the text operated, by specifying the institutions or social practices which brought it into being. Students of history might point to other social sites where the concerns evident in the text (or document) were also being articulated (traces found in the text studied, for example, of parliamentary debates or legislative campaigns, of protests or official reports, of the founding of institutions or the development of new everyday routines). They may subsequently be able to point to corroborative evidence for interpretations reached in seminars (especially where a text is taken as indicative of the development of, say, feminist or socialist consciousness). And the generalizations about cultural development that our textual readings promote might usefully be tested by historians against other accounts of the period under study. (One 'context' is the context of historical interpretation, which brings us back to our polemical goals.)

To specify possible 'specialist' contributions in this way is not to suggest they will always be made, nor to ignore the possibility that each group of students will be anxious about the range of their own skills. But to think of how likely a possible seminar text is to produce these echoes, to suggest these parallels (among literary students and historians) is to imply that the 'boundlessness' of the field neither entails nor legitimizes an arbitrary choice of material.

In asking students to attend to parallels we also seek (as the phrasing above would suggest) to promote ideas of 'context' that do not collapse into deterministic models of (historical) base and (textual) superstructure. To focus so insistently on texts for seminars means necessarily attending to their materiality (as signifying systems and as artefacts with a specific social circulation). Texts are never unproblematic, transparent transmitters of ideology – though seminar groups may sometimes try to read them as such. In the end, of course, there is a tension between the pedagogic goals discussed here (with their stress on problematizing and interrogating) and our recognition that 'courses' (which must, minimally, be a sequence of selected texts) inevitably do construct their own implicit histories, their own 'versions'.

However, a facile partisanship is, we hope, unlikely, not least because of an approach to the field which seeks to make central the *relationships* between different groups, different practices, different discourses in the culture(s). One key determinant over the selection of texts for study is our rejection of what might be called 'alternative canons'. These seem to us to rest upon essentialist notions through which texts in these canons are seen simply as the bearers of 'neglected' or 'repressed' values – the 'real' that the dominant tradition disguises or ignores. Such an approach returns the text to reflective passivity, whereas we want to insist that the discourse of which it is a part actively constructs and negotiates social and personal identities. Likewise the 'alternative canon' isolates the chosen texts from the conditions of their circulation and their status; we want to know the nature and means of its neglect, its repression, or subordination, questions that can only be posed by looking at the relative power of discourses in contention.

Not surprisingly, none of our courses is devoted to popular literature alone. In addition, in order to pursue the study of interrelated discourses, we examine texts from the dominant literary traditions and genres; texts usually seen in terms of the 'history of ideas'; texts referring or alluding to dominant literary traditions but which belong to historically specific and different traditions; subversive texts in self-conscious opposition to dominant traditions; and texts taken from historically important discourses.

Texts from the dominant traditions – Elizabeth Gaskell's Mary Barton[6]

Amenable as such a text is to straightforward 'oppositional' decoding – 'Whose point of view does *Mary Barton* adopt and with what consequences?' – there are, we think, more productive enquiries. For instance, why do such texts dominate contemporary (and to some extent subsequent) discussion of the 'human problems' of urbanization and industrialization? Is it because of their innate 'complexity' or through the power of the discourse to which they belong (if so, what are the sources of that power)? Such texts can then be used to focus discussion of the relative significance of 'literary value' as against 'context'. To pursue relations between literary value and context – or 'art' and 'ideology' – we examine the connections between literary form and ideological identity. In this text what ideological significance do we assign to such formal features as the shifting narrator, at once keen to publicize new conditions but uncertain as to their causes? Why is the narration arguably as engaging in its self-doubt as in its assertiveness? Or, we can focus on the texts shifting fictive genres (realism, melodrama). This last point (which any discussions of the literary 'unity' or the narrative 'assurance' of the text inevitably raise) in its turn leads to some general consideration of the difference between 'fictive' and 'documentary' texts (students will have already encountered early nineteenth-century descriptions of Manchester). Exploring the differences between such modes involves deconstructing what might be called the authenticating textures of the fictive and the metaphoric aspects of the documentary record. A comparison of modes, made possible by their justaposition in the course, should make for a sense of both their mutual borrowings and yet their separate and distinctive ideological address.

None of these approaches denies the relevance and the importance of a *thematic* analysis, but rather suggests that – undertaken in the light of these broader concerns – thematic readings will veer away from easy allegorical unmaskings and toward a recognition of the interior tensions of the text, the *effortfulness* of the discourse. (Not least, for example in trying to marry discourse on industry with discourse on the family, a puzzle that the early 'documentary' mode more wholly committed to the *public* sphere is less troubled by.)

'History of ideas' texts – The Rights of Man[7]

As well as Paine we also include extracts from such as Malthus, Darwin, Arnold, Ruskin, and so on. To label these works in this way is to accept, of course, that their *ideas* matter and need defining and discussing. But this course departs from a conventional 'history of ideas' approach to texts in two ways. Firstly, it is less concerned to locate texts in appropriate (usually highly-extended) 'traditions' than to consider their more immediate genesis, reception, and resistance. We aim, that is, to map the contours of the ideological ground of their day; to focus on the struggles between the contending values and interests articulated in response to the text. Secondly, where the text is located less immediately, in terms of 'traditions' rather than 'struggles', our particular interest is in how significantly it departs from or brings innovation to its discourse. Paine, for example, is studied (along with other late eighteenth-century and early nineteenth-century radicals) in terms of the development of a *vernacular* language in the field of political and social analysis.

Allusive or referential texts – artisan poetry[8]

Artisans, it might be said, made poetry, but not in conditions of their own choosing. The ways in which poetic traditions and conventions became available to artisan writers, the ways in which those to which they had access were used as models, provide necessary centres of interest. The force exerted by established connotations of 'poetry' and 'the poet' and how far these were adopted or challenged by the artisans provide another. The crucial matter is how knowingly artisans mobilized poetic conventions that can seem to us wildly at odds with their (assumed) subject matter (J. C. Prince's indignant *The Death of a Factory Child* is written in Augustan rhyming couplets).

In a complementary movement, we examine the responses made to such work by figures in the established literary culture of the time: how far do essays written by Carlyle and Kingsley about artisan writers direct, establish, or pre-empt their possible roles? In examining texts which refer or allude to dominant literary traditions but which belong to historically specific and different traditions (their own modes of publication, distinctive audiences, and so on) we inevitably encounter important aspects of hegemonic power. How is a culture negotiated between social groups? And how precisely are dominant modes and assumptions imposed?

Texts subverting the dominant traditions – The Political House That Jack Built, Chartist hymns[9]

The dominant traditions which many try to impose and some are forced to negotiate are, of course, sometimes resisted and a place must be found (whatever the views of an 'alternative canon') for recognizably radical texts. The examples cited here (and used in the course) intend to highlight different aspects of the 'subversive' text. This label itself needs explaining: for us it is perhaps more accurately applied to texts than the term 'oppositional' in that it suggests the determination exerted by the rejected mode or form. To oppose dominant traditions, this is to say, one has to take them up and take them on. In one respect cultural power must be confronted in some of those forms and modes that embody it. Hence the importance of radical parody and pastiche.[10]

The Political House That Jack Built (sited in the course, appropriately, after Blake's poetry) subverts by resituating an established genre. The nursery rhyme formula thus *now* articulates a mature and systematic social analysis; it is suited to extending the grasp of many in the audience who were newly literate (or illiterate) whilst simultaneously and by the same 'simplicity' debunking those who mystify their own power.

'Parody' seems less viable as a description of Chartist hymns (though they sometimes grimly rework some famous originals). Our interest here is in a different kind of resituating, where the context of consumption, especially performance, works fundamentally to challenge the assumptions underlying conventional hymns. To participate in their singing before or after a *political* 'sermon' was to affirm a very different sense of the function of religious belief (collective not personal, socially engaged not removed, and sometimes God-challenging rather than God-fearing).

Texts from historically important discourses – The Penny Magazine[11]

These texts foreground one of the course's polemical interests, here primarily testing *historical* interpretation rather than literary evaluation. An issue of, say, *The Penny Magazine* is read to explore arguments about the 'accommodation' of working-class radicalism. What can we learn from the mode of address, the type and distribution of items, the notions of participation allowed the readership, and from typology and illustration about the ideological complexion and ambitions of this publication? As this makes clear, whilst larger historical interpretations may be foregrounded (and the text read as a sort of test case) our judgement of them is not solely reliant on statistical and 'sociological' evidence about our chosen text but also draws on 'literary' concerns about style, form, and genre (the inductive piecing together of the 'reader' the text assumes). The inductive method is more perceptive and persuasive, of course, if part of a recurrent series, and if the opportunity is given (as the course does) to apply it to other examples from, say, the discourse of popular journalism (*Poor Man's Guardian* and *Tit Bits*, for example, see Hollis 1970).

Conventional 'popular' texts – the broadside ballad[12]

Lastly, we come to those texts that may seem most obviously 'our concern'. The classic defence of the study of popular literature is, after all, that whilst individual texts chosen may be unimportant, they belong to discourses of evidently broad social appeal. If we claim to study a culture then these must figure. Popular genres from which sample texts are chosen are assumed as significant for a number of reasons. Firstly, as 'barometric', as indicating in a more or less direct 'documentary' fashion the developing concerns of their public – about, say, such issues as the 'growth of the city', or the 'disappearance of the community', or 'rural nostalgia'. The difficulty here is that in terms of 'content', especially if narrowed to explicit or implicit 'view', the barometers don't necessarily coincide. Two contemporary ballads commenting on conditions of acute distress can (and usually do) offer very different responses. Another dimension to the problem of 'typicality' (concerning form rather than content or 'views') is, simply, how can individual texts be found to 'represent' a genre as extensive and diverse as the broadside ballad?

Secondly, a closely-related assumption is that popular literature offers an unmediated representation of popular feelings and emotions. Such texts it might be argued are more characteristic of ideologies of the day (because less removed, less polished, less refracted than sophisticated modes) and their ideologies are therefore more accessible ('closer to the surface'). True as this often seems to be, recent approaches to popular literature as the depiction of desires that cannot otherwise be expressed or socially realized (i.e. as *Utopian*) imply by their mobilization of the unconscious that we are dealing with displaced or transposed expression, so that important meanings of the text are latent rather than manifest.[13] In any event the notion of popular literature as the direct expression of popular feelings must be cast into doubt in view of the complexity of the publishing practices associated with, say, the broadside ballad (where the entrepreneurial, professional, opportunistic, and commercial dimensions of the production of such texts conflicts with the idea of the ballad as simple truth-to-experience).

Finally, even the simplest assertion about the significance of popular literature – it matters because of its numerical range and reach – needs a cautious response. As Altick argued thirty years ago there may not always be a direct match between the production, distribution, and consumption of the (allegedly) 'popular' text. His example (from religious tracts distributed in their millions but read by who knows how many) may seem a marginal case given the increasing commercialism of later nineteenth-century popular literature. But even where buying suggests that the artefact will probably be 'consumed', we might do well to be wary of assuming an easy unanimity of response or reception.

It is necessary, indeed essential, to read 'the popular' in literary/cultural studies but (as the questions raised above are meant to indicate) we must be careful not to sell 'the people' short. Better this cautious scrutiny than the idealist advocacy that abstracts 'the people' from real circumstances, that isolates a few of the works that seem to have mattered most into a new 'canon' or that imputes a mechanistic unanimity (here 'radical', there 'conformist').

The scope of the course, the choice of texts, and the debates between theoretical and particular which we have described so far, all indicate a movement away from explanations which work through simple oppositions. As teachers on these courses, we have increasingly wanted to question definitions of culture in which 'popular' is posed against 'high', working-class against middle-class or base against superstructure as mutually exclusive and defining pairs. Instead we have tried to explore the complexity of, for example, the ways in which class and gender intersect, or how economic and institutional practices shape and are shaped by struggles over language, narrative convention, or forms of entertainment.

One set of binary opposites, however, remains firmly in place. In higher education, where we work, teachers and taught face each other across the lecturer's desk, which represents the institutional and economic gap between them. It is true that, just as 'popular' and 'high' share the common term 'culture', so students and lecturers are both engaged in the process of 'education', but they are very differently positioned in it. The teacher's role is to be the dispenser of cultural values and truths, the student's to be the receiver. The theoretical debates and discussion of texts which we have described may enable us, as lecturers, to explore the complexities of nineteenth-century culture but what is the effect of these on the relation of teacher and taught within the process of 'education'?

Ironically, perhaps, there is a danger that the sub-text of all our texts continues to be that of the difference between the active lecturer and the passive student. The move towards complexity and greater theoretical sophistication can itself be threatening to students, especially because the language of some contemporary theory is so inimical. How does the teacher help the student to negotiate the difficult waters of poststructuralist theory, for example, unless with the kinds of supportive devices, the life-belts of over-simplified accounts, which discourage the students' own activity?

Besides this general point about theoretical sophistication, there is the way our courses have evolved historically, a history both particular and representative, in which certain differences between students and staff have been emphasized. In our department, as in many others, the cuts in higher education have meant that each year we teach more students without any new staff (there have been no new blood posts in polytechnics). A group of teachers have, therefore, been working together over a long period of time. The kinds of theoretical debate in which we have engaged about the cultural studies courses have been exciting for us as teachers. Collective work has produced, we believe, much better courses than we could have produced individually.

However, those same processes have inevitably widened the gap between the teachers and the taught. On one hand is a group of staff, engaged with each other over years, familiar with the material and the arguments. On the other, there are the students, whose situation is quite different. Obviously they have not been party to the collective discussion which has shaped the course. This means that they approach it not as part of a group but as individuals, because that is the nature of degree-level work. Even more importantly, they have in some measure to take the course as given, whereas to staff it is the product of a process in which they are still engaged. It would be very difficult for any of us who teach on these courses to have developed a belief in a popular alternative canon as an agreed body of texts. For us, the shape of the course, including the set texts, is fluid and at times – under the heat generated by argument – it evaporates altogether. For the students, however, the course, including the set texts, is solid and fixed. The reading represents, if not an alternative canon, then at least an alternative body of work which they are compelled to study.

This last point is important. Both our major degrees include a large compulsory element of cultural studies. We defend this in terms of a commitment to dialogue between literary and cultural studies. We believe they complement each other and, taken together, enrich the student experience in ways each on its own cannot. However, in practice some students perceive the compulsory nature of our cultural studies courses as repressive, indeed as even more repressive than the demand that they should follow certain literary courses.

We may argue that our courses liberate students from the constraints of the canon and of Literature as traditionally defined. But another way of reading them is to see these courses with their complex structure and carefully chosen texts as substituting for the authority of the canon the equally repressive authority of the teacher. All this seems to confirm rather than challenge the lecturer/student dichotomy which is central to the practice of higher education and to the expectations which students bring to the courses, including their understanding of how teachers behave.

Obviously students bring to the course assumptions and expectations which are the result of their own immersion in the education system and in contemporary culture. Student groups do not now (if they ever did) engage with lecturers in polemic about the content and structure of lectures. They sit quietly and take notes or else simply stay away. But students' demands are complicated, even contradictory. Those who, in late 1980s Britain, enter courses in the humanities and social sciences are, in some respects, already challenging the norms of Thatcherite culture. Of course, many of our students have a very instrumental view of their studies and it is important not to romanticize this. A degree is a degree is a degree. Many of them will have chosen to study English because there were no good science teachers at their school, or because at some level they realized that English was an acceptable subject for girls to do, or they may have come from Access courses or courses for mature students where the options were limited. However, they have – especially perhaps if they are men – made a choice which they may already feel they have to defend as unrealistic or alternative.

For some students, then, the choice of our course represents a resistance, often barely articulated, to certain of the dominant values of our culture in favour of another set of values, which are centred round the concept of literature. These contradictory currents flow together into the demand that teachers on courses like ours should initiate students into these values.

These values are not necessarily associated with a clearly defined body of writing. The particular experience of groups of our students who are mature entrants to higher education or who may come from under-resourced schools with poor libraries only reinforces that general departure from the idea of the canon which is evident in O level if not A level syllabuses. However, our students do have a clear sense of literature as something to which they can have direct access as individuals and from which they can get self-improvement, information, and truths about life, or even pleasure. A course which refuses to engage with what they understand as the best or the greatest literature may seem to be cheating them of precisely those values for which they chose it. Choice of texts is only one aspect of the problem. Perhaps even more confusing for students is the way the course examines and tries to deconstruct those ideas (truth-to-experience, for example, or pleasure) which they assumed would be its base and justification.

If those of us engaged in this kind of teaching claim, as I think we would, that what we are doing is liberating, that the widening of the range of culture we examine is potentially exciting for students, and that the course should enable and empower rather than confirm them in their passive role, then we need to address these problems. In seeking to do that, we have found that the tensions generated by the challenge to student expectation can be used creatively. The teaching strategy which we have found most useful in this has been group readings of particular texts. This is not to say that we have abandoned the formal lecture. Most of our courses consist of one hour's lecture and one hour's small group work per week. However, the central part of all our courses is the seminar in which students and staff focus on the close reading of texts.

This may seem a regressive strategy, a return to the bad old days of 'What do you think this passage means?' But at its best this method was always one of exploration of meaning. If this process is seen as a preliminary to the discovery or pronouncement of the definitive reading, then the student demand for a single truth can be met but only at the cost of reinforcing the passive student model. It is not easy for teachers to resist this, even with two of them from different disciplines in a seminar group and a variety of voices in the lectures. But if they can, then the reading of texts in a seminar can be seen as a collective process and one in which the group uses differences between them to make sense of texts, that is to produce meaning. The method of the seminar depends on exploring a range of possible readings. If the set text is a nineteenth-century radical newspaper we will move in discussion between the historical reader (who might have read this in 1831?), the reader positioned by the text (what does this piece imply by tone, by its assumptions about its readers?), and the reader coming to the text in the twentieth-century classroom. Any reading which the students are asked to make in this last role is informed by the historical and theoretical understanding which we hope the course develops but it also depends on their own ways of using that material to make sense of the text.

It may be that the texts on the course represent an authority which replaces the canon with the teacher. However, because so many of them are non-canonical texts they do not carry either the weight of critical importance or the mass of critical commentary which may come between the student reader and the great texts of the tradition. To the plaintive request, 'But what can I read that's about this book?', the answer on this course is 'You have to write your own'. There is pertinent historical material, there are theoretical discussions, and the students have to read the text in the light of these. This means that when it works, the course does enable students to use the contradictions and tension in the text productively and even powerfully.

The question we pose in every seminar, then, is 'How can we read this text?' The text, like the reader, is perceived as constructed by social and institutional pressures, by language and by conventions of form (narrative in the case of the text, and pedagogic in the case of the student), but the historical particularity of the text is confirmed, as is the historical particularity of the reader. This is a crucial part of that process of involving the student in making sense of the course. For the students are invited to make a reading informed by their participation on the course. However, the history from which they read is not simply defined by their role as 'student'.

Other kinds of difference than those of lecturer/student enter into the teaching situation; some of them emphasize those patterns of dominance which are central to our institution and to the society of which it is a part. The lecturers are all white, as are most of the students, though there are, in most classes, a few from ethnic minorities. More men than women teach on our courses; more women than men choose to study on them. Other differences, of age, of class, of sexuality, cut across the neat divide of lecturer from student. Such differences are irrelevant only if we assume that teaching goes on in a cultural vacuum empty of the differences of gender, class, or race. If we resist that assumption, then perhaps this diversity of difference can open up the possibility of questioning the simple teacher/taught pattern and of enabling students to offer readings which are both particular and informed by group differences.

One way in which this can happen has been evident in relation to the teaching of gender on these courses. In its original inception the course was centred on, though not exclusively concerned with the relationships between a dominant middle-class and a subordinate working-class culture. Subsequent revisions began to address the role of women and the nature of patriarchy as a cultural institution which intersects with class. Increasingly, this has been extended to considering the construction of gender. This has been a central part of that movement towards greater complexity which this paper has charted.

For students, this has meant a contradictory set of processes have been at work. On one hand, many of our students become deeply engaged with the discussion of gender and particularly, since the majority of our students are women, on the texts about female roles. They often seize on this material and relate it to their experience in a more or less direct way.[14] At the same time those other pressures which we have described are at work, moving them to question the ways in which their roles are constructed, whether as readers or as women or as reading women.

Here the theoretical and pedagogic concerns of the course come together. If we refuse to offer our students direct access to 'truth about life' vested in texts of received importance, we can at least offer them the opportunity to try out different kinds of readings in relation to various texts. In seeing how meaning is created in a distant historical situation and in relatively unfamiliar forms, perhaps they will be able to engage with questions of how meaning is created in the present. In trying out different roles as readers, they may perhaps see the variety of different social roles they occupy in a new way. Perhaps they and we may be enabled by the course to see these texts and these roles as subject not only to social forces but also as shifting, contradictory, and open to change.

In the end, whatever the complexities of our theory or the range of reading and knowledge we bring to the choice of texts, we may find that this is the most difficult aspect of these courses. How do we, as teachers and students find strategies for making of meaning across the differences, especially those of teacher/taught, which make us what we presently are?

Notes

The following notes document the kind of reading which has been important to our development of cultural studies courses over the years.

1   For the liberal dismissal of popular culture see D. Thompson (ed.) (1973) *Discrimination and Popular Culture*, Harmondswoth: Penguin; the orthodox Soviet line *c.*1934 is evident in speeches by Gorky, Zhdanov, and others quoted in G. Struve (1971) *Russian Literature under Lenin and Stalin, 1917–1953*, London: Routledge & Kegan Paul. The most famous 'immune' canons are to be found in F. R. Leavis (1972) *The Great Tradition*, Harmondsworth: Penguin, and G. Lukacs (1962) *The Historical Novel*, London, Merlin.

2   See, for the most celebrated statements, A. Gramsci (1971) *Selections from the Prison Notebooks*, London: Laurence & Wishart; L. Althusser (1984) *Essays on Ideology*, London: Verso; M. Foucault (1977) *Discipline and Punish*, Harmondsworth: Penguin.

3   For an account of the distinctive contribution of *Screen*, see A. Easthope (1982) 'The trajectory of *Screen*', *Essex Conference on the Sociology of Literature: The Politics of Theory*, University of Essex.

4   See, for example, the attention to Sherlock Holmes stories in C. Belsey (1980), *Critical Practice*, London: Methuen; and feminist analyses of such forms as gothic and romance, e.g. T. Modleski (1982) *Loving with a Vengeance: Mass Produced Fantasies for Women*, London: Archon and Methuen; J. Radway (1984) *Reading the Romance: Women, Patriarchy and Popular Literature*, Chapel Hill, NC: University of North Carolina Press.

5   Appropriate – and contending – historical accounts to which useful reference is made in this context include T. Tholfsen (1976) *Working Class Radicalism and Mid-Victorian England*, Beckenham: Croom Helm; H. Perkin (1969) *The Origins of Modern English Society*, London: Routledge & Kegan Paul; N. Kirk (1985) *The Growth of Working Class Reformism in Mid-Victorian England*, Beckenham: Croom Helm; J. Foster (1977) *Class Struggle and the Industrial Revolution*, London: Methuen.

6   The tradition of discussion of these novels as social problem documents is to be found in R. Williams (1963) 'The industrial novels', *Culture and Society*, Harmondsworth: Penguin, pp. 99–119. It has more recently been taken up, for example, in C. Gallagher (1985) *The Industrial Reformation of English Fiction*, Chicago: University of Chicago Press, and more briefly in P. Stoneman (1987) *Elizabeth Gaskell*, Brighton: Harvester Press, pp. 68–86.

7   O. Smith (1984) *The Politics of Language, 1791–1819*, Oxford: Clarendon, and E. P. Thompson (1963) *The Making of the English Working Class*, Harmondsworth: Penguin, provide an extended discussion of context here.

8   M. Vicinus (1974) *The Industrial Muse*, Beckenham: Croom Helm, and the appendix to L. James (1963) *Fiction for the Working Man*, Oxford: Oxford University Press, did much to open up this area of study. See B. Maidment (1987) *Poorhouse Fugitives*, London: Carcanet, for an extensive annotated anthology of this material and contemporary reactions to it.

9   E. Rickword (ed.) (1971) *Radical Squibs and Loyal Riposts*, Bath: Adams & Dart, reproduces and discusses some Hone pamphlets. Other relevant discussions are Maidment, op. cit., pp. 23–94, Smith, op. cit. 1984, esp. pp. 154–201, and Vicinus, op. cit. 1974, esp. pp. 94–139.

10 A. Louvre (1988) 'Reading Bezer; pun, parody and radical intervention in nineteenth century working class autobiography', *Literature and History* XIV(1) 1988, pp. 23–36. See D. Vincent (1982) *Bread, Knowledge and Freedom*, London: Methuen, for a full discussion of working-class use of the autobiographical mode.

11 On mode and influence of popular magazines, see R. Altick (1963) *The English Common Reader: A Social History of the Mass Reading Public, 1800–1900*, Chicago: University of Chicago Press, and L. James (1978) *Print and the People*, Harmondsworth: Penguin.

12 Helpful student introductions to these kinds of texts are not readily available. D. Harker (1985) *Fakesong: The Manufacture of the British Folk Song, 1700 to the Present Day*, Milton Keynes: Open University Press, gives a polemical account of the mediations of popular songs through its collectors and students, and anthologies like R. Palmer (1974) *A Touch of the Times: Songs of Social Change*, Harmondsworth: Penguin, and J. Raven (1978) *Victoria's Inferno*, Manchester: Broadside, contain useful material. A. L. Lloyd (1967) *Folk Song in England*, London: Panther is still very useful, as are the detailed readings in M. K. Booth (1981) *The Experience of Song*, New Haven: Yale University Press.

13 For a complex discussion of the notion of popular culture as 'Utopian', see the conclusion to Fredric Jameson (1981) *The Political Unconscious*, London: Methuen, and also his (1971) *Marxism and Form*, Princeton, NJ, Princeton University Press, esp. pp. 376–79; and (1977) 'Class and allegory in contemporary mass culture', *College English* (March) XXXVIII, 7.

14 For fuller discussion of the ways in which gender enters into the teaching situation in these courses, see M. Beetham, 'Influence of a teacher', in A. Thompson and H. Wilcox (eds) (1989) *Teaching Women*, Manchester: Manchester University Press.

Calendar: English in education 1988–9

The Conservative reform of education in the late 1980s has proceeded more rapidly, and with broader, more radical implications than any comparable initiative in the post-war period. Almost inevitably in these circumstances, further reports, speeches, and responses with special or indirect relevance to English have appeared after the time of writing and of the book going into production. These items are listed below without further comment in a calendar of relevant events between March 1988 and 1 April 1989.

17 March 1988: 'The Kingman Report' (The Committee of Enquiry into the Teaching of the English Language) recommends a model of language in use together with the teaching and assessment of linguistic knowledge, but rejects the idea of a return to formal grammar teaching. Kenneth Baker describes the report as 'interesting', as contributing 'to discussion about the teaching of the English language and about the importance of the grammatical structure of the language and of the correct use of the spoken word'.

17 May 1988: Motion for the abolition of ILEA passed in House of Lords.

7 June 1988: *Advancing A Levels* ('The Higginson Report') calls for leaner, tougher syllabuses in more balanced programmes of

five A and/or AS levels as the individual norm. It looks forward to more broadly defined recruitment and more flexible modes of assessment, tuned to academic and non-academic objectives.

29 July 1988: The Education Reform Bill, first published in November 1987, receives Royal Assent. This enables schools to opt out of local authority control and introduces the National Curriculum, which designates English, Maths, and Science as core subjects, with the addition of seven further foundation subjects, and with tests at ages 7, 11, and 14.

November 1988: 'The Cox Report' (The Report of the Curriculum Working Group on English 5–11) recommends five levels of attainment for the three curriculum profiles of speaking and listening, writing, and reading in primary schools and five additional levels for secondary schools. It gives a role to media studies, describes a 'cultural analysis' view of language providing a critical understanding of the world, and stresses the link between language use and cultural identity. Kenneth Baker's introduction speaks of the need for more emphasis on 'grammatical structures' in the study programmes and attainment targets.

20 December 1988: A document entitled 'Policy and Strategy' which recommends changes in lecturers' contracts requiring a thirty-seven-hour week and thirty days annual leave is endorsed by the PCFC (Polytechnic and Colleges Funding Council) Employers Forum.

6 January 1989: The Universities Authorities Panel offer a 3 per cent pay rise to university lecturers for 1988–9. Two-thirds of the AUT (the Association of University Teachers) vote to boycott the examination process from April 1989 in support of an improved offer.

5 January 1989: In a speech titled 'Higher education: the next 25 years' at Lancaster University, Kenneth Baker anticipates a greater role for private funding, a two-fold increase in student numbers to two million, and the separation of teaching and research functions.

15 February 1989: In a speech to the Association of Colleges for Further and Higher Education, Kenneth Baker recommends

that further education should introduce a core curriculum, straddling academic and vocational courses, and that employers should pay less to unskilled young people and offer more to those with a qualification as an incentive for young people to stay on at school or college after 16.

1 March 1989: The first annual report of the Senior Chief Inspector of Her Majesty's Inspectorate reports poor training and resources in preparation for the introduction of the National Curriculum and a particular shortage of teachers in both primary and secondary schools in the areas of maths, science, and technology.

2 March 1989: The National Curriculum Council consultative document on English in primary schools rejects proposals for the teaching of formal grammar and emphasizes the importance of skills in speaking and talking as well as in reading and writing.

17 March 1989: In draft orders to go before Parliament in May and for implementation in September, Kenneth Baker overrules the recommendation of the National Curriculum Council on English to insist on the rigorous teaching of spelling, punctuation, and grammar in primary school English and their inclusion in tests at age 7.

20 March 1989: The AUT (Association of University Teachers) rejects the offer of a 7 per cent pay rise over two years and declares its readiness to ballot its members and to continue the boycott of examinations.

22 March 1989: The CVCP (Committee of Vice Chancellors and Principals) demands that lecturers set and mark examinations after the Prime Minister declares the AUT's action 'irresponsible and unprofessional'.

26, 27 March 1989: The NUT (National Union of Teachers) rejects demands to hold a national campaign of industrial action to improve working conditions, but votes to boycott the use of untrained teachers.

28 March 1989: Government plans are unveiled to introduce increased student fees, loans, and vouchers, and to concentrate fundamental research in selected universities.

1 April 1989: The Education Reform Act becomes law.

1 April 1989: Eighty-nine polytechnics and colleges gain corporate status under PCFC.

References and further reading

The following list combines works referred to in the above articles with a selection of further relevant works. Information on journals which regularly debate the issues of English education and teaching practice or have taken these up in special issues is given at the end, and is followed by a list of useful addresses.

Adlam, Diana and Salfield, Angie (1980) 'The diversion of language', *Screen Education* 34: 71–86.

Aiken, Joan (1982) *The Way to Write for Children*, London: Elm Tree Books/Hamish Hamilton.

Altick, Richard (1963) *The English Common Reader: A Social History of the Mass Reading Public 1800–1900*, Chicago: University of Chicago Press.

Alvarado, Manuel (1981) 'Television studies and pedagogy', *Screen Education* 38: 56–67.

Alvarado, Manuel and Ferguson, Bob (1983) 'The curriculum, media studies and discursivity', *Screen* 24 (3): 20–34.

Alvarado, Manuel and Ferguson, Bob, with Gutch, R. and Wollen, T. (1987) *Learning the Media*, London: Macmillan.

Arnold, Matthew (1869, 1963) *Culture and Anarchy*, Cambridge: Cambridge University Press.

Auden, W. H. (1972) *Epistle to a Godson*, London: Faber.

Bakhtin, Mikhail (1973) *Problems of Dostoevsky's Poetics*, trans. R. W. Rostel, Ann Arbor, Mich.: Ardis.

—— (1981) *The Dialogic Imagination*, ed. Michael Holquist, trans. Caryl Emerson and Michael Holquist, Austin, Tex.: University of Texas Press.

Baldick, C. (1983) *The Social Mission of English Criticism 1848–1932*, Oxford: Oxford University Press.

Baldwin, Michael (1982) *The Way to Write Poetry*, London: Elm Tree Books/Hamish Hamilton.

Balibar, Etienne (1978) 'Literature as an ideological form,' *Oxford Literary Review* 3 (1): 4–12.

Ball, Stephen (1985) 'English for the English since 1906' in I. F. Goodson (ed.) *Social Histories of the English Curriculum*, Brighton: The Falmer Press.

Barker, Francis, Coombes, John, Hulme, Peter, Mercer, Colin, Musselwhite, David (1978) *1848: The Sociology of Literature*, Colchester: The University of Essex Press.

Barnes, Douglas and Barnes, D., with Clarke, S. (1984) *Versions of English*, London: Heinemann.

Barrett, Michèle (1987) 'The concept of difference', *Feminist Review* 26: 29–41.

Barthes, Roland (1977) 'Writers, intellectuals, teachers' in *Image–Music–Text*, trans. Stephen Heath, London: Fontana, 190–215.

—— (1983) *Selected Writings*, ed. Susan Sontag, London: Fontana.

Bates, Inge, Clarke, John, Cohen, Philip, Finn, Dann, Moore, Robert, Willis, Paul (1984) *Schooling for the Dole? The New Vocationalism*, London: Macmillan.

Batsleer, Janet, Davies, Tony, O'Rourke, Rebecca, Weedon, Chris (1985) *Rewriting English. Cultural Politics of Gender and Class*, London: Methuen.

Beetham, Margaret (1989) 'Influence of a teacher' in Ann Thompson and Helen Wilcox (eds) *Teaching Women*, Manchester: Manchester University Press.

Belsey, Catherine (1984) 'The politics of meaning', in Francis Barker, *Confronting the Crisis – War, Politics and Culture in the '80s*, Colchester: The University of Essex Press.

Bennett, M. (1988) 'Literature and anti-racist teaching; medium or vehicle?', *Wasafiri* 6/7: 21–3.

Bennett, Tony, Boyd-Bowman, Susan, Mercer, Colin, Woolacott, Janet (eds) (1981) *Popular Television and Film*, London/Milton Keynes: BFI in association with The Open University Press.

Bennison, Steve and Spicer, A. (1988) 'Challenging "A" level', *The English Magazine* 20: 30–4.

Berger, John (1972) *Ways of Seeing*, Harmondsworth: Penguin.

—— (1984) *And Our Faces, My Heart, Brief as Photos*, London: Writers and Readers.

Bergonzi, Bernard (1986) 'The Terry Eagleton story' in *The Myth of Modernism and Twentieth Century Literature*, Brighton: Harvester Press.

Betterton, Rosemary (1987) *Looking On: Images of Femininity in the Visual Arts and Media*, London: Pandora.

Bhaba, Homi K. (1988) 'The commitment to theory', *New Formations* 5.

Board of Education (1904) *Memorandum on Teaching and Organisation of Secondary Schools: Form 123*, London: HMSO.

—— (1910) *The Teaching of English in Secondary Schools: Circular 753*, London: HMSO.

—— (1938) *The Spens Report*, London: HMSO.

Booth, Mark K. (1981) *The Experience of Song*, New Haven, Conn.: Yale University Press.

Bourdieu, Pierre (1984) *Distinction*, London: Routledge & Kegan Paul.

Braidotti, Rosi (1987) 'Envy: or with my brains and your looks' in Alice Jardine and Paul Smith (eds) *Men in Feminism*, London: Methuen.

Brande, Dorothea (1983) *Becoming a Writer*, London: Macmillan.

Brathwaite, Edward K. (1984) *History of the Voice*, London: New Beacon Books.

—— (1987) *X/Self*, Oxford: Oxford University Press.

Brecht, Bertolt (1964) *Brecht on Theatre*, ed. and trans. John Willett, London: Eyre Methuen.

Britton, Julia (1973) 'How we got here', in N. Bagnall (ed.) *New Movements in the Study and Teaching of English*, London: Temple-Smith.

Brown, J. and Jackson, D. (1984) *Varieties of Writing*, London: Macmillan.

Burnett, John (ed.) (1974) *Useful Toil: Autobiographies of Working People from 1820s to 1920s*, London: Allen Lane.

—— (1982) *Destiny Obscure: Autobiographies of Childhood, Education and Family from 1820s to 1920s*, London: Allen Lane.

Burnett, Paula (ed.) (1986) *The Penguin Book of Caribbean Verse in English*, Harmondsworth: Penguin.

Bush, R. (1988) 'GCSE and multi-cultural concerns', *Wasafiri* 6/7: 18–20.

Cantor, N. F. and King, N. (eds) (1984) *Notebooks in Cultural Analysis – An Annual Review*, Durham, NC: Duke University Press.

Casterton, Julia (1979) 'In the kitchen: problems of women's studies courses', *Red Letters* 9: 45–8.

CCCS Education Group (1981) *Unpopular Education: Schooling and Social Democracy since 1944*, London: Hutchinson.

Chambers, Iain (1986) *Popular Culture. The Metropolitan Experience*, London; Methuen.

Chatwin, Bruce (1987) *The Songlines*, London: Cape.

Clarke, John, Critcher, Chas, Johnson, Richard (eds) (1979) *Working Class Culture*, London: Hutchinson.

Cohen, Anthony (1982) *Belonging*, Manchester: Manchester University Press.

Colls, Robert and Dodd, Philip (eds) (1986) *Englishness: Politics and Culture 1880–1920*, London: Croom Helm.

Connell, Ian (1983) '"Progressive" pedagogy?', *Screen* 24 (3): 50–4.

Cook, Jon (1986) 'Critiques of culture: a course', in David Punter (ed.) *Introduction to Contemporary Cultural Studies*, London: Longman.

Culler, Jonathan (1983) *On Deconstruction*, London: Routledge & Kegan Paul.

—— (1988) *Framing the Sign. Criticism and its Institutions*, Oxford: Basil Blackwell.

Culley, Margo and Portuges, Catherine (1985) *Gendered Subjects: The Dynamics of Feminist Teaching*, London: Routledge & Kegan Paul.

Curzon, L. B. (1985), *Teaching in Further Education*, London: Cassell.

—— (1987) *Higher Education – Meeting the Challenge*, London: HMSO.

Dabydeen, David (ed.) (1988) *A Handbook for Teaching Caribbean Literature*, London: Heinemann Educational Books.

Davies, Tony (1978) 'Education, ideology and literature', *Red Letters* 7; reprinted in Tony Bennett (ed.) (1981) *Culture, Ideology and Social Practice*, London/Milton Keynes: Batsford/Open University.

de Castell, S. *et. al.* (1986) *Literacy, Schooling and Society*, Cambridge: Cambridge University Press.

de Lauretis, Teresa (1984) *Alice Doesn't: Feminism, Semiotics, Cinema*, London: Macmillan.

Department of Education and Science (DES) (1975) *A Language for Life: The Report of the Committee of Enquiry*, under the chairmanship of Sir Alan Bullock (The Bullock Report), London: HMSO.

—— (1980) *Examinations '16–18'*, London: HMSO.

—— (1984) *English 5–16*, London: HMSO.

—— (1985a) *Education for All: The Report of the Committee of Inquiry into the Education of Children from Ethnic Minority Groups*, under the chairmanship of Lord Swann (The Swann Report), London: HMSO.

—— (1985b) *GCSE The General Criteria*, London: HMSO.

—— (1985c) *GCSE The National Criteria for English*, London: HMSO.

—— (1986) *English from 5–16: The Responses to Curriculum Matters 1*, London: HMSO.

—— (1987) *The National Curriculum 5–16: A Consultation Document*, London: HMSO.

—— (16 Jan 1987) *Press Release*.

—— (1988a) *The National Curriculum Working Group on English: Terms of Reference*, London: HMSO.

—— (1988b) *The Report of the Committee of Enquiry into the Teaching of English Language*, under the chairmanship of Sir John Kingman (The Kingman Report), London: HMSO.

—— (24 April 1988) *Press Release*.

Doyle, Brian (1982) 'The hidden history of English studies', in Peter Widdowson (ed.) *Re-Reading English*, London: Methuen, 17–31.

Eagleton, Terry (1983) *Literary Theory. An Introduction*, Oxford: Basil Blackwell.

—— (1984) *The Function of Criticism*, London: Verso.

—— (1985) 'The subject of English', *The English Magazine* 15: 4–7.

—— (1986) *Against The Grain*, London: Verso.

Easthope, Anthony (1982) 'The trajectory of *Screen*, 1971–9', *Essex Conference on the Sociology of Literature; The Politics of Theory*, Colchester: University of Essex Press.

Education and Science News (12 January 1988) *Press Release*.

Fairbairns, Zoë (1987) 'I was a teenage novelist', in Z. Fairbairns, *More Tales I Tell My Mother*, London: Journeyman Press.

Fairfax, J. and Moat, J. (1981) *The Way to Write*: London: Elm Tree Books/Hamish Hamilton.

FEU (1979) *Active Learning – A Guide*, London: Further Education Curriculum Review and Development Unit.

FEU (1981) *Experience Reflection Learning*, London: Further Education Curriculum Review and Development Unit.

FEU (1982) *A Basis for Choice*, 2nd edn, London: Further Education Curriculum Review and Development Unit.

Feuchtwang, Stephan (1987) 'Fanonian spaces', *New Formations* 1 (Spring): 124–30.

Foucault, Michel (1972) *The Archeology of Knowledge*, trans. A. M. Sheridan Smith, London: Tavistock.

—— (1977) *Discipline and Punish. The Birth of the Prison*, trans. Alan Sheridan, Harmondsworth: Penguin.

—— (1980) *Power/Knowledge: Selected Interviews and other Writings*, ed. Colin Gordon, Brighton: Harvester Press.

Gaine, Chris (1987) *No Problem Here*, London: Hutchinson.

Gallagher, C. (1985) *The Industrial Reformation of English Fiction*, Chicago: University of Chicago Press.

Gilroy, Paul (1987) *There Ain't No Black in the Union Jack*, London: Hutchinson.

Grace, G. (1978) *Teachers, Ideology and Control*, London: Routledge & Kegan Paul.

Gramsci, Antonio (1971) *Selections from the Prison Notebooks*, ed. and trans. Quentin Hoare and Geoffrey Nowell-Smith, London: Lawrence & Wishart.

Green, Michael (ed.) (1987) *Broadening the Context*, London: John Murray for the English Association.

Green, Gayle and Kahn, Coppelia (eds) (1985) *Making A Difference: Feminist Literary Criticism*, London: Methuen.

Griffith, Peter (1987) *Literary Theory and English Teaching*, Milton Keynes: Open University Press.

Gundara, Jaqdish, Jones, Crispin, Kimberley, Keith (eds) (1986) *Racism, Diversity and Education*, London: Hodder & Stoughton.

Gunner, Elizabeth (1984) *A Handbook for Teaching African Literature*, London: Heinemann Educational Books.

Hall, Stuart, Hobson, Dorothy, Lowe, Andrew, Willis, Paul (eds) (1980) *Culture, Media, Language*, London: Hutchinson.

—— with Slack, J. D. and Grossberg, L. (1989) *Cultural Studies: An Introduction*, London: Macmillan.

Hamil, S. and O'Neill, G. (1986), 'Structural changes in British society: the implications for future consumer markets' *Journal of the Market Research Society* 28 (4): 313–24.

Hargreaves, David H. (1982) *The Challenge for the Comprehensive School: Culture, Curriculum and Community*, London: Routledge & Kegan Paul.

Harker, D. (1985) *Fakesong: The Manufacture of British Folk Song, 1700 to the Present Day*, Milton Keynes: Open University Press.

Harlow, Barbara (1987) *Resistance Literature*, London: Methuen.

Hawthorn, Jeremy (1984) *The British Working-Class Novel in the Twentieth Century*, London: Edward Arnold.

Heath, Stephen (1987) 'Male feminism', in A. Jardine and P. Smith (eds) *Men in Feminism*, London: Methuen.

Hechter, M. (1975) *Internal Colonialism – The Celtic Fringe in British National Development, 1536–1966*, London: Routledge & Kegan Paul.

Hollis, Patricia (1970) *The Pauper Press: A Study in Working Class Radicalism of the 1830s*, Oxford: Oxford University Press.

Holmes, Edmond (1911) *What Is and What Might Be*, London: Constable & Co Ltd.

Hoyles, Martin (ed.) (1977) *The Politics of Literacy*, London: Writers and Readers.

Humm, Peter, Stigant, Paul, Widdowson, Peter (eds) (1986) *Popular Fictions. Essays in Literature And History*, London: Methuen.

Hunter, I. (1987) 'Culture, education and English', *Economy and Society* 16 (4): 568–98.

—— (1988) 'Setting limits to culture', *New Formations* 4.

Irigaray, Luce (1985) *Speculum of the Other Woman*, trans. Gillian G. Gill, Ithaca, NY: Cornell University Press.

—— (1985) *This Sex Which Is Not One*, trans. Catherine Porter, Ithaca, NY: Cornell University Press.

James, Louis (1978) *Print and the People*, Harmondsworth: Penguin.

Jameson, Fredric (1977) 'Class and allegory in contemporary mass culture', *College English* XXVIII (7).

—— (1977), *Marxism and Form*, Princeton, NJ: Princeton University Press.

—— (1981) *The Political Unconscious*, London: Methuen.

Jardine, Alice (1987) 'Men in Feminism: odor di uomo or compagnons de route?', in Alice Jardine and Paul Smith (eds) *Men in Feminism*, London: Methuen.

Jardine, Alice and Smith, Paul (eds) (1987) *Men in Feminism*, London: Methuen.

Jones, M. and West, A. (eds) (1988) *Learning Me Your Language: Perspectives on the Teaching of English*, London: Mary Glasgow Publications.

Kaplan, Cora (1986) *Sea Changes. Culture and Feminism*, London: Verso.

Kappeler, Susanne and Bryson, Norman (eds) (1983) *Teaching the Text*, London: Routledge & Kegan Paul.

King, Noel (1987) 'The Newbolt Report re-examined', *Literature and History* 13 (1): 14–37.

Kitchen, Paddy (1981) *The Way To Write Novels*, London: Elm Tree Books/Hamish Hamilton.

Klein, Renate D. (1987) 'The dynamics of the women's studies classroom: a review essay of the teaching practice of women's studies in higher education', *Women's Studies International Forum* 10 (2): 187–206.

Labov, W. (1972) *Language in the Inner City: Studies in the Black English Vernacular*, Philadelphia, Pa: University of Philadelphia Press.

Lee, Victor J. (ed.) (1987) *English Literature in Schools*, Milton Keynes: Open University Press.

Leitrim, Anna (1979) 'Me and my history', in Paul Ashton and Michael Simons (eds) *Our Lives: Young People's Autobiographies*, London: ILEA English Centre.

Levitas, Ruth (1986) *The Ideology of the New Right*, Cambridge: Polity Press.

Lloyd, A. L. (1967) *Folk Song in England*, London: Panther.

Lodge, David (ed.) (1988) *Modern Criticism and Theory: A Reader*, London: Longman.

Lusted, David (1986a) 'Introduction. Why pedagogy?' *Screen* 27 (5): 2–14.

—— (1986b) 'Media studies and media education', *Papers from the Bradford Media Education Conference*, London.

MacCabe, Colin (1987) 'The state of the subject (1) English', *Critical Quarterly* 29 (4): 5–8.

—— (1988) *Futures for English*, Manchester: Manchester University Press.

Macherey, Pierre (1977) 'An interview with Pierre Macherey', *Red Letters* 5 (Summer): 3–9.

—— (1978) *A Theory of Literary Production*, London: Routledge & Kegan Paul.

Macherey, Pierre and Balibar, Etienne (1978) 'On literature as an ideological form', in Robert Young (ed.) (1981) *Untying the Text: A Post-structuralist Reader*, London: Routledge & Kegan Paul.

Maidment, Brian (1987) *Poorhouse Fugitives*, London: Carcanet.

Marxist-Feminist Literature Collective (1978) 'Women's writing 1848', in Francis Barker, John Coombes, Peter Hulme, Colin Mercer, David Musselwhite (eds) *1848: The Sociology of Literature*, Colchester: The University of Essex Press.

Masterman, Len (1980) *Teaching About Television*, London: Macmillan.

Mattelart, Armand, Delcourt, X., Mattelart, Michelle (1984) *International Image Markets*, London: Comedia.

Medway, Peter (1980) *Finding A Language*, London: Writers and Readers.

Meek, Margaret and Miller, J. (1984) *Changing English*, London: Heinemann.

Metcalfe, Andy and Humphries, Martin (1985) *The Sexuality of Men*, London: Pluto Press.

Miller, Jane (ed.) (1984) *Eccentric Propositions*, London: Routledge & Kegan Paul.

Miller, Nancy (1985) 'Mastery, identity and the politics of work: a feminist teacher in the graduate classroom', in M. Culley and C. Portuges (eds) *Gendered Subjects*, London: Routledge & Kegan Paul.

Modleski, Tania (1982) *Loving with a Vengeance: Mass Produced Fantasies for Women*, London: Methuen.

Moi, Toril (1985) *Sexual/Textual Politics*, London: Methuen.

Montefiore, Jan (1987) *Feminism and Poetry: Language, Experience, Identity in Women's Writing*, London: Pandora.

Moore, R. (1987) 'Education and the ideology of production', *British Journal of Sociology of Education* 8 (2).

Morley, Dave and Worpole, Ken (eds) (1982) *The Republic of Letters: Working Class Writing and Local Publishing*, London: Comedia/Minority Press Group.

Mulhern, Francis (1979) *The Moment of 'Scrutiny'*, London, New Left Books.

Mulvey, Laura (1975) 'Visual pleasure and narrative cinema' *Screen* 16 (3), in Tony Bennett, Susan Boyd-Bowman, Colin Mercer, Janet Woolacott (eds) (1981) *Popular Television and Film*, London/Milton Keynes: BFI and Open University Press, 206–15.

Munby, S. (June 1978) 'Bored and angry', *Marxism Today*, 185.

Nelson, Cary (ed.) (1986) *Theory in the Classroom*, Urbana and Chicago, University of Illinois Press.

Nelson, Cary and Grossberg, Lawrence (1988) *Marxism and the Interpretation of Culture*, London: Macmillan.

Nichols, Grace (1983) *I is a long memoried woman*, London: Karnak House.

O'Connor, Errol (1979) 'Jamaica child', in Paul Ashton and Michael Simons (eds) *Our Lives: Young People's Autobiographies*, London: ILEA English Centre.

Owen, J. (1984) 'TVEI: Future control', *Perspectives* 14, TVEI Exeter University, 11.

Paice, E. (1981) *The Way to Write for Television*, London: Elm Tree Books/Hamish Hamilton.

Palmer, R. (1974) *A Touch on the Times. Songs of Social Change*, Harmondsworth: Penguin.

Parker, Rozsika and Pollock, Griselda (1981) *Old Mistresses: Women, Art and Ideology*, London: Routledge & Kegan Paul.

Parrinder, Patrick (1987) *The Failure of Theory*, Brighton: Harvester Press.

Peim, Nick (1986) 'Redefining "A" level', *The English Magazine* 17: 10–17.

Phillips, Anne (1987) *Divided Loyalties: Dilemmas of Sex and Class*, London: Virago.

Prescod, Colin (1985) 'Keynote address: Black artists, white institutions conference', delivered at Riverside Studios, 4 November 1985; published in *Artrage* 12 (Spring 1986): 32–6.

Protherough, Robert (1986) *Teaching Literature for Examinations*, Milton Keynes: Open University Press.

Punter, David (ed.) (1986) *An Introduction to Contemporary Cultural Studies*, London: Longman.

Radway, Janice (1984) *Reading the Romance; Women, Patriarchy and Popular Literature*, Chapel Hill, NC: University of North Carolina Press.

Raven, Jon (1978) *Victoria's Inferno*, Manchester: Broadside.

Rickword, Edgell (ed.) (1971) *Radical Squibs and Loyal Riposts*, Bath: Adams & Dart.

Rose, Jacqueline (1984) *The Case of Peter Pan*, London: Macmillan.

Rowbotham, Sheila (1973) *Hidden From History: 300 years of Women's Oppression and the Fight Against It*, London: Pluto Press.

Rushdie, Salman (1988) 'Minority literatures in a multi-cultural society', in K. H. Peterman and A. Rutherford (eds) *Displaced Persons*, London: Dangaroo Press.

'Rutherford, Mark' (William Hale White) (1881) *The Autobiography of Mark Rutherford*, London: T. Fisher Unwin.

Sandra, Margaret (1981) *Teaching London Kids* 19, n.p., 40 Hamilton Road, London SW19.

Scheman, N. (1980) 'Anger and the politics of naming', in Sally McConnell-Ginet, Ruth Borker, Nelly Furman (eds) *Women and Language in Literature and Society*, New York: Praeger.

Scholes, Robert (1985) *Textual Power – Literary Theory and the Teaching of English*, New Haven, Conn.: Yale University Press.

—— (1987) 'Reading like a man', in A. Jardine and P. Smith (eds), *Men in Feminism*, London: Methuen.

Schor, Naomi (1987) 'Dreaming dissymmetry: Barthes, Foucault and sexual difference', in Alice Jardine and Paul Smith (eds), *Men in Feminism*, London: Methuen.

Segal, Lynn (1987) *Is the Future Female? Troubled Thoughts on Contemporary Feminism*, London: Virago.

Showalter, Elaine (ed.) (1986) *The New Feminist Criticism*, London: Virago.

Showalter, Elaine (1987) 'Critical cross-dressing: male feminists and the woman of the year', in A. Jardine and P. Smith (eds), *Men in Feminism*, London: Methuen.

Simon, Brian (1988) *Bending the Rules*, London: Verso.

Simons, Mike and Raleigh, Mike (1981) 'Where we've been. A brief history of English teaching. Part one, 1920–1970', *The English Magazine* 8: 23–8.

Smith, Olivia (1984) *The Politics of Language*, Oxford: Clarendon Press.

Spivak, Gayatri Chakrovorty (1987) *In Other Worlds: Essays in Cultural Politics*, London: Methuen.

Tallack, David (ed.) (1987) *Literary Theory at Work*, London: Batsford.

Tallis, Raymond (1987) *Not Saussure. A Critique of Post-Saussurean Literary Theory*, London: Macmillan.

Terrell, T. (1977) 'A natural approach to second language acquisition and learning', *Modern Language Journal* 61: 325–37.

Thompson, E. P. (1963) *The Making of the English Working Class*, Harmondsworth: Penguin.

Toffler, Alvin (1980) *The Third Wave*, London: Collins.

Traves, P. (1987) 'Anti-racist, multi-cultural and socialist education', *Wasafiri* 6/7: 14–18.

Trease, Geoffrey (1961) *The Young Writer*, London: Thomas Nelson.

Treichler, Paula A., Kramarae, Cheris, Stafford, Barbara (eds) (1985) *For Alma Mater: Theory and Practice in Feminist Scholarship*, Urbana and Chicago: University of Illinois Press.

Vicinus, Martha (1974) *The Industrial Muse*, London: Croom Helm.

Vincent, David (1982) *Bread, Knowledge and Freedom*, London: Methuen.

Voloshinov, V. N. (1986) *Marxism and the Philosophy of Language*, trans. L. Matejka and I. R. Titunik, Cambridge, Mass.: Harvard University Press.

Walcott, Derek (1965) 'Some West Indian poets', *The London Magazine* 5 (6): 252.

—— (1970) 'What the twilight says; an overture.' *Dream on Monkey Mountain and Other Plays*, New York: Farrar, Straus & Giroux.

—— (1984) *Midsummer*, London: Faber.

Walters, Margaret (1979) *The Nude Male: A New Perspective*, Harmondsworth: Penguin.

Weed, Elizabeth (1987) 'A man's place', in A. Jardine and P. Smith (eds) *Men in Feminism*, London: Methuen.

Weissman, J. (1987) 'Masters of the universe: deconstruction and the yuppies', *The Syracuse Scholar*, Supplementary Issue, Syracuse University, NY: 11–23.

Weldon, Fay (1985) *Letters to Alice on First Reading Jane Austen*, London: Coronet.

White, A. (1975) 'From culture to culture: the disputed passage', *Cambridge Review*: 128–32.

Widdowson, Peter (1980) '"Literary value" and the reconstruction of criticism', *Literature and History* 6 (2): 138–50.

Widdowson, Peter (ed.) (1982) *Re-Reading English*, London: Methuen.

Williams, Raymond (1961) *The Long Revolution*, London: Chatto & Windus.

—— (1965) *The Long Revolution*, reprint, Harmondsworth: Penguin.

—— (1973) *The Country and the City*, London: Chatto & Windus.

—— (1979) *Politics and Letters*, London: New Left Books.

—— (1980) *Problems in Materialism and Culture*, London: New Left Books.

—— (1984) *Writing in Society*, London: New Left Books.

Wolpe, Anne Marie and Donald, James (eds) (1983) *Is There Anyone Here from Education*, London: Pluto Press.

Woolf, Virginia (1929, 1977) *A Room of One's Own*, London: Granada.

Wordsworth, William (1977) *Poems. Volume 1*, ed. John O. Haydon, Harmondsworth: Penguin.

Worpole, Ken (1984) *Reading by Numbers: Contemporary Publishing and Popular Fiction*, London: Comedia.

Magazines

Dragons Teeth
English in Education
Literature and History 13:1 (1987); 14: 1 (1988)
LTP (1981–7) issues 1–6
Multicultural Teaching
Multi-Ethnic Education Review
News from Nowhere

Radical Teacher
Red Letters (1980) no. 10; (1981) no. 11; (1982) no. 12
Screen (1983), 24, 3; (1986) 27, 5
Screen Education (1980) no. 34; (1981) no. 38; (1981/2) no. 40
The English Magazine
Wasafiri

Addresses

The English Association, 1 Priory Gardens, London W4 1TT.
The ILEA English Centre, Sunderland Street, London, SW1.
For the London Association for the Teaching of English (LATE) contact Chris Nevin, 153 George Lane, London, SE13.
For LTP and back nos contact Helen Taylor, School of Humanities, Bristol Polytechnic, Fishponds, Bristol.
For publications from the National Association for the Teaching of English, write to Birley School Annexe, Fox Lane, Frecheville, Sheffield, S12; Tel.: 0742 390081.
For *News from Nowhere* contact Tony Pinkney, Oxford English Limited, 16 Southdale Road, Oxford, OX2 7SD.
For *Radical Teacher*, contact Susan O'Malley, 150 Lafayette Avenue, Brooklyn, NY 11238.

Index

275